Raechel's Eyes

Raechel's Eyes

The strange but true case of a human - alien hybrid

Helen Littrell
and
Jean Bilodeaux

Preface by Dr. Richard Boylan, Ph.D.

Wild Flower Press
P.O. Box 1429
Columbus, NC 28722

Third Edition

Library of Congress Cataloging-in-Publication Data
Littrell, Helen E.
Raechel's eyes : compiled evidence of a human-alien hybrid/
Helen Littrell and Jean Bilodeaux -- 1st ed.
p. cm. -- (Star kids chronicles ; v. 2)
ISBN 0-926524-60-7 (pbk. : alk. paper)
1. Human-alien encounters--United States. 2. Nadien, Raechel.
I. Bilodeaux, Jean. II. Title. III. Series.
BF2050.L58 2004
001.942--dc22
2004026012

Cover Artwork: Noah J. Crissey
Manuscript Editor: Brian L. Crissey
Manuscript designer: Pamela Meyer

Author contacts:
Helen Littrell helen5thworld@aol.com
Jean Bilodeaux jeanb@hdo.net

Printed in the United States of America.

Address all inquiries to:
Wild Flower Press
an imprint of Granite Publishing
P.O. Box 1429
Columbus, NC 28722

Order via email to orders@5thworld.com
or visit http://5thworld.com/Raechel

DEDICATION

To
Marisa,
Raechel,
and
anyone else who,
because they are different,
has ever felt alone.

ACKNOWLEDGEMENTS

Due to the controversial nature of the topics discussed in this book, the names of many who contributed their time, memories, and skills, shall by their choice remain anonymous.

The authors, who are solely responsible for the interpretations contained in this book, wish to express appreciation for the contributions of Michael Brein, Rick Coimbra, and Paul Von Ward to the early research on this project. Our thanks go to our publishers, Brian Crissey and Pamela Meyer, who believed in us for a very long time, and to Dr. Richard Boylan whose enthusiastic support for the project has made a difference.

A special thank-you goes to Dr. June Steiner, psychotherapist and hypnotherapist, with a specialty in anomalous events of all kinds. She is president of OPUS, an organization that helps people to a better understanding of the overall nature of unusual/anomalous personal experiences and supports those who have them.

Our gratitude goes out to our many friends who encouraged us along the way.

We thank all of you.

Table of Contents

Part II

Preface

In all my years of research into UFOs, Star Visitors, and the transformations humans experience as a result of Star Visitor encounters, I have hardly read a book which advanced my understanding beyond what I was getting from my own pioneering research work. But *Raechel's Eyes* is a book from which I gained new and valuable information and insights.

People have wondered what happens to the hybrid children whom the Zeta Reticulans have fashioned from their genes and mixed with a few human genes. *Raechel's Eyes* gives the answer. They grow up, and in the case of teenager "Raechel," help crew starcraft, including one which crash-landed on the Nevada desert in 1956.

This book tells the gripping story of how a compassionate Air Force officer on a Perimeter Security Team befriended a Zeta Reticulan survivor who happened to be a hybrid teenage girl. His subsequent daring experiment, authorized by the National Security Council through the Air Force's Aerospace Technical Information Command, to adopt Raechel and let her try living a normal life as a college student as a roommate with the author's blind daughter, makes for an account that is poignant, strangely familiar, heart-wrenching, and full of pathos.

Raechel's Eyes also provides an accurate picture, less the usual disinformation, as to what really goes on below the surface of the heretofore undisclosed "Four Corners" base, which is sister to and apparently north of the better-known Area 51 facility in the central Nevada desert. "Four Corners" (which is deliberately misleadingly not anywhere near the real Four Corners, AZ/UT/CO/NM) is actually a U.S. Government-run Star Visitor Reception Area and Ambassadorial Interface Facility for representatives from the interstellar Federation. And it also serves as an integration tutoring place for those Star Visitors who want to fit in and be able to walk around and observe Earth while passing for human.

Raechel's Eyes closely parallels information about the underground activity at Area 51, leaked by Army Command Sergeant-Major Robert Dean, the NSC's Dr. Michael Wolf, former [Area 51] Site S-4 physicist Robert Lazar, and USAF Colonel Steve Wilson. I found the day-to-day struggle of hybrid Raechel in trying to get accepted in the human world to be an Nth-degree case of the basic struggle so many Star Kids (and Star Seed adults) experience in trying to define themselves, and be openly who they are without the rejection, ridicule and avoidance too many humans dish out to someone who is different.

The Star Kids are hybrids, too, only not as dramatically obvious as the Zeta Reticulan hybrid who Raechel is. This book is a "must-read" for any person who wants to be informed about the amazing developments behind the scenes in the saga of government interaction with the Intergalactic Council, and the decades of quietly facilitating curious Star Visitors walking among us virtually undetected, and getting to know us better.

Needless to say, every experiencer, Star Seed, Star Kid, and serious UFO enthusiast should be sure to read this book. Do it as soon as possible, and be prepared for upcoming further developments in human-Star Visitor relations.

Richard Boylan, Ph.D.
Director, Star Kids Project, Ltd.

Introduction

We have eyes but do not see. Marisa is legally blind; she sees with her heart. Raechel can see; her eyes hold secrets. Helen's eyes are mother's eyes that once saw hate and despair; they now see hope and love.

This is the true story of two girls determined not to let their physical handicaps stifle their dreams. Striving to overcome the obstacles of being different, they serve as an inspiration to others who may find themselves in similar situations.

Searching for the truth can present a challenge, especially if the events in question began thirty years ago and continue to this day. This difficulty is compounded when vested interests do not want the truth known. As our research delves deeper into the secrets of the past, the ongoing truth is exposed. This is the story of sinister people with powerful, lying eyes, intruding on the lives of the innocent, hiding secrets, and controlling their destinies.

This is the story as Marisa's mother Helen remembers it. Conversations are reconstructed, the main characters are real, and all the names except Raechel's and Helen's have been changed.

This book invites the reader to expand his vision, to see the individual, the soul, the world, and the universe through the eyes of a blind girl, her mother, and most importantly, Raechel's eyes.

Part I

Chapter 1

Initial Meeting
Marisa, Raechel, and Harry — 1972

"Okay, Marisa, you're standing in front of the counselor's door. Just reach out and knock," Bobby urged.

Marisa's hand reached through the darkness until she felt the smooth coolness of the door. Tapping on the wood, she heard a voice, "Come in."

Bobby gave Marisa a quick hug, saying, "You'll do great, Marisa. I have to run to class now."

Hearing his words of encouragement, she gently pushed the door open and entered. A voice from somewhere in front of her said, "Hello, Marisa. Please sit down, there's a chair about five feet to your right. What can I do for you?"

"Mrs. Ross, I live with my mom and stepfather, and they fight almost every night. He drinks too much and they end up yelling and screaming at each other. Sometimes he gets so drunk he beats her up. Mom's even had to go to the hospital several times. We can't tell the police because he's in law enforcement himself. We did once, but it didn't do any good. Mom's afraid of him, and I am, too. It's so noisy in the evenings I can't study. I need a quiet place to live. Would you help me find an apartment near campus? I can't afford anything expensive because I only get a small Social Security check, but I just can't stand it anymore. I don't want to flunk out. Would you help me?" Marisa pleaded to her counselor.

It hadn't come out quite like she'd rehearsed in her mind. She'd wanted to hide the tendrils of uncertainty and panic that were pulling her downward, threatening to drown her dreams in a pool of despair. Silent tears welled up in her eyes, threatening to reveal the emotional turmoil raging in her heart. Brushing her tears away, she crossed her fingers, hiding her hands within the folds of her favorite yellow skirt.

Please, Jesus, please let her help me, she prayed repeatedly in her mind.

Studying the slightly built eighteen-year-old blind girl across her desk, Lyla Ross could see the tension in her face. *She's not telling me everything,* she thought, *but no matter. The girl needs help.*

Several years earlier, she had been assigned as a counselor to the handicapped students who were attending Lost River Community College. Her total caseload was less than a regular counselor's, but the challenges seemed greater.

"It'll be okay, Marisa. I'll see what I can find close by," Lyla said, hoping she sounded more confident than she felt. Housing was at a premium. Quickly scanning her list of student housing, the only place available was a small, two-bedroom apartment in a large complex. It was within walking distance from campus and most of the tenants there were students at the college.

"Here's one. The rent's a little high for one person, Marisa," she continued, "but it's available now, and, if I can find you a roommate to split the costs, it would be a real bargain. Let's walk over there and see if you like it. There's money in the office slush fund that I can loan you so you can move right in. You can pay it back later. I don't want you to get behind in school your first semester. I'll start hunting for a roommate for you today."

Walking the short distance across campus to the apartment complex, they entered an attractive group of older, but well-kept white buildings shaded by huge oak trees set in neatly manicured lawns. The fragrance of climbing yellow roses filled the courtyard, delighting Marisa's heightened sense of smell. Inside the apartment, the furniture was old but comfortable, and the carpet was slightly threadbare, but the rooms smelled of fresh paint and everything was immaculate.

Walking through the apartment, Marisa could barely make out the shapes of the rooms. Although legally blind, her vision had begun to improve slightly, fluctuating daily, always worsened by stress. Some days she saw only darkness, other days shapes and sometimes colors. But seeing is not always with the eyes, and she knew she'd feel safe and comfortable living there, plus there was no need to buy anything. It was fully furnished, right down to linens, dishes, pots and pans. Sitting on the couch, she ran her hands over the fabric. Feeling the worn cloth she asked, "This couch is yellow or orange, isn't it? Yellow is one of my favorite colors. I can feel yellow, it's warm and pleasant."

"Yes, Marisa, the couch is yellow and orange," Lyla smiled at the blind girl's tactile perception of color. So many times she had seen her handicapped students develop their other senses far beyond that of their non-handicapped peers.

"Oh, it's a sign that this place is for me," Marisa exclaimed, her voice full of relief and happiness. It smells so clean and fresh. All I'll need to do is pack my clothes and move in."

Filling out the application for Marisa, Lyla handed the manager enough cash to cover the security deposit. Marisa paid the fifty dollars she'd been saving towards the first month's rent, and made arrangements to pay the balance when she moved in the following Saturday.

Walking back to the campus, Marisa thought, only a couple of days and I'm free. I'm going to make it. I'll get through college and on with my life! Bubbling with excitement, each step loosened the hold that despair had on her. She felt as if a giant hand had reached down and saved her from drowning.

Smiling with gratitude, she thanked Lyla. "I'll be able to pay you back a few dollars each month. I don't know how I would have managed if you hadn't helped me."

"Don't worry about the money, Marisa. Just pay what you can when you can. I'm just thankful I was able to help you. The important thing is that you'll be away from the tensions of your home in only a few more days," Lyla replied, "I'll find the right roommate for you, you'll see. It might not take very long at all. You just never can tell. Things seem to be falling into place. Come on, I'll walk you to your next class."

Lyla knew the roommate would have to be a very special person. Marisa had special needs but things had already worked out well with finding her a tutor. She still marveled at the coincidence of Bobby signing up at the counseling office for a part-time tutoring job on the same day Marisa had come in needing help with her schoolwork. All three of them were surprised when they discovered that Bobby and Marisa had the same class schedules. Since he was going to class anyway, he volunteered to guide Marisa to her classes. Bobby got the part-time job he needed to help pay his expenses, and Marisa was getting a bright, conscientious tutor. Few of her tasks went quite that smoothly. Bobby read Marisa his class notes from each day's lectures, and made sure her homework was completed on time. It was working out perfectly for both of them and, besides, they were becoming good friends. Lyla was pleased that she'd been able to help them both.

After leaving Marisa at her class, Lyla returned to her office, poured herself a cup of tea, settled back in her chair, and began looking over the list of students who wanted to share housing. It didn't look promising. Most of the girls wanted to party every chance they got, and Lyla suspected that some were involved in drugs. No one on the list seemed right for Marisa. She'd have to look elsewhere. Sighing, she dropped the list back in the folder and closed her desk drawer.

A knock on the door interrupted her thoughts. She had no appointment scheduled. A tall, casually dressed man stood in the doorway with a thin, frail-looking girl at his side. She wore wrap-around sunglasses and a broad-brimmed hat that seemed much too large for her face. The girl appeared to have or be recovering from some ailment.

"Come in. I'm Lyla Ross. What can I do for you?"

"I'm Colonel Harry Nadien, and this is my daughter, Raechel. She's just registered for classes and we were sent over here to see if you might help her find a roommate. I was just transferred to Masters Air Force Base and I've been looking for housing in the area, but Raechel would really like to try living with someone her own age. We've been stationed at a little military base out in the desert where she was the only young person around, so she's never interacted with kids her own age or been on her own before. I can live in the BOQ and be nearby in case she needs me. Anyway, the registrar's office said you may be able to help us find something for her."

As they talked, Raechel's head turned first to her father, then to Lyla. Appearing to be afraid to say anything lest her father change his mind, she just watched silently.

"Well, Raechel, I do have quite a few people looking to share expenses. One girl in particular, Marisa, just left the office. She might be just the kind of roommate you're looking for. She's quiet and serious about her schoolwork. She's legally blind and looking for someone who is fairly quiet, too. Since she's on a limited income, she needs someone financially responsible. Although a tutor comes in every day to help her with her work, she spends a great deal of time studying by listening to tapes, so she can't have a lot of loud music, parties, and that sort of thing going on around her. She needs someone really dependable. You'd each be responsible for providing and cooking your own food and for taking care of your room. You could split the general cleaning chores. Does that sound like something you might want? Or maybe you're looking for a little more excitement?"

Lyla stopped talking, afraid she'd painted too dismal a picture for Raechel. *Why am I rambling on so,* she wondered. *After being isolated on a military base out in the desert, Raechel is probably looking for more social life.*

Glancing briefly at her father, Raechel spoke directly to Lyla, "No, it sounds just right! I eat a special food that does not require cooking. And I am slow with my studies, and I need to concentrate on what I read, so I really do not care to have people around me most of the time. That is probably from spending so much time alone. I need someone who will not be too critical of my ways. And because my mother has never lived with us, I am used to picking up after myself and taking care of my room."

"Money's not a problem," Harry interjected. "In fact, since Raechel has a light schedule this semester, registering late like this, she'll probably spend more time at the apartment than Marisa. So I'm willing to pay all of the utilities and half the rent. That would be fair, under the circumstances. The main thing is that Raechel is happy and the girls are compatible. Could we meet her?"

Lyla studied the middle-aged man and his thin, odd-looking daughter, then she picked up the phone, dialed and spoke briefly. Hanging up, she smiled and said, "Marisa will be here in just a few minutes. If you girls think it could work out for both of you, we can go over and look at the apartment. I think you'll like it, but let's be sure. We just might be able to get this all settled today and you can start moving in this weekend."

Harry liked Marisa the minute he saw her and was sure Raechel did, too, because she reached out to touch Marisa's hand when Lyla introduced them. Raechel never extended herself to anyone unless she sensed they'd be able to accept her as she was.

Marisa couldn't see what Raechel and Harry looked like but she immediately felt comfortable with them. It was obvious that Harry was very concerned about his daughter's comfort and happiness, wanting her to find just the right place to live. How lucky Raechel is, Marisa thought, to have a father who cares so much about her.

"Well, girls, what about it? Think this might work for both of you?" Lyla asked hopefully, "It sounds to me like it could be the perfect arrangement."

When Lyla told Marisa about Harry's offer to pay half the rent and all of the utilities, Marisa didn't hesitate, "Yes, Raechel, I'd love to have you as a roommate. I wish I had more time to talk and get to know you better, but I've got to get to my next class. Why don't you go see the place and tell Mrs. Ross what you decide? I'll stop by later to find out."

Turning to the father as she started to leave the room, she added, "Thank you, Colonel Nadien. I hope I'll get to know both you and Raechel better very soon."

That did it. Harry's mind was made up. This was perfect. A blind girl would be the perfect roommate for Raechel, and the girls seemed to hit it off like sisters. However, he did want to look at the apartment to make sure it was clean and large enough.

Harry was impressed with Raechel's new home, and was sure she'd be happy and contented. Marisa was even more than he could have hoped for as his daughter's roommate. He sensed that she'd be a good friend and teacher for his daughter; the first young friend she'd ever had. Sitting down at the kitchen table, he wrote out a $200 check. Handing it to Lyla, he said, "Here, this'll cover

Raechel's share of the rent for a couple of months. Be sure to tell Marisa to call me as soon as the utility bills come in, and I'll take care of them, too."

Raechel added, "It is perfect, Harry. I am sure I will be happy living here with Marisa."

When they returned to the campus, Raechel and Harry headed for the parking lot, and Lyla went straight to her office. *What a day,* she thought. *It's amazing how everything fell into place so precisely, almost as if it had been planned in advance. There's something different about Raechel, though, a little unsettling. I can't quite put my finger on it. Maybe it's her voice and the way she deliberately enunciates each word, almost in a mechanical monotone. The way she never uses contractions made her sound so stilted. Raechel's features are a little unusual, too. And when she smiled at her dad, she had such a small, tight smile, almost as though her mouth couldn't stretch wide enough for an easy smile. And she'd called her father by his first name. Not many girls do that. Yes, she's an odd one, all right. Oh well, kids do strange things nowadays. But none of this makes any real difference. Raechel's looks won't matter to a blind girl. Both girls seem well brought up, quiet and considerate. And both are on a special diet, so the matter of food won't be an issue either. Yes, it's a match made in heaven.*

Closing the door to her office, she kicked her shoes off under her desk. Leaning back in her chair, she pondered again the amazing coincidences of the day and how they'd all worked out. The girls were going to be good for each other. She was sure of it.

Chapter 2

Marisa Escapes a Bad Situation — 1972

Marisa went home, letting herself in the front door. The smell of stale tobacco smoke and warm beer from the night before still hung in the air. Dirty smells, carrying with them a flood of unhappy memories.

And that's what they'll soon be, she thought. *Just memories. Thank goodness I had the courage to talk to Mrs. Ross. This morning I was worried about finding an apartment, and now I not only have an apartment, but a roommate to share expenses with.*

After she'd finished doing the dishes, Marisa said, "Mom, I'm feeling a little tired tonight. I think I'll go to bed early and listen to some music."

Her mom hadn't suspected anything unusual, having already expressed concern over how pale and tired her daughter had been looking lately.

Slipping quietly into her room, Marisa carefully locked the door behind her and double-checked it to make sure. There could be no accidental discovery of her plans. The quiet click of the lock signaled the door closing on her past, allowing her to focus on her future.

Dropping on her bed, Marisa started working on her next plan. Mrs. Ross and Bobby had both offered to help her move. They wouldn't tell anyone, so there would be no chance her stepfather, Jon, would find out. She knew that if he did, he'd try to stop her. He wanted to control her life just as he did her mother's. She could feel his mounting frustration at her growing independence.

No more, she pondered. *Never again. Not after tomorrow. Nothing will stop me from getting a college education. I'll never find myself trapped in a sick marriage, unable to afford to escape. I'm going to become an occupational therapist specializing in visual rehabilitation and helping others. Nothing will stop me, not Jon, my blindness, or my diabetes. Although leaving Mom will be difficult.*

Marisa thought back to all the times when her mom had done her best to shield them both from Jon's drunken rampages. It was no use. The situation was out of hand, and had been for a long time. On countless nights, Marisa had fled to the safety of her room, locking herself in to escape the emotional and physical abuse being inflicted on her mother. It didn't help; she still heard everything that went on in the rest of the house.

Cradling her head in her hands, Marisa sobbed, shedding tears for her lost childhood, the happiness that seemed always just beyond her reach, and her real father who was never there for her. Tears for her mother trapped in an untenable marriage. The screaming and fighting had gotten worse, almost every night now. She had to get out. She couldn't sleep. Each night graphically reinforced the pressure of having to succeed in college, to never be in her mother's position. She took a deep breath to shake off the sorrow and regret. *Think of the good things,* she told herself. *Five days a week at college, the couple of hours each afternoon when Bobby takes me home from school, us laughing together as he helps me with my homework. Too few precious sanity-filled hours before Jon comes home drunk from work, bringing the insanity with him. Oh, how I crave a peaceful, safe environment twenty-four hours a day, where I can study and lead a normal life.*

In a few weeks, after I've had a chance to sort out my feelings, I'll call Mom to let her know I'm okay. Once she scrapes the money together she'll escape too. In two or three months, she's due to test for a promotion at Highland Air Force Base. She'll be gone, too, just as soon as she gets her raise. Enough thinking about Mom. I need to be ready for tomorrow. Bobby will be here early in the morning, just after Mom and Jon leave.

Turning up the volume on her tape player, the haunting sounds of her favorite song, Simon and Garfunkle's "Bridge Over Troubled Water," filled the room. She smiled. "Troubled waters are my life story. At least the sound will cover any noise I might make."

Opening the closet door, she removed the empty boxes she and Bobby had stashed there earlier. Putting them on the bed, she gently pushed Bo aside. "Bo, you big sweetie, I'm going to miss you most of all," she murmured quietly to the purring cat. The big tiger cat was her best friend and she was his favorite human. He'd follow her around the house, climbing on her lap whenever he had the opportunity. Every time the drunken fighting would start, Bo would hide under Marisa's bed. They were two fugitives, hiding in the relative safety of each other's presence. Sleeping on her bed every night, he would snuggle up in the curve of her knees, his soft purring transformed into a lullaby that brought peaceful sleep to his frightened human. She wanted to take him with her but pets were not allowed in the complex.

"Mom loves you as much as I do, Bo. She won't let anything bad happen to you," she whispered reassuringly to the sleepy cat.

Sliding open her dresser drawers, she began placing her clothes in her cedar chest and the cardboard boxes. As she filled each box, she carefully taped it up and hid it back in the closet. Soon she was finished.

Laying a set of comfortable clothes on the top box, she closed the closet door. Tomorrow would be tiring, both physically and mentally. She needed to be as comfortable and rested as possible.

Peering around her room as best she could, she could distinguish two rectangular gray shapes on the wall — a photograph of her grandparents and an old, faded print of Jesus. She could still remember what they looked like from back when she could see. Taking down the picture of her grandma and grandpa, she whispered to their images, "Why did you return all my letters and hang up the phone whenever I called? Just because I wanted to move to California with my mom was no reason to shut me out of your lives. Your stubbornness and cruelty cheated all of us out of all the love and happiness we could have shared."

Cradling the photo against her chest she whispered, "I still love you. Why can't you love me?"

Wiping her tears from the photo, she carefully wrapped it in a woolen scarf and placed it in her cedar chest, cushioning it between some sweaters.

Taking down her treasured print of Jesus, she cringed at the memory of how, when she and her mother had attended Sunday services at the Holy Grace Baptist Church just across the street from their house, Jon would stand in the front yard drinking beer and sneering contemptuously at the congregation as they walked past him to get to their cars after services. What made it worse was that the congregation had become the family they'd both longed for, a family willing to accept them as they were. It was a warm, comforting feeling, a respite from the hate-charged atmosphere at home, and they both looked forward to the Sunday services.

Marisa winced when she recalled that occasionally, they couldn't attend church because Jon would be on one of his tirades about religion, threatening them with physical violence if they left the house. Winter or summer, the church left its windows and doors open and the sounds of joy and praise could be heard the length of the block; so on those days, her mother would throw open the kitchen window to let the sounds of the congregation's singing fill the house.

Marisa remembered how she'd known that Jesus was watching over her, helping her, and it didn't matter to Him whether or not she was actually in the church. She knew that if she couldn't go to Him, He would come to her, no matter where she might be. He had taken care of her so far, and she knew He always would. He was the most important thing in her life, and she could take Him with her.

Shaking herself back into the present, she reached in the closet for the special cardboard mailer she'd saved, put the print in it, and carefully placed it in the chest. *Tomorrow, you'll be first out, and together we can unpack the rest,* she mused.

After checking the dresser drawers a final time, she turned off the tape player and listened a moment. The house was quiet. Her mother had probably gone to bed, and Jon would be home at his usual 2:00 A.M. when the bars closed. Sighing, she thought, *It's no longer my problem. By noon tomorrow, I'll be in my own apartment, and this place will belong to the past.*

Now for the most difficult task of all. A note to Mom. I hope she'll understand why I have to leave like this. Sitting on the edge of the bed, she held her magnifying glass in her left hand while she wrote with her right so that she could see the words and not run off the edge of the paper. Squinting through the lens to see the words, she read the note and whispered, "It could be better phrased, Mom, but it'll have to do."

She placed it on top of her cedar chest and planned on putting it under an antique moustache cup on the freezer in the morning. *I know you'll be shocked, but you'll handle it. Hopefully it'll spur you to get the hell out of here yourself. We're both survivors, you and I.*

She undressed, slipped on her nightgown, climbed into bed, and pulled the covers up carefully so as not to wake the already sleeping Bo. He stretched lazily in his sleep. Reaching over to the lamp on the night stand, she felt around for the switch and turned out the light.

Lying in the darkness, she took Bo's paw in her hand. His ears twitched on her cheeks as she murmured, "Bo, I'm going to miss you so much. I love you, Bo."

Chapter 3

Harry Enlists in the Air Force — 1955

"You'll be forced to associate with undesirables or be killed in some war," Harry's father told him over the mashed potatoes. "Why can't you do something you can take pride in? Be an attorney or a physician. Do something that would be a real credit to the family. We want to be proud of you. No one else in the family has ever joined the military. It isn't a normal life. You get sent to terrible places to live and it pays nothing."

"It's not like I'm going to prison. I've enlisted in the Air Force. That's all," Harry muttered to his parents as he stabbed at the food growing cold on his plate. He knew his decision conflicted with the plans they had for his future. Ever since he could remember, they'd been at odds, and he'd had to endure constant lectures. "Do this, don't do that." Like a broken record, the litany went on and on, while they wrinkled their faces in disapproval.

Sitting at the table, he watched as his mother poured herself a cup of coffee. Compressing her lips into a thin, tight, downward curve, she pretended she hadn't heard him. As she sipped her coffee, he couldn't help but wonder if it was still warm, considering her icy demeanor.

"Pass the gravy, please," his father said to the space above Harry's head, reaching across the table and forking two of the largest pork chops off the serving dish and onto his plate. The discussion was clearly over. Other than the initial disapproval, there was no acknowledgment of what Harry had just said, no argument, no debate, no anything. It was as if he hadn't spoken, as if he wasn't there. This was his parents' typical response to anything that went against their wishes. To them, enlisting in the Air Force was open defiance. They were the parents; he was the child. They gave the orders; he was expected to follow them. If he disobeyed, his punishment was being ignored.

Shit, Harry thought. *I'm not a little kid that they can order around. I'm legally an adult, and what I do with my life is up to me.* He continued, breezily, *I'm leaving for basic training on Friday. It's near San Antonio, Texas. I just need to get away from here. With Annie gone, there's no reason to stick around. I'm not ready for college yet. I don't even know exactly what I want to do for a career. This will give me some time to figure it out and get paid at the same time.*

Watching their stony faces across the table, part of him wanted to laugh at their childish reaction. Another part of him wanted to scream out in rage at the way they'd treated him all his life. He wasn't brain-dead as far as he knew; he could make intelligent decisions on his own. He realized they weren't picking on him specifically with their behavior. They dealt with any situation they couldn't control by sulking. Refusing to talk about something, while maintaining their dignity and pompous attitudes, was just easier than confronting the problem.

"Excuse me," he said, getting up from the table. As he left the room, their eyes focused on their food, as if he didn't exist.

Out on the patio, Harry made a couple of circles around the yard, then lay down on the grass. Stretching out on his back, he felt the life-giving coolness as it soothed his body, cleansing it from the day's stifling heat. Watching the stars as they took their appointed places in the evening sky, he asked the sky, "I wonder if anyone in any of those other worlds out there has problems with their parents, too?" He sighed. Only a few more days and I'm free.

Three days later, he returned to the recruiting office and picked up a bus ticket to the military intake processing center in Boise, Idaho. Once there, after passing his physical, he and about thirty other enlistees boarded an Air Force bus heading for the long drive to San Antonio, and Lakeland Air Force Base.

Shortly after arriving at the base, he suffered the routine head-shave haircut that proclaimed him official U.S. Air Force property. Issued a set of uniforms and assigned to a barracks, he was ready for the upcoming eight weeks of basic training.

The rigors of boot camp and the camaraderie of the other recruits were a joy compared to his last encounter with his parents, and the time went by quickly. After basic, he was given seven days' leave, and headed back home to try to mend things with his folks. However, his reception was even more frigid than before. He tried making small talk with them, asking about their jobs and what had happened in the two months he'd been gone. His father only muttered, "Not much," in reply and continued reading his newspaper, completely uninterested in anything concerning his son.

Christ, why did I even bother? he thought. *It doesn't take a rocket scientist to figure out I'm no longer a member of this family. At least the Air Force wants me. I may have to follow their orders, but they talk to me, even if I don't always like what they say.*

All his old buddies were wrapped up in the petty dramas of their own lives, still pumping gas or waiting tables at the pizza parlor. At night, they'd hang out in the park, drinking beer and boasting about their latest amorous conquests. To them, Harry was a deserter, and they were distant with him. The only person who supported him was a sheriff's deputy who stopped by the park for a beer. He'd served a tour in Korea, and said, "Yep, the Air Force is a man's world all right. Them Asian girls'll do anything for a man in uniform. Wish I could do it all over again, son. Better'n this graveyard of a town, I tell ya."

Later that night in his room, his fiancée, Annie, looked down at him from her photo on the wall. "Why, Annie? Why did you leave me?" He pulled out the newspaper clipping and read it for the hundredth time. DRUNK DRIVER KILLS LOCAL GIRL. The article detailed how, two months before her graduation, Annie had been crossing the road, was hit by a drunk driver running a red light, and killed instantly. "Thank God you didn't suffer," he said to her photo.

He was still haunted by the closed casket at her funeral. "Remember her as she was in life and not by what's in there," the funeral director had said.

"It will be a very, very long time before I let myself love anyone like I loved you," he confided to her photo. "Without you, I don't fit in here anymore. Might as well cut my losses and leave them behind before I go crazy."

In a short note to his parents, he told them he'd decided to get an early start for his new temporary duty station at Crawford AFB in Nebraska. Tossing his few belongings in his old Chevy, he slipped behind the wheel. Turning the key, he broke all ties with his past, started the engine and a new life.

Chapter 4

ATIC Training School on ETs and Spacecraft — 1955

The long, straight road shimmered in the heat of the Nebraska afternoon, mirages playing tricks on Harry's eyes, as miles of farmland rolled by his open window. *I wonder what SAC does, anyway. "Strategic Air Command" sounds more impressive, though.*

Never having been to Colorado, Kansas, or Nebraska, he was using his five remaining days taking his time getting to Crawford. Sitting back and relaxing as he drove, he enjoyed the flat scenery and did a lot of thinking. "Annie, if things had turned out the way we planned, you'd be sitting here beside me. I still can't believe you're gone. I reckon I did the right thing enlisting in the Air Force, though. It's time to put some distance between me and Nampa. Too many memories."

He pulled his orders out, glanced at them again, and continued his monologue to Annie. "What the hell is a Technical Information Investigation School? The fancy words don't tell me a thing about what I'll be doing. Probably military jargon for becoming some kind of cop. And then on to the Aerospace Technical Information Command (ATIC), whatever that is. And how is it connected with Masters AFB in California? It all seems very cryptic and melodramatic. Why can't the Air Force speak English? Talk about alphabet soup.

"Hope I can handle it. What if there's a lot of physics and trigonometry? I'll be in deep shit. Guess I scored pretty high on the aptitude tests, though. At least high enough to be assigned to this technical investigation school thing. But why was I the only one out of the entire intake group to be selected for ATIC?

"I know they ran a routine background check on all of us, but why was my clearance Top Secret and not just Secret like all the rest of them? And why did the lieutenant say, 'You'll need it, where you're going?' Hell, I could have figured that out by myself.

"Maybe it's standard for all airmen assigned to SAC, with all the spy planes, state-of-the-art communications systems, secret aircraft, and other things I don't even know about. But why won't anyone even talk about it? And why did the lieutenant say, 'Never heard of ATIC, airman. You probably read your orders wrong.'"

The answer had seemed too quick and rehearsed, especially when the lieutenant's face changed almost imperceptibly to a blank expression before turning away and calling the next name on the list. "Well, I'll just have to wait and see. They should know at Crawford. They're the ones who are going to teach me whatever it is I need to know for assignment to ATIC. Damn this alphabet soup," Harry moaned. "I'm sick and tired of all the initials that no one knows anything about, or claims not to."

Harry reported to Crawford AFB Sunday afternoon, and the duty officer told him, "Your class begins at 0700 tomorrow. Room 108. There'll be six of you. Don't be late."

He figured he was the youngest of the six and the only new recruit. All the others had been in the service for several years and had volunteered for the school and their eventual assignment to ATIC. At 0700 prompt, a lieutenant entered the room and all six airmen jumped to their feet. "At ease, men. I run a casual ship, so no more saluting. The first order of the day is that everything you hear in this room stays in this room. You do not breathe a word of what you learn here to anyone. Do not even discuss it among yourselves or you will end up as coyote food out in some godforsaken wilderness. Am I making myself clear?"

"Yes, sir," the six said in unison.

"Okay, pick up your pens and put that answer on paper. Read and sign this Nondisclosure Statement. Make sure you understand the full implications, gentlemen."

An hour into the class, Harry understood the secrecy and, by the end of the first week, he thought his brain would explode. ATIC was the Air Force organization that oversaw the investigation of extraterrestrial landings and crashes, and the recovery of the alien occupants. The CIA and several other covert civilian intelligence agencies were equally involved in the operation.

He learned that his first duty station would be located at one of the areas where a number of these crashes and landings had occurred in the past and were still continuing to happen. He was assigned to a duty station called Four Corners, a detachment of Masters AFB. No other explanation was offered, not even which state it was in.

One morning the instructor handed each of the airmen a small pamphlet stamped with the words: TOP SECRET/ORCON. "ORCON stands for Originator Controlled information, and remember that from now on, you are still under strict orders not to discuss anything you see or hear in class with anyone outside this room. Not even with each other. Am I understood?"

Going through the pamphlet with them page by page, their instructor carefully explained each classified project in detail, who was responsible for carrying it out, and exactly what its function was. "At the highest level of security is MAJI, or Majority Agency for Joint Intelligence. It controls all projects dealing with alien entities, concocting and distributing deliberate misinformation as a cover-up. The Director of MAJI, usually the Director of the CIA, is designated as MJ-1. He reports only to the President of the United States."

Harry learned that the Majestic-12 was a group of experts in various scientific, political, and espionage fields who were responsible for evaluating the information gained from alien life forms, then making recommendations based on this information. Each member worked independently, never meeting as a group. Moreover, each member was given only the information that pertained to his individual specialty. This information was provided strictly on a need-to-know basis. The members of this group carried a security clearance called MAJIC, or MAJI-controlled. They, too, were also responsible only to the President.

The instructor looked over the roster he'd just been handed. It was a list of the names and assignments of the six airmen. He began reading aloud, "Nadien, you're assigned to the detachment of Masters AFB located at Four Corners. It's not the real Four Corners you're expecting. You won't find it on the map. The rest of you are going to Area 51, or Dreamland, as some people call it. It's located at Groom Lake in Nevada. Don't look for any roads leading there. There's a few, but the place is so classified that it's authorized personnel only. Anyone unauthorized, civilian or military, going there disappears. No explanation given. The government knows nothing and tells nothing. As far as they're concerned, the place doesn't exist, and neither does anyone that sneaks in."

Handing each man a copy of the roster with a set of his own individual orders attached, the men actually saw the name of their next duty station printed in black and white. It added a touch of reality to the surreal scene that had been painted for them. The instructor went on, "Okay, men, now you know what the orders say, but you still don't know exactly which project you're going to be working on. Look in that white space in the middle of the page. You'll see either Project Luna or Project Pounce typed there."

Harry's orders said Project Pounce.

"Seems you airmen are going to the two projects that deal face-to-face with the alien life forms and their craft. We'll go over the rest of the projects briefly so you'll get an overview of how they all fit together. It's a real tight fit, too, just like a brand-new jigsaw puzzle. It's very critical that you know exactly what part each one plays."

Looking up from his papers the lieutenant asked, "Ready?"

"Yes, sir," they answered in unison.

"Let's go back to MAJI," the lieutenant said, "This is where everything started. Back in the late 1940s, MAJI and Project Plato established a secret treaty with the Intergalactic Council composed of planetary governments from several of the more progressive planets. Under the terms of the treaty, the aliens agreed to share scientific, medical, and technological information with us. In return, we agreed to keep their presence here on Earth a secret, and to allow them to conduct experiments on animals...and humans.

"Some of you may have heard of the so-called animal mutilations that have been occurring all over the world. I won't go into details other than to say that the animals are found with various surgically-sharp incisions, certain body parts removed, and without any blood left in their bodies. These are some of the experiments we agreed to let them conduct. Bovine DNA is very close to human DNA, and they use it in some of their cloning research. They also use it to create an artificial atmosphere conducive to raising hybrids in liquid-filled tanks. God knows what else they're doing. If any of you want to know more, I've got plenty of photographs and printed information you can read.

"MAJI also agreed to let the aliens carry out a limited number of human abductions. In return, the aliens were to provide accurate, current lists of those being abducted. Lately the lists seem to be getting smaller, but more and more people are claiming to having been abducted. There are increasing reports by abductees who are credible, responsible individuals who refuse to be silenced by the government. They suspect they're being abducted and being forced to participate in some kind of interspecies reproductive experiments where hybrid alien-human beings are created. I do know that one of these, the Humanization Project, is being conducted at Four Corners, but I don't know the details."

Pausing, the lieutenant's gaze rested briefly on each of the six students. "Everyone still with me? Any questions? Okay, there's lots more to cover. Project Aquarius is what you might call the umbrella for all the other projects. It's responsible for collecting all scientific, medical, and technological information from alien life forms, and their vehicles. Aquarius then shares this information with other intelligence agencies and with NASA for use in its space probes. This project absorbed all the projects that were established prior to it, and is 100% funded by confidential CIA funds — no appropriated government funds — no way to trace where the money comes from, or how it's spent. There are no restrictions placed, no explanations given. No questions asked. The general public has no idea it even exists. If anyone finds out, everything is denied. It's one of the blackest of the so-called black projects. Eventually the National Security Agency, or NSA, took over the management of Aquarius.

"All you airmen single? Nobody's got a wife or fiancée back home, right?" the lieutenant asked.

They looked at each other, wondering what he was getting at. How did he know? Why was that important?

"Each person assigned to the Aquarius project has to remain single during his or her tour of duty. It's always unaccompanied status. A wife left at home alone, not told anything about a husband's duty station or even where he is, is a big security risk. She feels she's entitled to know where her man is. This can't happen. Tell anybody anything about where you're stationed or what you're doing, and you're automatically guilty of a security breach and will be terminated. In plain words, gentlemen, you disappear, never to be heard from again.

"This is serious stuff, men. You've each got a Top Secret clearance. As soon as you check in at your detachment you'll be handed your MAJI clearance."

Something clicked in Harry's mind. *So this is why I got this assignment. When they ran the background check on me, they discovered that Annie and I were engaged and that she had been killed in an accident, that I didn't have much in common with my old buddies, and that I was a loner. Being practically thrown out of my family for joining the Air Force must have earned me extra points too. Things are beginning to fall into place. It's clear the NSA knows everything about me.*

Harry's reverie was interrupted by, "Nadien, let's talk about your new job on the project." The lieutenant continued, "I'm going to read what it says here in my manual. It's a little more detailed than the booklets you men have."

Harry focused on every word. "Now, Pounce was the project established to recover all crashed or safely landed crafts and aliens. Military personnel assigned to Project Pounce were stationed in several detachments located in remote areas in the southwest, including Nevada, Utah, Arizona, and New Mexico.

"The project gave out cover stories and explanations meant to satisfy local residents who witnessed the incidents and had experienced close encounters. When private citizens refused to accept the explanations given by base security, they were taken to remote locations by military police and subjected to mind manipulation. Some of these people knew what they'd seen and refused to change their accounts. They were then injected with a chemical that caused short-term memory loss, and returned to their homes. A meeting would be arranged with local and sometimes national media, where they'd issue official statements that the whole thing was a hoax.

"In addition, just to tie up any loose ends, all of the original written reports and photographs of the sightings or incidents in possession of local law enforcement officials or civilians were seized and supposedly destroyed. In reality, agents attached to Project Pounce confiscated all written records, photographs, and any physical evidence.

"This is an ongoing thing, men. It's too bad we've got to treat innocent bystanders like this, but this stuff's way too classified to take any chances. We just follow orders from higher up."

Clearing his throat, the lieutenant continued, "Project Luna is a code name that designates at least two alien underground bases that have been established with the knowledge and aid of both government and civilian agencies. One of these, Dreamland or Area 51, is located in a remote area in the Nevada desert. A smaller detachment connected with it, dealing with even more exotic spacecraft and extraterrestrials, is located at Papoose Lake, not far from Dreamland.

"The other base is called Four Corners. Both bases are heavily guarded by Delta Force personnel from the National Reconnaissance Organization, or NRO. These guys really mean business. Trespassers are shot on sight, and no explanations are required or given. The NRO has absolute responsibility for the security and welfare of all aliens or alien-connected projects wherever they are located. They make their own regulations, and answer to no one but the President."

Harry's body stiffened. *No wonder everybody I asked was so damned evasive. They were under orders not to say anything, and they weren't taking any chances. They simply didn't want to face the consequences of disclosing this information. I don't blame them.*

"Now we'll give the rest of the projects a quick once-over. If you need to know more, it's all in your pamphlet," said the lieutenant. "Or you can see me anytime before you ship out on your assignments. I'll be glad to fill you in on the details the best I can."

It's going to be hard to top Projects Pounce and Luna, Harry thought. *God, I can hardly believe I'm being exposed to all this information that the government claims is a total pack of lies. And I'm going to be perpetuating these lies.*

"Okay, men. Project Gabriel originated from German technology obtained during and after World War II. It was involved with the research and development of very low-frequency sound waves designed to disable the control systems of alien craft, and weapons. For years, residents of several states in the southwestern area of the United States have reported low-frequency humming that's not so much heard as felt. It's even been called the Taos Hum. Residents who complain are told they have overactive imaginations. Many living in these areas suffer all kinds of physical, emotional, and neurological disabilities as a result of this continuous low-frequency humming caused by this nonexistent project. When the residents become too vocal about it, the government simply circulates more disinformation, like it's probably humming air conditioner motors, just something that they've got to learn to live with. This way, we undermine the credibility of the complaining residents.

"Project Excalibur is responsible for research and development of a nuclear-powered weapon that can destroy the alien underground bases in case things get out of hand."

What do they consider "out of hand," Harry wondered. *This is truly mind-boggling. How has the government been able to keep this stuff secret for all these years?*

The lieutenant continued, "Project Garnet controls all the information on genetic manipulation being carried on by aliens. I find this one really hard to believe myself, but the aliens claim to have created the human race by hybridization, using Rhesus monkeys, and that the existence of RH-negative blood is their proof. I do know for a fact that they have been and are carrying out experiments creating hybrid human/alien life forms using human ova and sperm that they extract during abductions.

"They combine these extracts, then raise the fetuses in large tanks that look like aquariums. They use a solution of nutrients to sustain life until the hybrids are fully developed. This particular aspect of the Humanization Project is one of the conditions the government agreed to under the terms of the treaty. It's been going on for many years. I myself have seen this several times. One or two hybrids are even working in the underground labs with our scientists right now."

Looking around the class, the lieutenant's gaze lingered on Harry. *Does he mean there are some hybrids at Four Corners,* Harry wondered, his thoughts racing. *This gets crazier all the time. The real craziness is that it's all true. The aliens have been here among us for many, many years, possibly thousands of years. We've been lied to all this time. We're told we're only imagining the things we know we've really seen and experienced. All the time, nothing we could possibly imagine even comes anywhere close to the bizarre truth. And I thought my parents were controlling. No wonder this is such a well-kept secret. The few government officials and military personnel who do leak information are 'terminated,' vanishing without a trace.*

The lieutenant continued, "Sometimes the informants 'commit suicide,' always under conditions that are quickly explained in believable detail. Elaborate cover stories are immediately issued to downplay or explain away any of the leaked information. They don't discriminate — the rules of absolute silence apply equally to high-ranking government officials and lowest enlisted men alike. It's government policy."

Slowly shaking his head, the lieutenant finished, "This is a dangerous game we're playing, men. The government holds all the aces, they...we...are manipulating the destiny of the whole human race. We're not allowed to warn people about it, and we sure as hell can't let them know we're a part of it. Okay, let's continue."

By the end of the third week, they had finished the in-depth exploration of each project. Closing the manual as he finished, the lieutenant asked, "Any questions?"

If any of them had questions, no one dared voice them.

I'm glad this part of the class is over, Harry thought with relief. *My mind is saturated. Three weeks ago, I would have thought the content of the pamphlet was pure science fiction. Now I know that everything I've ever imagined before is absolutely true. And soon I'm going to be part of it, very soon.*

"I know you're all anxious to hear about the 'little green men.' You'll be learning about them next week," the instructor said, with a hollow laugh.

The six airmen smiled faintly in return. Seeing actual photographs of spacecraft and whatever or whoever was piloting them was not a subject they were prepared to deal with yet. Their senses were still reeling from what they'd learned up to this point.

Right now, a weekend break sounds good to me, thought Harry. *A couple of days' rest for my poor boggled mind and about fifty laps in the Airman's Club pool might clear my thinking a little. Geez, I can't remember ever feeling more confused. Is the military just playing the same games my parents do, pretending their problems don't exist, or eliminating them when they do appear? All the time controlling their family on a larger scale, a cosmic scale? What about these hybrids at Four Corners? Are they a part of this family, my new family, too?*

Getting up from his seat, Harry walked slowly out of the classroom and into the Airman's Club. In the changing room, he stripped the clothes off his muscular six-foot four-inch frame, and tried to shed the thoughts weighing heavily on his mind. The act of swimming seemed mundane after what he had been learning all week, but he needed to do something physical, something that required a minimum of concentration. His mind and body both needed some cooling off.

Chuckling to himself, Harry recalled words on the recruiting office poster back in Nampa, "Join the Navy. See the World."

Well, I joined the Air Force instead of the Navy, he thought, *but I'm going to see this world, and cold, hard evidence of several other worlds, too. Being on the inside of the greatest secret ever is sort of thrilling in a way. Scary but thrilling. Just knowing this stuff has certainly changed my life. Nothing will ever be the same.*

His body knifed into the liquid coolness, slicing away the concerns and apprehensions of the last few weeks as he entered the aquatic world. For a good half-hour, he focused on his breathing and strokes, becoming a single-pointed swimming machine.

Showering afterwards, the thoughts began again. *One thing's for sure. The Air Force is right in saying there are no such things as unidentified flying objects. We've identified every single one of them. And there are aliens living on Earth, interbreeding with us, establishing a new hybrid species. We've hidden them at our bases and helped them, guarding them with our most elite security forces.*

We're interacting with them, not hesitating a second to kill any of our own people who talk about it. Are the extraterrestrials more important than U.S. citizens? I sure hope the technology we're getting in return justifies the experiments and the killings. And have aliens struck the same deal with other countries? If so, we've got to keep up, or someone else will become the dominant force on this planet.

In just a few more weeks, I'll be seeing my first aliens face to face. Christ, the more I think about it, the more it seems like I'm in some kind of weird dream. Only I hope this dream isn't steadily, relentlessly, and uncontrollably edging into a nightmare.

Chapter 5

Assignment: Four Corners — 1955

Early Monday morning Harry was back in the classroom. Part of him was eager to begin the next phase of his training, but another part was apprehensive about what he'd learn.

The instructor began, "This week will be devoted to the various types of craft recovered, including those that have landed without mishap. NASA conducts extensive laboratory analyses of recovered craft, and their findings are backed up by labs at MIT and other universities. The outcome is always the same—materials and alloys unknown. Likewise, the method of propulsion is a complete mystery, although the aerospace engineers are convinced that more than one method is used, depending on the design of the individual craft. They've tried retro-engineering because there seems no other way to figure out the propulsion systems. But the government's equipment lacks the proper degree of sophistication to accomplish anything definitive. To complicate things, many times extremely high levels of radiation extend far into the surrounding area.

"Most of the crashed craft explode and burn on impact, incinerating both vehicle and occupants. Those shot down either by accident or intentionally by the Air Force are nearly always in the same condition. Only rarely are the occupants of a craft recovered alive. Those who live through the landing almost never survive for any length of time.

"All you men will begin your new tour of duty as part of the security team at the projects. Your jobs will be to pick up the pieces of craft found at the crash site once the medical team has recovered its crew. If there are any live aliens, they'll be picked up and transported to the medical lab before you're allowed to go in. If they're dead, you'll still have to wait until they're put in body bags and taken to the pathology lab for analysis."

Pausing, the lieutenant looked around the room to see how his students were handling this information. They silently waited for him to continue.

"You'll have a grid map of the area, and you'll be assigned to check each grid, one by one, until you're sure you've picked up every last trace of wreckage. Most of the time, you'll have to wait until the heat dissipates. Sometimes the heat is so intense you can't touch a thing for hours afterward. There's not that much urgency connected to that part of the investigation—it can take as long as necessary.

"You'll be undergoing a couple of days' orientation on these things as soon as you get to the detachment. They'll tell you exactly what to do, and how to do it. The crew you'll be assigned to has been there a few months, and it doesn't take long to get lots of experience. They'll clue you in on whatever you need to know."

Harry's mind wandered from picking up pieces of crashed craft to images of what an intact vehicle might look like. Focusing in again, he realized that was exactly what was now being discussed in class.

The lieutenant was explaining, "These craft come in all sizes and shapes, from small ovals fifteen or twenty feet in diameter to long, cigar-shaped craft the size of a football field, or larger. A few are triangular in shape and very shallow in depth, but none of these have ever made a witnessed landing, and we can only speculate on the extraterrestrial life forms that might pilot such exotic-appearing craft. Every craft has two things in common: materials and method of propulsion unknown.

"Some project members theorize that the differences in appearance of the craft may be related to the purpose of its expedition to Earth. Larger craft with several inner compartments containing medical facilities and equipment are used in the abduction of humans, and animals, allowing ample space to run their experiments. Smaller ships are believed to be used for reconnaissance. All this is strictly conjecture. No one knows for sure. The hybrids participating in the exchange projects at Area 51 and Four Corners arrive in craft of the smaller type.

"We never find food supplies on board a vehicle. However, we often find plastic-like bottles containing a liquid resembling water which we assume to be some type of nutritional supplement.

"The crews on some of the ships have an insect-like appearance. Chemical analysis has determined that they're chlorophyll-based life forms that seem to require a type of liquid nutrition, which they absorb through their skin because they lack a discernible digestive system. This may explain the containers of liquid discovered on their craft."

Day after day the class studied photographs and plans of the various types of craft. Their heads felt as if they would explode with all the mind-boggling information. On Friday afternoon, the instructor finally said, "That's enough for this week. I'm sure your brains need a rest. But men, take my word for it, you ain't heard nothin' yet. The best is yet to come," he added with a knowing grin.

Sitting back in his chair, Harry was both fascinated and stunned by what he'd learned. This stuff was the real thing. All the stories he'd heard for years about UFOs and extraterrestrials were confirmed. So much for the public dismissals of UFOs as weather balloons, swamp gas, the planet Venus, or worse yet, someone's half-baked hallucination.

He'd trusted the image that life's mirror had reflected back to him. Now he knew it was an illusion, a two-way glass, reflecting what he perceived, but with much more going on behind it. As class progressed, his feelings of uneasiness had increased. He was overwhelmed with differing emotions. Excitement over all this incredible information, resentment at being lied to, embarrassment at not having seen through the lies, anger at having been taken as a dupe, disgust at how his government deliberately made fools of innocent, unsuspecting people, and empathy for the ordinary citizens who really had seen spacecraft or extraterrestrials and conscientiously reported their sightings, only to be publicly ridiculed. All the while the CIA, other intelligence agencies, and the military carried out their highly classified investigation of each incident — working side by side with the aliens. Harry asked himself, *Which is worse? The honest activities and intentions of the extraterrestrials or our double-dealing government? And now I'll be one of them.*

Even the President himself, several of them in fact, had sat in the White House, controlling the whole damned operation, instructing the military to fabricate whatever stories would sound most plausible to fit each incident as it occurred.

The lieutenant was winding things down for the day. "One last thing. On every craft and on every extraterrestrial's uniform, we've seen a triangle with three horizontal lines running through it. We call it a trilateral insignia. We think it must be some kind of universal symbol, representing a federation or large group. Over the weekend, try to relax and have a little fun. There are plenty more photos and drawings of craft and their pilots to discuss. The material you'll be getting next week will have details on dimensions, and what specifics we've gleaned from our investigations. Just bear in mind that once you're out on the site, you'll probably see quite a few that aren't in the book. Okay, men. Dismissed. See you Monday."

Arriving early for his last week of class, Harry could barely contain his enthusiasm. He was eager to learn more about what other forms of extraterrestrial life looked like. He wanted to get to his new duty station at Four Corners, where he'd be face-to-face with the real thing.

Smiling at Harry, the lieutenant handed him a booklet bearing the words: TOP SECRET/MAJIC and the trilateral insignia on the cover. It was much thicker than the other booklets had been.

The lieutenant took advantage of being alone with Harry to ask, "Nadien, you seem more interested in the subject matter than the others. You tested higher than average, and you're the youngest in the class. How'd you manage to get assigned to ATIC straight out of basic?"

Harry was at a loss about how to answer, and the lieutenant sat down on the next desk. "At ease, airman. This is between you and me. Off the record. I can see you've got a special interest in this whole thing. Special aptitude, too, from what I can tell by your work in this class. I'm going to recommend through channels that you spend only six months on the perimeter team instead of the normal two years. Then you'll be assigned directly to the Blue Team. They're the outfit that goes in first to investigate all the incidents that take place at Four Corners. They recover the live crew members, and escort them to the underground facility for medical treatment if it's needed. They also carry out interrogations right at the site whenever possible. In short, you'd be part of the welcoming committee."

Glancing toward the door, he continued, "It's part of my job to keep an eye out for any airmen who show special interest in the projects. You appear to have the right qualifications to join the Blue Team. Some guys do great in class, but they don't have what it takes to handle the emotional trauma of dealing with aliens face-to-face. I reviewed your background check, and it shows you've been successfully dealing with some heavy-duty personal problems for a long time. You don't let anybody step on you, and you keep a cool head no matter what. I've already talked to Headquarters at ATIC and Colonel Walker, the commander at Four Corners, and they want you on the Blue Team as soon as possible."

He looked Harry straight in the eye and asked, "What do you think, Nadien?"

Realizing he'd been singled out for a very special assignment, Harry was caught completely off guard. He managed to express his gratitude the best he could. "Thank you, sir. That's quite an honor. I hope I can handle it okay. I expected I'd have to work my way up like everybody else."

The words seemed totally inadequate, but it was all he could manage for the moment. Smiling, the lieutenant assured him, "You'll do just fine, Nadien. Maybe one of these days you'll be the one I talk to at Four Corners to recommend a sharp young airman for the Blue Team. Who knows?"

Harry was in a state of complete shock. Things seemed to be accelerating rapidly. He thought, *I don't know if I'm ready. I feel as if I'm on a runaway horse and have just dropped the reins. I've got a feeling this is going to be one hell of a ride.*

The day flew by. There seemed to be as many different kinds of extraterrestrials as there were craft. He'd been prepared to be repulsed, maybe even disgusted at the sight of living, breathing nonhuman beings but on the contrary, he was fascinated with everything he learned, awestruck by the sheer diversity in appearance of these space travelers. They ran the gamut from insect-like, to plant-like, to mutated humanoid, to the offspring of experimentation in the hybridization of humans and extraterrestrials. He was even more impatient for the training to be finished so he could actually see some of these entities in real life.

The instructor explained, "The big Greys, so-called because of their height and gray-blue skin color, frequently appear threatening, and are extremely difficult to communicate with, but, to date, none of them has posed any physical danger to Blue Team members. This particular group of extraterrestrials never remains on the ground long, emerging from their craft for only short periods. They never allow team members to approach closer than thirty feet, which is probably just as well because they give off an unpleasant, dank body odor, similar to the smell of wet cardboard, or an old cellar that's been closed up for a long time. We believe that these Greys are responsible for the majority of human abductions and animal mutilations. They usually travel in craft of enormous size, sometimes the size of a football field, maybe even larger."

Harry hoped his first encounter with aliens wouldn't be with them, but he guessed he wouldn't have a lot of choice in the matter. He'd have to handle whoever, or whatever, whenever they arrived.

For the next five days, the lieutenant told the class all that was known of each type of extraterrestrial race that had visited Earth, and towards the end of the last day, Harry had decided he'd rather deal with the smaller ones whose skin was a yellowish-green color. According to the book, their appearance was more insect-like and they moved in a jerky, awkward way. But they appeared much more friendly and, on every landing, had been the first to initiate a thought-transference type of communication. Many of them had long, thin, spindly arms and legs that reminded Harry of a praying mantis.

These were the extraterrestrials who had offered to share their knowledge with humanity, and were presently working with government scientists in the underground laboratories at Four Corners and Area 51. According to the treaty established between the U.S. Government and the Intergalactic Council, a rotating schedule had been set up where a few of the most outstanding researchers from various galaxies spent several months at a time at Four Corners. Then, returning to their homes, they were replaced with a new group.

Harry thought, *What the heck, we're all part of the same family. Everyone has some strange-looking relatives in their family tree. This assignment is definitely going to be the most interesting thing that's ever happened to me. I'm as ready as I'll ever be for ATIC and the Blue Team.*

When the course ended, it was time for Harry to leave Crawford for his new post. *The subject matter's been intense,* he thought, *and it's a relief to have it all behind me now. I'm looking forward to just kicking back and taking it easy while I enjoy the scenery during a leisurely drive up to Four Corners. My poor mind sure needs a rest before I have to face the reality of dealing with extraterrestrials. I feel as if I've just stepped through the looking glass door of reality. I hope it's not a one-way mirror.*

Chapter 6

Jon's True Nature — 1971

"Okay, guys, drinks are on me," Jon exclaimed, bursting through the door of the Drop Inn, a neighborhood bar near his home. "I'm gettin' close to a new job. Let's celebrate."

Marisa's stepfather had no real friends, just booze buddies. Deep down he knew their friendship lasted only as long as he kept paying for their drinks, but this was something he didn't want to admit to himself. Unable to relate to people at all unless he was drinking, he wanted them to be drinking too. Considering himself superior to others, he'd gone to great lengths to cultivate a cynical, sardonic manner which he considered a social asset, but in reality ended up turning most folks off.

Hurrying home from classes at Foothill Junior College where he was majoring in police science, he'd stopped by his house only long enough to drop off his books and put on a clean shirt. He was a fanatic about cleanliness, but mainly he wanted to appear fresh when he got to the Drop Inn so as to impress the hookers who hung out there.

"By God," he'd brag, "women really go for a man with clean clothes. Makes 'em fuckin' hot. Think you dressed up special just for them. Put on a buncha Aqua Velva too. Gets their damn hormones ragin'. Can't keep their hands off a man when they get wind of that."

Nodding, the barflies agreed, "Yeah, Jon, it does make all the difference in the world," all the while thinking to themselves,

The big difference is if we agree with you, you buy us more booze. Sucker, you can look like Mickey Mouse and smell like Miss Piggy as long as you're buyin', we don't care.

The smiling hookers congregated in the back of the room hoisted their glasses in mock salute of Jon's profound wisdom. They had put the word out to the regulars at the bar that Jon couldn't get it up any more and, on those rare occasions when he did, it was lost in a hurry. He was an easy mark for them, the easiest john any of them had ever found. All they had to do was keep telling him how great he was in bed, and he bought it hook, line, and sinker. *Stupid fucker,* they thought. *Easy money.*

"Pompous ass, why doesn't he realize everyone here knows the details of his sex life, or the lack of it?" one hooker whispered, not too quietly, to another.

"Shhhh. He's good cheap entertainment for the bar. We all get free drinks as long as his money holds out."

"Simple bastard, he's so stupid he doesn't have the slightest idea that people are laughing at him. Can't even feel sorry for him, he doesn't deserve it. A fool and his money...."

"Come on, gals. Snuggle on up to Big Jon, I'm gettin' lonely," he yelled towards the hookers. Turning to the bartender, he spoke loudly. "People like a man who'll buy for the bar. Line 'em up again."

That was their cue. The girls would sidle up, sit at the bar with him, making sure he got really smashed. Then one or two, sometimes three of them, depending on how many twenties he'd flashed, would help him out the back door and around the back of the building where they had a few rooms reserved for their trade.

Once he was in their room, he would pass out as soon as he hit the bed. The girls, taking their usual twenty each, plus any extra ones, fives, and pocket change, would pull his boots and pants off, leaving him in the room to sleep it off. They didn't have to do a thing for their money other than sit there and wait for a few minutes until they were sure he was out cold. Then they'd go back to the bar and laugh. When he came to, he'd see that his pants were off and figure he'd made out like a stud.

"Jeezus, I must have been pretty damn good! Made myself pass out," he'd tell himself after waking up, completely oblivious to what had gone on. *Wonder why they're always gone when I wake up. But, hey, if they took my money, I must have made out with 'em. They'd never cheat me. They're good honest girls, work hard for their money, by God.*

He treated them right, and he was sure they did the same by him.

The hookers all liked to see him come in. Always drunk on his ass by the time they got him to the room, he was the easiest trick they'd ever had. It was nothing short of a miracle, though, that he never figured out he spent all that money for nothing. "His loss is our gain," they joked amongst themselves. The next time they saw him in the bar, they'd call to him, "Hey, Jon, you were really great last time. What a stud! Can't wait until next time."

He lapped up their lies as fast as he did the booze.

His routine was to stagger home, barge into the house making as much noise as possible, and turn on all the lights as he headed for the bedroom. He usually woke Helen to see if she had anything to say about where he'd been, and why he'd been out so late.

Bracing herself when she heard his pickup door slam, Helen would turn over in bed and face away from the bedroom door, hoping he'd think she was asleep. She didn't want to risk another beating from him. Usually if she just lay still and didn't answer him, he'd flick her bedroom light on and off a few times, then stagger down the hall, muttering loudly, "What a fucking bitch."

The kitchen was next to catch hell. He would slam dishes around, bang the refrigerator door, then turn on the television full blast to see if that would get a rise out of his wife. Walking back to his bedroom, he'd stop outside Helen's door, rattle the doorknob a few times, and call her a few more ugly names. Then he'd stagger into the guest bedroom, slam the door until the windows rattled, and pass out on the bed. Except for his snoring, that would be the last Helen would hear of him for the rest of the night.

These days he was on a power trip. He was in his last year of police science at the local junior college. Part of the program included volunteer duty riding on patrol with deputies from the sheriff's department. He loved the excitement of the midnight to eight shift he was assigned to on weekends.

He was in total agreement with the unwritten rule of law enforcement, observed by almost every one of the deputies in the department—that family disputes and incest reports took last priority as far as investigation went. Women and children were a man's property and what he did with them was his own business. As for protecting them against the man of the house, no fuckin' way.

Hey, a husband beats up on his wife and kids, who gives a fuck? he thought. *Goddamn woman probably got mouthy, and deserved a beating. Old man's got a right to keep her in her place. So what, if she gets all banged up. Next time she'll think twice about gettin' on his case fer screwing around. Shit, a man's gotta have a little fun, ain't he?*

He'd heard most of the deputies say something to this effect time after time, and loved it.

Rape? Incest? Who gives a damn? Way most women act and dress, they're just looking fer it. Kids, too. Goddamn jailbait. Got no right to turn the old man in. All he does is just give 'em what they're looking for!

After his first weekend riding on patrol, he knew he'd picked the right career, and boasted to a drinking buddy, "I can drink on duty, arrest a hooker and get all the free pussy I want in exchange for letting her go. And once I get hired in the right department, I can go on the take. And best of all, 'cause all the bosses do the same thing, I'll never get busted for any of it. Yep, law enforcement definitely takes care of its own. Gives us officers whatever keeps us happy. It's almost too damn good to be true."

Chapter 7

Marisa Reflects on her Past — 1972

Waking early Saturday morning, Marisa ran her fingers over the raised characters on her Braille alarm clock, 3:30.

Excited and apprehensive, she lay in the darkness, her mind racing through the day's plan. First, Mom and Jon will leave the house around six-thirty. Then Bobby will be here around seven. Have I forgotten anything? What will it be like living in my new apartment? It's going to be so much fun getting to know Raechel. I think I'm all packed and ready. I've got to try and relax for a couple of hours until my alarm goes off. Sleep's definitely out of the question, though.

Marisa's mind raced on. What about Mom? We don't always agree but, no matter what, she loves me. I'm going to miss her, and I know she'll miss me. We've become so close lately, since my older brothers moved out. But nothing and no one are going to keep me here. Mom's tough and she'll understand once she gets over the initial shock. She'll be relieved to know I'm starting a new life on my own.

Marisa remembered her mother telling her, "I was born and raised on a farm. My family scraped by. Mom and Dad had wanted a boy, and they weren't pleased at having a girl, something they never let me forget. I had to do heavy farm work just as if I'd been a boy. My father needed an extra, unpaid hand and I was that hand. I wanted to earn his approval and did my best, but it did no good. Work was his love, and his god, and he worshipped it faithfully every day. And I was just a goddamned girl who barely paid her way."

Lying in bed, the softness of the covers brushing her chin, Marisa remembered her mother telling how it felt to grow up with her mother or father never once saying they loved her, never having felt loving arms around her, or the comfort of a hug or a kiss. On the few occasions when she had tried to take her mother's hand or kiss her goodnight, she'd invariably been brushed away and told that she was making a spectacle of herself. Her mother's disapproving looks were the only response she'd ever received.

She had not been allowed to laugh, or to cry out loud. "Emotions are to be held back and kept under control," her mother had said. "Never let anyone know how you feel. What will people say? What will they think?"

"As a little girl, I developed a hard, unemotional shell that protected my aching heart," her mother once confided. "Soon I didn't care much at all about what people said, and even less what they thought. Inside, though, I knew there was something dreadfully lacking in my life. But what was it? Love? Emotion? I didn't know. I envied other children when I saw them being hugged when their mothers picked them up from school. And when they dropped their kids off in the morning, they'd say 'I love you' to them."

Hearing this had brought tears to Marisa's eyes, as her mother had continued, "Early on, I decided that when I left home and made a life for myself, I would express exactly how I felt, no matter what my parents or other people might think. Living like a robot, without love, was something I'd never do again. I lavished all my affection on the farm animals, especially the horses and cats. I had to be discreet, though, because my father would beat me if he caught me being 'foolish' as he called it."

Marisa reached out and stroked Bo. He was only animal they had now, and they both talked to him as though he were a person who might take an active part in their conversations. They knew that he understood what they said to him, at least most of the time.

To the still-sleeping cat, Marisa whispered, "Mom will never abandon you, Bo. She won't leave you in this god-forsaken house when she makes her escape."

She felt sorry for her mother. She hadn't planned for her life to turn out like this. "I only wanted to help Jon through his drinking problem," she once confessed. "It didn't work out that way, though. But I'll pick up the pieces of my life once I get away from him.

"I've wanted to leave and take you with me, but locked into that job as a file clerk at the base, there was no way I could support both of us. When I checked with Welfare to see if they could give me some assistance, they told me I made too much money. If I'd been a drug addict or an alcoholic who refused to work, or if my skin were a different color, Welfare would have helped me in an instant. 'To hell with the system,' I told them as I stomped out of the office. I resolved to do it on my own. It might take me a little longer, and I'll have to put up with a little more abuse, but one day we're going to make it out of this hell-hole.

"I've been taking Air Force correspondence courses, and night classes at the junior college to prepare myself for a higher-paying job as a buyer in the Procurement Division. I'll take the proficiency test in a month or so and, if I score high enough, I'll be eligible for a big promotion. I've already talked to the division director about it, and he said I could have the job if I pass the test and get my name on the roster. Until then, I'll have to keep out of Jon's way as much as possible, and put up with his drunken rages.

"It's not easy to handle Jon's provocation and antagonism, but I've learned to tune him out, and let him rant and rave, and slam dishes, pots, and pans until he gets tired. Whatever he does to the house doesn't really matter any more. I've given up on ever making it a home. Nothing much matters to me any more except you, Marisa. My life is on hold until I can leave the son-of-a-bitch. Nobody's going to help me. I've already found that out the hard way. The protective shell I developed in my youth still serves me well.

"To escape the miseries of my home life, I married young, having mistaken sex for love. I divorced your father after a few years and married Jon, ending up in an even worse mess. Both marriages have been nothing but empty shells. All my life, I've been cheated out of the one thing I desire most. Love."

Marisa remembered her mom even calling the police a few times after being beaten. The responding officers didn't seem to care. They just sat around the kitchen table drinking beer with Jon while they made a big show about questioning her and writing down her complaint. In the few instances they actually filed a report, she was described as unstable, her husband coming up smelling like a rose, a hero trying to subdue his hysterical wife. The police never took photographs of her bruises and cuts, using lame excuses such as, "Sorry, ma'am, but someone on the previous shift must have taken the camera out of our squad car or forgot the film."

Her mom had told her, "It seemed they would screw up the evidence on purpose, one time telling me, 'A physical examination isn't necessary.' Or they'd conveniently forget to read Jon his rights. They had supreme power, made their own rules, and nearly everyone played by them. The few new recruits who showed some compassion to victims were denied promotions, and their lives made a living hell until they either moved on or knuckled under."

"I once attended an Al-Anon meeting because I'd heard they provided emotional support to people who lived with alcoholics. When I got home that night, Jon forced me to tell him where I'd been and I got the worst beating of my life, ended up in the emergency room with two black eyes, a big bruise on my cheek, and two stitches in my forehead. So much for Al-Anon. There was no way they could possibly ever give me enough emotional support to make me risk another beating like that."

Marisa recalled that about a month later, in sheer desperation, her mother had attended an afternoon church meeting across town that advertised help for people with troubled marriages. After explaining her situation, the church counselor told her, "According to the Bible, a wife is always subject to the will of her husband in every way. You must be doing something wrong to incur your husband's wrath. You must repent, mend your ways, pray to God for forgiveness, and everything will be fine."

Once back home, her mom had confided in her, "I walked out of that meeting muttering to myself, 'You religious bastard. Using the old guilt trip. Make the victim believe she caused the crime. So much for your help.'"

"Oh, Mom, you're tough, you'll make it. And I will too," Marisa whispered into her pillow. Reaching for her clock once again, she felt the raised characters on the dial. It was almost time to get up, another half hour.

Snuggling with Bo in the early morning quiet, she felt the familiar swish of his tail against her leg. He was waking up and in a few minutes he'd be wide awake, in full attack mode, playing with her toes.

Forcing herself to relax a few moments longer, Marisa remembered what her mother had told her when she'd come back from the church meeting, *They say God helps those who help themselves. I'll do whatever it takes to get away from that sick, perverted son-of-a-bitch. No matter what he does to me, I'll keep my sanity, and I'll be a success in spite of him. If I can just hold on a little longer, this nightmare will be over. We'll be safe, and he can go straight to hell. Well, they would both escape, just not together.*

Thinking of the faded print of Jesus, she determined, *I'm taking you with me, Jesus, and I know you'll help me no matter what happens. With your help, no one is ever going to stop me from reaching my goals.*

Bo stopped his attack on her toes and started purring as he cuddled close to her side. Marisa's mind drifted back to when she was very young, maybe five or six, and her real father had lived with them back east. He'd been a country musician, very handsome, and had always dressed in expensive custom-made western suits trimmed with rhinestones and fringe so that he'd look good on stage. Now she realized that he'd wanted to look good to the girls in the audience.

Teenage girls called the house at all hours of the day or night. Age or looks didn't matter, he gave his phone number to any female who asked for it. Whenever Marisa answered the telephone, the girls always sounded upset when she told them her father wasn't home, and even more upset when she asked, "But would you like to speak to my mom?"

Marisa remembered the time the three of them had gone out to dinner. Two flashily dressed women, obviously fans, came over to the table and asked for his autograph. They looked at the woman and girl also at the table and asked, "Who are they?"

Her dad replied, "Uh, that's my sister and my niece. We're having dinner before they fly home to Chicago tonight. Give me your number and I'll call you as soon as I get back from the airport."

Marisa still remembered the hurt and humiliation she saw on her mother's face when he said that. She'd wanted to cry right there at the table, but didn't. She just sat quietly, glancing back and forth from her mother to her father.

Out in the parking lot, he told them, "I said that so they'd think I was single. Shit, I never wanted to be married in the first place, and I couldn't have any fun if women knew I had a wife and kid. Such a pair of goddamn frumps, too. I'm going places, and it won't be with either one of you. What I need is a woman who's a real looker, one who looks like she knows how to give a man a good time. God, a family is such a drag."

At that time she didn't know what the word "frump" meant, but from the expression on her mother's face, she knew it wasn't anything good. She'd had no idea of what was going on then, but she understood perfectly now.

Marisa didn't see much of her father after that. He moved out of the house and in with one of his girlfriends a week later. Finances became a real problem after he left. He didn't leave them any money, just huge credit card bills for his fancy clothes and extravagant gifts for his girlfriends. Marisa realized that her father didn't love her any more, if he ever had. He never once asked if she needed more insulin or needles, or the little blood sugar test kit she had to have for her diabetes. Or even whether they needed money to pay for her monthly checkups at the doctor's office.

Reflecting on all these things as she lay in bed waiting for morning to arrive, she saw clearly just how selfish and cruel her father had been. She'd never once heard from him in all these years, not at Christmas, or on her birthday. She wondered if she'd ever meet him again, or if she even wanted to.

Chapter 8

Harry Arrives at Four Corners — 1956

Stowing his duffle bag in the trunk of his old Chevy, Harry carefully laid his uniform-filled garment bags on top of it. The sergeant in personnel had told him, "Nadien, travel in civilian clothes, keep yer uniforms out of sight. Don't tell anybody yer military. Don't tell nobody where yer headed. Jest change the subject if someone tries to get nosy. Most of the time, it's jest some local tryin' ta strike up a conversation, then again it might not be."

Closing the trunk solidly, he took one last look around the base, thinking this might be the last traditional military installation he'd be seeing for a long time. Things could get wild from here on out.

Picking up his travel orders, he drew his pay and an extra check to cover travel expenses. The sergeant handed Harry a piece of paper with a telephone number scratched on it and instructed, "When ya get to Ely, stop at a phone booth and call this number. It's the detachment where yer going. Ely's a couple hunderd miles north of where yer headed, but when ya start gittin' closer, ya'll have to take some back roads. And watch for the landmarks they tell ya about. There won't be any signs to where yer goin', so ya need ta write down whatever directions they give ya and follow 'em real close. It's big country out there and ya don't wanna get yerself lost."

The sergeant's voice dropped a couple of notes, and his tone turned dead serious, "This is off the record, Nadien. Yer life ain't never gonna be the same once ya leave here. I wish to God I was goin' with ya, but Four Corners ain't no place fer an old man. Take care of yerself, Nadien. Good luck."

"Thank you, sir," Harry said, saluting the grizzled old sergeant. Turning, he walked outside and climbed into his car. He drove to the Credit Union, cashed the expense check and got travelers checks in exchange for his paycheck.

He'd checked the oil and battery earlier that morning. The tires still boasted a hint of tread, hopefully enough to get him to the detachment. He had three days to make the trip, so he could take it easy.

He drove south, picking up sections of Interstate 30 and 80, which were under construction, for the long drive west. As the miles rolled by, he thought about his parents. After getting the cold shoulder when he'd returned home after basic, he'd written them a few letters, and gotten no response. Now he was headed to a detachment where communication with family was forbidden. His parents had just beaten him to the punch when they cut him off, so the guilt was all on their shoulders, not his.

The thought of Annie drifted into his mind. *Damn,* he thought. *I wish I could come to terms with losing her. She was the one person who truly understood and loved me, and now she's gone.* When the loneliness was about to drive him crazy, she came to him. Just as he awoke in the morning, he'd catch the scent of her perfume on him, as if she had been in his arms. He could shower off her scent, but he couldn't, wouldn't, wash her memory out of his mind.

After crossing into Wyoming, Harry pulled off the road for a pit stop in Cheyenne. With a meal inside him and a full tank of gas, he was ready to tackle the 400-mile run to Salt Lake City.

After six hours, he'd almost made the Utah border but exhaustion forced him to call it a night.

Sunday he awoke refreshed, and after breakfast he navigated Salt Lake City and headed out across the Great Salt Lake. It was a long, boring stretch, but offered the reward of a little gambling at one of the many truck stops in Wendover. He left the Interstate and headed south on Highway 93 to the town of Ely, a dot on the map and home to about 5,000 souls. Immediately he ran into the spectacular sight of red rock buttes scored by deep canyons. The signs proclaiming OPEN RANGE. WATCH FOR CATTLE weren't fooling. There were more cattle than cars on the road.

He assumed the occasional dirt road branching from the highway, snaking off out of sight over the hills, meant there was a ranch somewhere in the vicinity. Once he noticed a homemade sign by the roadside, "5-Bar Cattle Company," then ten miles further down the road, another one that proclaimed "Black Rock Ranch." Sometimes there was just a sand-blasted and sun-bleached board lying in the dust, a remnant of someone's failed dream.

Gradually the Earth's scenery gave way to a lunar-like landscape of steep, forbidding mountain ranges with stark, barren peaks, sliced by deep canyons hinting at silent sentinels guarding hidden mysteries within. With the air clean and crisp, he could see clear to the distant horizon that beckoned him on, enticing him into his future.

In a blink-and-you-miss-it town, he found the only motel and wondered which it had the most of—fleas or slot machines. After a meal washed down with a beer in lieu of the undrinkable coffee, he turned in, determined to make an early start in the morning.

Rising before dawn on Monday, he felt like a child on Christmas morning. He realized this was the day he'd been subconsciously anticipating all his life. Tossing his overnight bag in his Chevy, he walked across the street to the local café for breakfast. The greasy odors turned his stomach, so he turned and left. On the edge of town, a sign announced: ELY 57. Glancing at his watch, he thought, *It's nearly seven, I'll be there by nine easy for a real breakfast. Should have plenty of time to get to my destination in the daylight, too. No sense in driving around in the dark trying to find a place that doesn't exist.*

Parking at the Lucky Coin Casino, he walked in through the front door. A row of vacant telephone booths lined one wall, facing a row of slot machines on the other. Making his phone call, he wrote down the directions, then read them back to make sure he'd gotten them correct. Crossing the lobby to the Sagebrush Grill, he ordered the house special, a sixteen-ounce steak, fries, and trimmings.

Finishing his meal, he walked back into the casino, and bought a roll of nickels from the cashier. Idly strolling around the large room, stretching his legs, he saw a vacant slot machine with three coins lying in its tray. Picking a nickel out of the tray he fed it into the machine and pulled the handle. Three bars slid around, aligning themselves on the center line. Lights began flashing and bells ringing, signaling a $10 jackpot. He played three more coins, and more bells and lights signaled a $30 win. Looking at his watch, he saw it was almost one. Damn, just when I was on a roll. Anyway, I'm under twenty-one, and they'll confiscate my winnings if they catch me. Quit while you're ahead, kid, he told himself.

Scooping his winnings into the plastic bucket provided between the machines, he took the coins to the cashier's cage and cashed them in. Stuffing the $40 into his pocket, he thought, *I hope that's a good omen.* He filled his car with gas and headed back out into the lunar landscape. As he continued down Highway 93 through the surreal scenery, he felt mounting excitement at entering another world. *An isolated, secret world far from prying eyes and probing questions,* thought Harry. *A world the average*

Joe knew nothing of, and would probably scoff at. God, real aliens who had piloted real spacecraft across countless light years to this planet. And tomorrow, I'll be meeting them...maybe.

He slipped the paper with the directions into the slot in the center of the steering wheel so he wouldn't have to take his eyes off the road when he read it. "Exactly 135 miles south of Ely," the voice on the phone had said. As the numbers rolled up into place on the odometer, he looked to his right and saw the remnants of an old cattle-loading chute. If he hadn't been looking for a pile of lumber next to an unpaved road overgrown with scraggly weeds, he certainly would have driven right past without giving it a second thought.

Pulling off onto the nondescript dirt road, he dropped the transmission into second and drove at about fifteen miles an hour. Huge billows of dust poured out from behind his vehicle. Half a mile from the highway, he geared down to first, creeping carefully over a ridge. Cresting the hill, the overgrown, nearly impassable dirt track transformed into a wide gravel road that had obviously been graded recently. It snaked around in corkscrew fashion for no apparent reason for exactly five miles from the main road, just as the directions said.

Approaching a fork in the road, he chose the left path. As he reached the summit of the next hill, an eight-foot high fence told him he'd arrived. Constructed of heavy-gauge steel mesh topped by concertina-like coils of razor wire, it stretched as far as he could see in either direction. Attached to each side of the wide gate that spanned the road, large signs read, "PROPERTY OF U.S. GOVERNMENT. DO NOT ENTER. USE OF DEADLY FORCE AUTHORIZED."

Just outside the gate on either side of the road stood two enormous guards in unmarked fatigues, each wearing a double holster around his waist and carrying an MP6 assault rifle. Beside each man sat the meanest-looking dogs Harry had ever seen. *Christ, they look like they eat railroad spikes, not dog chow,* he thought. *What breed are they? They look like a mix of Doberman, English mastiff, pit bull, and lion. Don't think I'll be petting those critters. Looking from the dogs to the MPs, he figured it was a toss-up as to which looked more menacing. God, I hope they don't ask me to get out of the car.*

Several hundred yards on the far side of the gate, he saw what appeared to be an old abandoned ranch house and several long, weathered barns with swayback roofs. Parked behind one of the barns was a five-ton truck with a camouflage paint job.

As the MPs and dogs walked up to his car, he rolled the window down, opened his briefcase, and removed his orders. A guard and dog team approached the driver's side. The dog's bloodshot eyes glowed a dull red as it peered through the open window, lips curled back, revealing menacing fangs. Transfixed by the creature, Harry gazed back into its flaming eyes, thinking, *Christ, it doesn't even look like a dog.* His near panic was broken by the MP asking, "Can I help you, sir?"

"Airman Nadien reporting for duty!" he said bravely, handing the orders to the guard who scanned them briefly, handed them back, and waved him on through, his demeanor softening immediately.

"Straight ahead to the barn and park beside the truck. Colonel Walker's expecting you. Welcome to Four Corners!"

The guard and the creature from hell took a few steps back while the gate slowly swung open. Harry noted that the guard hadn't activated the gate, so he assumed it was operated remotely by someone he couldn't see. There was more here than met the eye.

He inched his car through the gate toward the derelict buildings. As the gate swung shut behind him, the guards and dogs assumed their original positions.

"Well, I'm finally here," Harry muttered. *Doesn't look much like I expected, though. Everything's falling down. And there aren't enough structures here even for a platoon. Christ, the buildings look like they'd collapse if I breathed hard on them.*

Suddenly he felt exhausted, both emotionally and physically. "Well, Nadien, for better or worse, this is it," he told his reflection in the rear-view mirror. "Your new family awaits you. I hope you're ready to meet them."

Parking beside the large truck, he got out of the car, took a deep breath, and knocked on the door. Heavy footsteps approached on the other side, and the door opened to reveal a scene completely at odds with the building's exterior—an enormous room that looked like a combination dining hall and dayroom, complete with couches, television, pool tables, and vending machines for soda and candy bars.

"Welcome ta Four Corners, Airman Nadien!" A large, burly man in a khaki T-shirt and camouflage pants tucked into combat boots stuck out his hand. "Colonel Walker! C'mon in, yer just in time for chow."

Confused, Harry ignored the hand and saluted; after all, that's what you do with colonels. Harry's confusion was apparent. "It's okay, Harry, this is ATIC. We might still be Air Force but there's no formality here. No salutin' required, and we're informal as all hell. Considerin' the nature of the job, we don't stand on a whole helluva lotta ceremony."

The colonel ushered Harry inside where several other men dressed casually in T-shirts and fatigues had just entered the room from a stairway that seemed to come from somewhere beneath the barn.

"New man's here," the colonel announced. "Let's make him welcome. C'mon over and introduce yerselves. We go strictly by first names here. If yer yellin' for help, titles and last names are really useless. My name's Bill, by the way."

Harry was dazed. *On first name terms with a full bird colonel? This doesn't make sense,* he thought, *but then nothing does since I left basic training. I'm in the middle of nowhere, somewhere in the Nevada desert, inside what looks like a derelict barn from the outside, but is a modern facility on the inside. And my CO, a colonel, wants me to call him Bill. And he doesn't even talk like an officer.*

A bell sounded near a small panel in the wall next to the stairway. "Chow's here," Bill announced. Two of the men slid the panel back, revealing a dumbwaiter loaded with food. They ferried the pans and platters to the others who placed them on the long table. Plates, glasses, and silverware were already laid out on a large serving cart at the far end of the table. Pitchers containing milk, lemonade, and iced tea awaited, sweating their coldness onto the table top.

"Siddown, Harry, over here 'cross from me so's I kin clue ya in on what we got planned for tomorrow," Bill said. "First thing in the mornin', I'll give ya a grand tour of El Rancho Grande here. Under these old shacks is a maze of tunnels that'd make a rat dizzy."

The aroma of baked pork chops, stuffing, and mashed potatoes made Harry realize he was hungry. It sure didn't look like cafeteria cooking.

"It's all cooked in the main kitchen under the barn here," Bill explained, as if reading Harry's thoughts. "We've got three professional chefs contracted to us. They wanted to work someplace interestin' and we wanted good chow. ATIC made 'em an offer they couldn't refuse and got security clearances for 'em. Now they're makin' big money, got all the excitement they kin handle, and we're eatin' like kings. Everybody's happy."

After the meal, Bill showed him the barracks beneath the old machinery storage shed next to the barn. The entrance led off the stairway that went down at the rear of the dining hall from where Harry had seen the airmen emerging when he first arrived. A short underground tunnel connected the two buildings.

When they got into the barracks area, Harry saw two long hallways with small rooms off to each side. There was one bed in each room, and each room had a bath with a shower.

"Duty here's got a lot of stress connected with it. Ya see such hellish things that sometimes ya need a place to be alone," Bill told him, "It helps to get yerself back together. The regular Air Force would give their eyeteeth to have private rooms like this. ATIC treats us real special, kinda lets us do our own thing out here."

As they reached the end of the second hallway, Bill said, "This one's yers, Harry. There's no one across the hall yet; the guy oughta be here in about a month." Colonel Walker turned to leave, then stopped, adding, "See ya at five. We get started early while it's still cool."

Harry looked around the little room. It was immaculate, as was the bathroom, not at all like the drab-looking barracks he'd become accustomed to in basic and then at Crawford. The fluffy white towels and enormous bars of soap reminded him more of an upscale motel than a military barracks. The bed was soft and comfortable, sure as hell a lot better than the room he'd paid good money for the night before. That place had been a real fleabag, and he would never forget that coffee. He didn't see a television set anywhere, but that was fine. He much preferred listening to music where he could choose his own entertainment. He'd brought his radio and that would be good enough for now.

Needing to bring in his gear, he walked back up the stairs and outside to his car. Jake, the airman he'd sat next to at dinner, helped him carry his gear back downstairs and into his room.

"I'd stay and talk a while, but you look beat. Get some Z's, but set your alarm for four-thirty. Chow's at five sharp. Soon as I wake up, I'll knock on your door and make sure you're up."

Harry hung his uniforms at the back of the closet, thinking, *I certainly won't need these anytime soon. T-shirt and fatigue pants will be great. The hot desert's no place for uniforms, anyway.*

Too exhausted to unpack everything, he took out a clean khaki T-shirt and camouflage pants, smoothed out the wrinkles a little, and set his boots by the chair. He'd put the rest of his things away tomorrow. Bill had told him they didn't have daily inspection, although they were expected to keep their rooms clean and neat.

God, I'm tired from three days of driving, he thought. After a long, relaxing shower, he fell into the soft, comfortable double bed, groaning in satisfaction. As he drifted off to sleep, he imagined Annie lying next to him and said aloud, "Well, so far, so good. My new family seems friendlier than my real one."

Chapter 9

Dealing with Diabetes and Blindness — 1960

Lying in bed, an hour from freedom, Marisa thought back on the terrible and turbulent years that had transformed her from a bright and healthy eight-year-old into a blind student on the run, just starting junior college.

"There you go, I've set a special place for you at my birthday table," Marisa had said to the doll she hoped to receive, the doll who wasn't there yet. Excited about the prospect of getting the doll she wanted, Marisa could hardly wait for her eighth birthday. "The closest thing to a real baby," the ad had promised. "It wets its diaper and has skin that actually feels real." Together, she and her new doll would celebrate the occasion with lots of cake and ice cream.

Balloons, sweets, happiness, and laughter had mixed together to make the day special. Her new doll didn't feel quite as real as advertised, but in every other aspect it was all she'd wished for. It would be the little sister she'd always wanted.

Awakening the morning after the party, Marisa had felt tired. "It must be all the candy and excitement of yesterday," her mom said. As the days went by, she didn't feel any better, no matter how early she went to bed. In fact, she felt more tired each day. She'd always been the skinny one in the family, but her clothes seemed to be fitting more loosely. And no matter how much water she drank, she was always thirsty. Finally her mother took her to the doctor.

After getting the results of the lab tests, the doctor had explained what was going on. "Marisa, you have what we call *diabetes mellitus*. Children sometimes get this when they're your age. It's difficult to treat because you're still growing. But that's what's making you so tired. We can't cure it, but we can control it. To feel better you'll have to take insulin injections every day for the rest of your life, beginning today."

He'd paused to let that sink in and continued, "I'm going to put you in the hospital for a few days so we can figure out just the right insulin dosage you'll need so you won't be so tired and thirsty all the time."

Her only response had been, "Can I take my sister doll with me?"

After the first few days in the hospital, she had felt better. She spent her time trotting up and down the halls in her pajamas and robe, talking with other children, and playing with them in the sunroom at the end of the corridor. If she sat still for too long, the nurses would remind her that she had to keep moving to get the exercise she needed to balance the insulin dose that had been calculated.

She hadn't minded the stay at all. Playing with the other kids had been fun, and there'd been so many rooms to explore. She did miss her mother, though, and looked forward to her daily visits.

Sometimes, after the other children were in bed for the night, she would go down the hall to the nurses' station and talk to them until she got sleepy. They usually drank coffee while they discussed the patients and went over the charts, and they would make her a cup of chamomile tea to drink with them. She remembered how sleepy she always got after she drank the tea. It wasn't until now as she lay on her bed thinking about the long-ago events in the hospital that she understood the connection between drinking the tea and feeling drowsy.

One afternoon when her mom had come to visit, Marisa told her she had a special friend in the room across the hall. Excitedly, she had led her mother into the room and pulling back the curtain drawn around the crib, pointed to the child lying there.

"It's a baby that looks like a rat! Look, Mom," Marisa had said. Helen was speechless. Lying in the crib was a baby with a horrendous birth defect. It had the facial features of a rat, and tiny hands and feet resembling a rat's paws. Its fingers and toes were fused together about halfway down and, where its little fingernails should have been were partially formed claws. Its eyebrows were thick and bushy, tapering down to a thin line of hair across the bridge of its nose. The rest of its body, its arms and legs—what they could see sticking out of its pajamas—looked human.

Looking up at her mom, Marisa had explained, "Sometimes when she cries and the nurse doesn't come right away I go in and tell her not to be afraid, and she stops crying. She's my new friend."

The next day when Helen came to visit, Marisa was worried. "Mom, my new friend's gone. She's not in her room. Do you think she died?"

"They've probably just moved her to another room. I don't think she died," Helen had reassured her daughter, and changed the subject. Marisa wondered, but never mentioned it again.

After two weeks, the doctor had told Marisa, "Your daily dose of insulin has been adjusted and you're almost ready to go home. You'll have to be careful about what you eat. You're going to have to learn how to give yourself the insulin injections. I'll have the nurse come in and show you how. You can practice on an orange until you get the hang of it."

The doctor had her practice on an orange until it resembled a pincushion, then finally she got brave enough to try it on her arm.

When the time came for the real thing, the doctor had stood beside her, encouraging her. It wasn't nearly as bad as she had anticipated. The idea of it was far worse than the actual feeling of the needle entering her skin. She hated the morning ritual, and it never got easier. "Even to this day, every time I smell or see an orange, I still smell the hospital and see needles," she would joke with her friends years later.

A short time later, the dietitian had come into her room and had handed her a list of foods she could eat and how much. They went over how to make food exchanges and the "forbidden list" of foods she was not allowed to have at all. When Helen came in to take her home, they all went over both lists one last time.

Marisa sighed as she thought back to how diabetes had changed her life. Coping with it hadn't been easy, for nothing showed on the outside, as with measles or a broken arm. And much worse than that, it was forever. She'd just had to learn to live with it.

Through the years, Marisa had come to learn the hard way. Sneak a candy bar, a soda, or even a spoonful of ice cream and she risked ending up in the hospital with a hyperglycemic reaction. If she took her insulin shot and then didn't eat for an hour or two, or if she got the flu or even a minor infection, she could have a hypoglycemic reaction. Either way, if she wasn't careful, the result could be coma or death. Watching what she ate was difficult, but the alternative was even worse. She made up her mind that she'd do whatever it took. It might be inconvenient, but the diabetes would never control her life.

Shortly after her seventeenth birthday, Marisa had wakened one morning unable to see out of one eye. Frightened, she called out, "Mom, something's wrong! I can't see anything out of my left eye. When I look, everything's all red, like there's blood there, but I don't think it's bleeding. I didn't bump it or scratch it or anything. Can you see what's wrong?"

Rushing into her daughter's bedroom, Helen examined Marisa's eye. "Your eyes look okay to me, both of them," her mom told her. "Just lie still and I'll call Dr. Parks." The ophthalmologist had warned them of the likelihood that she could experience a sudden loss of sight. Marisa could still remember the shakiness in her mother's voice as she'd talked to the doctor on the phone.

Half an hour later they were in his office. Marisa hoped he might find a speck of dirt or an eyelash in her left eye and remove it, and she would be able to see again. But that was not to be. After a careful exam of both her eyes, Dr. Parks told them the one thing they had hoped never to hear.

"Your left retina is bleeding and causing you to lose vision in that eye. The blood is making everything look red to you. It's pooling at the back of your eye, waiting to be absorbed. We've talked about this before, and how it often happens to juvenile diabetics. I'm afraid your vision loss will probably be permanent. Eventually your right eye may also be affected. They may improve a little from time to time. I know that doesn't make any sense, but it can happen. If it does, you'll probably be able to see enough to get around by yourself, maybe read large print with a magnifying glass. But it will depend on how good your diabetic control is, how much stress you're under, and on any number of things going on in your life at that particular time."

Dr. Parks' voice softened, "I know that's not much consolation right now. It's times like this I feel so helpless. I'm supposed to be able to help you, but there's not much I or anyone else can do for you. Marisa, I'd give anything not to have to tell you this, but the outlook is not very promising."

Marisa had burst into tears. Taking the tissue that the doctor offered, she'd wiped her eyes, not seeing that he took one for himself.

Helen and Marisa were both silent on the way home. Neither knew what to say. They'd been aware that this could happen right from the first day, and that it probably would happen, but they'd both hoped that it was one of those things that only happens to other people, to strangers, or bad guys, and never to you.

Then there was the day that she was told by the head nurse at the hospital where she was working, "You're one of our best and most faithful candy-stripers, Marisa. Our patients are always asking about you, but considering your medical problems, you may want to start considering some other way to volunteer."

"I understand, Mrs. Hancock, but going blind in one eye isn't contagious. I can still work just as hard as before," responded Marisa, attempting to deflect the verbal blows hammering away at her dreams.

"The doctor told you your disease is progressive and untreatable. Quitting as a volunteer is as much for your own health as for that of our patients," the nurse explained in a cold, unfeeling tone of voice.

Forcing me to give up what I enjoy doing most in life doesn't seem especially beneficial to my health, Marisa thought, as she replied, "I understand your concerns, but there must be something I could do to continue helping the patients."

"Well, we might be able to think of a few things, but only for another month or two. You must start coming to grips with the inevitable. I'm sorry you are going blind," the nurse said with a tone of finality.

Three weeks later Marisa had awakened unable to see out of either eye. Now she was totally blind. She didn't bother calling out this time. There was no use. When Helen got up to make coffee, she always looked in Marisa's room on the way to the kitchen. That morning when she'd seen her daughter lying in bed sobbing, she knew.

Not waiting for regular office hours, Helen had called Dr. Parks at home. "There's no real point in your coming to my office," he'd said. "There's absolutely nothing I can do, but there is something I'd like to have you try. One of my old classmates from Yale has moved to the area and is specializing in laser surgery. Sometimes the laser can improve diabetic retinopathy, which is the medical term for Marisa's condition. I've already discussed the case with him and, although we both believe that it's unlikely that laser treatments will work in her particular case, there's nothing to lose by trying."

Grasping the slim possibility that the treatment might restore even limited vision, Helen set up an appointment for that morning. As soon as they arrived at his office, Dr. Riley took Marisa into his examining room. "Marisa, if you and your mom are willing, I'd like to try a couple of laser treatments to see if there'll be any regression in the damage that's already done. I can't promise you that it's going to work," Dr. Riley said. "We'll need to do at least two treatments, about seven days apart, and then check to see if there's any improvement. If there is, then we can schedule more. If there isn't, then there's nothing else we can do."

Helen numbly signed the consent forms without reading them. Who cares what the fine print says, she'd thought. I'm willing to chance almost anything at this point to restore my daughter's sight.

Receiving her first laser treatment that morning, Marisa had gone home filled with hope, but the next day there was only total blackness, no light, not even the faint red glimmer. She groped and stumbled her way around the house, touching familiar doorways, walls, and chairs to find her way from room to room, all the while fighting the darkness that threatened her future.

"Mom, I'm going to take the second treatment but, if I still can't see anything after that, I don't want to try anything else he or anyone else suggests. I can't bear to get my hopes up and then not have it happen. I'd rather just forget about the whole thing. I can learn how to do things the way other blind people do."

Marisa felt her mother's arms encircle her, holding her, willing her love and strength to get through this ordeal. Knowing her mother felt the pain of her blindness almost as much as she did, Marisa hugged back in return.

Wanting to soften the impact of her blindness, her mom had offered, "Honey, you don't have to do the dishes in the evenings. I can do them for you."

"Mom, I can still do the dishes," Marisa replied, somewhat offended. "I'll have to do dishes for the rest of my life, blind or not. Just check them for me and, if they're not clean, put them back in the sink and I'll do them over."

Marisa couldn't see the tears that her bravery and courage prompted.

The following Monday they'd returned to Dr. Riley's office. Again he checked her retinas. "No improvement, I'm afraid, but we'll proceed with the second treatment, although there's little likelihood that it will be of any benefit."

Marisa nodded, hoping against hope that some kind of a miracle would take place. The next day, Marisa saw nothing but total darkness, and the final exam on Friday still showed no improvement.

Dr. Riley's voice could not disguise his sadness. "The arterioles have stopped bleeding and there hasn't been any further damage. But I can't see any improvement either. We gave it our best shot, Marisa, and it simply isn't working. It's the latest thing medical science has to offer, but it doesn't always help, especially in cases like yours. It's frustrating for me to have to tell you this, but there's nothing more I can do for you."

Marisa could still feel the warmth of Dr. Riley's arms as he'd comforted them both. The three had stood in silent communion, their embrace saying all that needed saying.

She'd left the doctor's office in shock. She was blind, with no hope of ever seeing more than blurry shapes, if she were even that lucky.

Lying in bed, she felt numb all over again as she remembered that day. Although it had been the biggest blow she'd ever suffered, she'd already decided that if the laser treatments didn't work, she'd finish high school and go on to junior college. Then on to the University of California and obtain a degree in visual rehabilitation. *It will take extra time,* she determined, *but I will achieve my goal and nothing will stop me. I'll use my blindness to help others like me.*

Then she recalled how, just the week before that pivotal day, she'd bought a ticket for a fund-raising raffle held by her junior class. The first prize had been a restored Ford Mustang and she'd told her friends, "I can drive with one good eye. This car will be great when I go to college...if I win."

Crossing her fingers for good luck, she'd done a little dance down the high school hallway, laughing with her friends.

A few days after her second eye had gone blind, the winning ticket had been drawn—hers. Only now it didn't matter, for she'd never be able to drive again. Disappointed, she sold the Mustang to a classmate for $25, depositing the money into her college fund.

Transferring to a high school that offered special classes for visually handicapped students, she had struggled to get through her last year of high school. Her textbooks were all recorded on audiotape, and she often had to listen to an entire chapter in order to glean a single needed fact tucked away in one paragraph—an extremely time-consuming process—but there was no other way. Complaining wouldn't have helped, so she just did her best.

Taking notes was completely out of the question because she couldn't see where she was writing on the paper and couldn't have read them afterwards. She managed to keep her grades up by listening to the tapes every night and remembering the information as best she could for the oral quizzes. When graduation time finally came, she walked out on the platform on the arm of the class president to receive her diploma. The student body had risen and given her a standing ovation. Many of the students who understood the obstacles she'd overcome in order to graduate cried in joy.

Apprehensive about how she would manage in junior college, and knowing there were no special classes for blind students, she'd talked with Mrs. Ross, the counselor assigned to her, about her concerns. And Mrs. Ross had introduced her to Bobby, who agreed to tutor her.

One by one, she'd faced all of her fears head-on and, one by one, each had fallen away when faced with her resolute determination to succeed. Lying in bed, less than an hour from freedom, she analyzed her apprehensions about the day ahead, confident that it would turn out okay, as had everything else. Slowly her apprehensions melted into anticipation, and her alarm went off. A new chapter of her life was begining.

Chapter 10

Helen Discovers Marisa's Move — 1972

Helen was not happy about having to take Jon to the police benefit breakfast at the campus cafeteria this morning. She and Marisa had made plans to go to the Saturday flea market and look for bargains when it first opened at 6 A.M. Even though Marisa's eyesight was almost nonexistent, she still loved doing the same things she'd always done. Abandoning these plans in order to accompany Jon filled Helen with resentment, but it was less trouble than the beating she'd get if she said no.

Someday, Marisa and I will be free of that controlling bastard, she thought, *sipping her morning coffee. He'll probably want to play golf with his buddies afterwards, so at least Marisa and I can hit some garage sales together later.*

On the way back from dropping Jon off at the clubhouse, Helen planned the day's activities. *Anything we do will be fun,* she thought. *We enjoy each other's company and the freedom we feel when we're together.* Walking through the front door, she tensed. "Something's not right," she told the welcoming Bo. She was overwhelmed with a sense of foreboding. Even Bo was acting strangely.

"Marisa?" she called. "We need to get going if we're going to do the garage sales. You have to get your shot and eat something before we leave."

Puzzled at her daughter's silence, thoughts raced frantically through her head. *Maybe she's still sleeping. Probably her bedroom door is closed, and she can't hear me.*

"Marisa, get up! I'll make some toast and bacon while you're getting dressed, so we can eat and get going." She called again, louder.

Turning on the coffee-maker, Helen took two cups down off the shelf. As the aroma filled the room, she poured a cup of the steaming liquid for each of them. *Marisa will enjoy having coffee in bed,* she thought. *We can chat a few minutes, then get started on the day.*

While carrying the mugs down the hall towards Marisa's room, she saw that the door was closed. "Something is definitely not right," she told herself.

Glancing to her right, Helen saw the old chest freezer she had put there because there was no place else it would fit. Her gaze locked onto the odd placement of a cast iron skillet turned upside down on the top of the freezer. Then on top of the skillet was a neatly-folded square of paper held securely in place by the antique moustache cup she and Marisa had bought last year at a garage sale.

Her hands shook as she removed the note and saw the words, "Mom, I love you, Marisa." Staring at the note clutched tightly between her fingers, she dreaded opening it. She had a feeling that something terrible had happened. Shoving the folded note into her pocket, she looked around.

She knocked, and opened the door. The room was empty, completely empty.

The bed was neatly made and looked as if it hadn't been slept in. But it had been, because she had peeked in to check on Marisa earlier that morning. She'd left the door ajar so Bo could get out if he wanted to. Seeing her looking in, Bo had jumped off the bed and run into the kitchen for his morning milk.

As she gazed around the room, her knees turned to jelly and she felt weak all over. The cedar chest she'd given Marisa when she'd graduated from high school was gone. The dresser was bare except for the dresser scarf that Marisa had embroidered and given her as a Christmas gift the year before she'd lost her eyesight.

As she walked stiffly to the closet, she knew even before she touched the sliding door that it would be empty too. She was right. All the clothes, the boxes of mementos, albums filled with photographs, everything was gone. Marisa couldn't see the pictures anymore, but refused to part with them because, she said, "Maybe someday I'll be able to see them again."

Marisa had to have planned this in order to get herself and all of her things out of the house in such a short time, Helen thought. *Why had she been so secretive about running away? Was this the reason she'd seemed so withdrawn and quiet, spending more time than usual in her room? What in God's name was going on?*

Helen's head began to buzz and she felt light-headed. "Please don't let me pass out," she prayed to anyone who might be listening. Walking unsteadily to the bed, she sat down.

Pulling the note from her pocket, she opened it with shaking, white-knuckled hands. Tears flowed down her cheeks as she read.

"Mom, first, let me tell you that I love you with all my heart. But I'm leaving because I can't stand the drunken fights and incessant noise. I don't want to hurt you, Mom, but I need to succeed in college. I can't study here at home. I don't want Jon to throw a fit or try to stop me. Some friends found me a place to live near school that's safe, so don't worry. I'll call you at work and let you know where I am in a couple of weeks. Bobby is helping me move, and he'll come to the new place to help me with homework and shopping. Take care of yourself and Bo. I love you, Marisa."

Collapsing onto the bed, Helen lay still for a moment and tried to think what to do first. *No wonder Marisa has been so quiet the past few days. I should have known something was up. But then Marisa hasn't been feeling well; she's had the flu. And now she's gone and we're both alone, her in her new apartment and me with Jon. There'll be no one to share my troubles with, no one to take my side after the fighting and arguing. Jon's wrecked my life with his damned drinking. My sons both left home as soon as they could enlist in the military. Only my daughter stayed, and now she's gone, too. After every beating I hope and pray each will be the last, that somehow, some way, God will figure I'd suffered enough to finally be allowed to have a happy home life. Jon's drinking has driven all hope for a decent life from me. He's finally won. What do I have left? He's taken it all.*

Walking unsteadily to the kitchen, she poured the now lukewarm coffee into the sink, and made herself a cup of tea. Sipping the comforting beverage, she sat at the kitchen table, staring into the nothingness of her life. Tears fell unchecked.

Slowly, a plan born of frustration and despair began to materialize. *I'll be picking the stupid, miserable bastard up later this afternoon. I'll tell him that since it's such a beautiful day, we should go for a ride in the country, to some place pretty and quiet, out along the levee where we can sit and talk. That should do the trick. I'll remind him that we haven't done that for a long time. I'll smile and be calm and pleasant. I won't say a thing about Marisa.*

Once we've parked, I'll ask him to get the beer I brought out of the back so we can have a drink together. When he does this, I'll reach into my open purse and take out his police Smith and Wesson .357 Magnum, slip up behind him, put the barrel against his head and watch it explode. There's no way I can miss at point-blank range.

I'm glad he insisted on taking me out to the shooting range and making me practice until I was a crack shot. "You gotta be able to protect yourself," he'd said. Well, that's exactly what I plan to do now, protect myself against any more of your bullshit and abuse. She smiled at the memory of what a .357 Magnum once did when she shot at a pumpkin from close range.

"Why, officer, you know how hysterical I can get. Remember when I called you right after Jon beat me up the last time? Why, I could hardly make myself coherent trying to talk while breathing through my broken nose."

"Hysterical," they'd called her. Well, I'll show them hysterical!

Thoughts raced crazily through her mind. *Got to hit the side of his head, or the splatter will make a hell of a mess in the car. I'll dump his body in the river. I'll need some rope and weights, or as soon as his body starts to decompose, it'll rise to the surface.*

I'll teach him, beating me up, screwing around on me, and driving my kids away.

Helen got up out of the chair, put her cup in the sink, and walked back into Marisa's room. The emptiness hurt her heart. Nothing remained of her beloved daughter. Only the faint scent of Marisa's flowery cologne lingered in the air. Taking a deep breath, she imprinted the scent on her memory. "I will never forget this scent, or any of the wonderful things we've done together. Always and forever I will love you."

She checked the closet once again, hoping in vain that Marisa's clothes might have magically reappeared, and everything would be okay again.

Sunshine streamed into the bedroom through the lace curtains. Marisa had chosen lace because she said the texture felt beautiful to her hands. She said she could remember what lace looked like, and that was what she wanted for her room. Even the pale yellow wallpaper was fresh and dainty like Marisa herself. It had little wildflowers all over it in a delicate pattern, and, when the sunlight came in through the open window the way it did today, the room was filled with the hope and beauty of spring.

Noticing that the old, tattered print of Jesus was gone, she couldn't help but wonder if even Jesus could help Marisa and her out of this mess.

Helen sat on her daughter's bed, trying to collect her thoughts. She was going to have to do everything just right and in exactly the proper sequence from now on. Her entire future hinged on how she handled things during the next few hours. Shooting Jon was definitely the best way to get rid of him once and for all. She'd probably end up in jail for a few months. But with a good attorney, and a copy of the report from her last emergency room visit, together with the pictures they'd taken of the cuts and bruises he'd inflicted on her, she could probably get off with a light sentence, maybe just a couple of years' probation.

The mere decision to kill him had a calming effect on her. Both she and Marisa had been through far too much already and they didn't need any more stress in their lives. Besides, Marisa was gone, hopefully in a safe place. There was no way that bastard would ever hurt her again.

Walking across the hallway into her room, she opened the top dresser drawer and stared at the police issue .357 Magnum in its heavy leather holster. She kept it in the dresser in the guestroom where she'd been sleeping for the past several months. It was always loaded in case someone broke into the house at night. Unsnapping the small safety strip of leather, she pulled the revolver partially out to make sure the chambers were full. They were.

She stared intently at her ticket to freedom for several minutes, sighed, and pushed the gun back into the holster. She snapped the safety strap securely and replaced the gun in the drawer, saying to it, "You're not the answer. My self-esteem is gone. Lost that a long time ago. But I haven't lost all of my integrity."

She suddenly remembered that Jon had a job interview for a deputy's position in a small town about eighty miles away and a new plan formed. *He knows the answers to their questions cold and is sure to get the job. The chief's main concern is whether the little wife will be happy living in a small town, and he'll interview me after Jon, so whether or not he gets the job will ultimately depend on me.*

I'll put on a good show at the interview and convince them that I'm a loving, supportive wife whose sole ambition is to move to a tiny country town and never see city lights again. I know I can pull that off. They'll need him to start immediately, so I'll stay behind to put the house on the market and get packed for the move. Then, as soon as he's out of the house, I'll start looking for an apartment I can afford, and he can go to hell. Once they hire him, though, there's nothing they can legally do if I refuse to move there with him.

I'll still drive him out by the river, park the car, and tell him about Marisa leaving. Then I'll tell him, "I planned to blow your brains out with your own gun. Somehow that seems fair payback. You destroy my life, I'll destroy yours."

I'll watch him sweat and squirm for a while, then I'll tell him, "On second thought, I've got a better idea. Do you want to make a deal? I'll help you get that the job and you give me my freedom. Oh, and if you expect me to cooperate with the job deal, you've got to start treating me like a human being. Otherwise, you can kiss your precious job good-bye. I'll spill the beans at the interview and tell them all about your drunken rages, how you beat your wife, and how you're looking forward to going on the take. I'm sure they'll find that very interesting."

Chapter 11

Helen Makes a Deal with Jon — 1972

"Jon, it's still early, and such a beautiful day. Why don't we take a ride out by the river? It might be fun just to sit out there. We can talk and have a beer. There isn't any real hurry to get home," Helen suggested as soon as Jon got in the car.

Jon grudgingly agreed. He'd actually planned on having her take him straight to the Drop Inn, but since she was driving, he didn't have much of a choice. "You're the driver, guess I gotta humor you," he said, but there was no humor in his voice.

Big deal, Helen thought as she pushed the pedal to the floor. *Take a half hour off from your whoring and go with your wife. Watch out, sucker, I still have Plan A.*

A few miles along the levee, she came to a wide circle in the road that looped around a giant oak tree. Turning off the roadway, she parked in the shade. Placing her handbag on her lap, she made sure the top was open. Then she smiled at Jon, hoping it was a pleasant smile, one that he couldn't read.

Jon surprised her by asking, "So how did your day go?" She knew he didn't give a damn how any of her days went, or her nights either, and the feeling was mutual.

"Marisa and I had made plans to go to some garage sales, but we weren't able to go because she's run away from home," she said casually.

"So, the blind brat's finally gone! That's one less mouth to feed," he responded flippantly. "And don't expect me to be sorry.

She's your kid, someone I just had to put up with to keep you happy."

God, the SOB is even more of a lowlife than I realized. Marisa's always been nice to him. I should have brought the damned gun after all, Helen thought. *Calm down. Don't let him get to you.*

She took a couple of slow, deep breaths and said, "Do you want to know why I really suggested coming out here?"

"I guess you're gonna tell me, whether I care or not."

Putting her hand in her open bag, she said, "I really drove you out here to kill you and dump your body in the river. I'm tired of your drunken rages, the beatings, and the humiliation. You've destroyed my life and driven away my boys and now my daughter. I'm fed up with you. You make me sick. And I want you dead."

She hoped she sounded more in control of the situation than she felt. She got a perverse pleasure in watching him squirm and bluster as he tried to figure out if she meant it.

"You've seen me handle a gun. And you know I hate you so much that I could pull the trigger," she added to make him sweat a little more.

"They'd know it was you. You'd never get away with it."

"Come on, Jon. My medical records are full of details about all the stitches I needed after the beatings, and photos of all the bruises. With a battered wife defense, I'd maybe get probation. Hell, I could even fake you beating me up now and then claim self-defense. They wouldn't even file charges. Everyone knows what a temper you've got."

She let him sit and sweat, wondering how soon she'd pull the trigger. Helen thoroughly enjoyed the power of the moment.

"Before I kill you, is there anything you want to say?"

"Look, you know how I get after a few drinks. Don't mean none of it. I'm sorry. Let's let bygones be bygones and start over, okay?"

But he didn't look sorry at all and she knew he wasn't. Never had been and wasn't now.

"What are you sorry about, Jon? For destroying my life, or that I'm going to kill you?" she asked.

When he didn't answer, she went on, "There is a way you can stay alive. I'll help you get that job next week and and after you're set up there, I'll tell them we're splitting up and I won't be joining you. Then it will be too late to fire you. So you get the job and I get my freedom. How do feel about that? It's up to you. I don't care. Either way I win and you're out of my life."

It was almost as if she were listening to someone else's voice, some other person making the offer.

"Look," he said, "I admit I need you in order to get that job. If you'll help me, I'll leave you alone. I'll never touch you again, okay? Shit, I won't even talk to you, if that's what you want."

Helen knew he would agree to anything just so he didn't end up murdered with his own gun, in his own car, by his own wife. "Okay, we have a deal," she said coldly, starting the car.

They drove home in silence, and when they arrived, she tossed the keys into her purse, and walked into the house. *I'm keeping the keys,* she resolved, *and if he doesn't like it, tough. He can crawl on his hands and knees to the Drop Inn, or to hell, for all I care. From now on, I don't give a damn what he does or where he does it, as long as it isn't to me.*

Helen went to the kitchen sink and splashed her face with cool water. She walked out to the patio. Bo was curled up on a lawn chair, enjoying the late afternoon sun. Sitting down in the chair next to him, she began to plan her next move. He looked up at her through heavy-lidded eyes, blinked, and started to purr. Gazing sleepily up at her, he stretched and yawned. Then he gave her hand a gentle nudge with his head to let her know he loved her. Helen wished her life was as simple as his.

Chapter 12

Harry's First Encounter with an ET —1956

On Harry's second night at Four Corners, the eerie, high-pitched wailing of a siren signaled an approaching craft. The night shift Perimeter Security Team, or PST, to which he'd been assigned had been relaxing in the rec room. Hearing the siren, the men scrambled, donning fatigue jackets, synchronized like a well-oiled machine.

The Blue Team would go in first while the PST worked the perimeter at a distance. They were happy not to be exposed to the blast-furnace heat that emanated from some of the crashed vehicles.

PST members wore heavy one-piece oversuits with several layers of protection underneath, including specially made boots, gloves, and a hood to protect them from the intense radiation that was nearly always present. The Blue Team wore suits of similar, but much lighter-weight material, since their exposure was shorter.

Pinned to each suit was a meticulously calibrated dosimeter, which measured the exact amount of radiation they were exposed to during an incident. Each team member turned in his meter after each incident and received a new one.

Earlier that day, Bill had briefed him on what to expect, and had Harry sign a statement releasing the government from all liability in the event of any possible future illness arising from radiation exposure. "It's simply a formality, Harry. They tell me there's no danger connected with yer duties. It's jest government red tape and ya know how that goes. We all put up with it."

"What if I don't sign it?" Harry had asked.

"Well, since it's a direct order, refusal constitutes disobeyin' an order, and that'll get ya a court martial and a season ticket to Leavenworth."

Harry signed, even though he felt uneasy. *I can't believe that the intense radiation levels we're exposed to can be harmless. If it's so safe, why do we have to wear the heavy, cumbersome suits? And dosimeters? Hell, all of the team members look healthy enough, but how long have they been here? How many incidents have exposed them to this supposed safe level of radiation? No danger, yet all these precautions. Isn't there a contradiction here?*

The wailing siren ceased and a loudspeaker in the barracks announced, "Craft approaching grid five from the southwest."

Harry joined the rest of his teammates running up the steps and throwing themselves into their assigned five-tonner. The main gate swung open and the caravan raced out into the moonlit desert while the passengers donned their protective gear.

Peering through the truck's side window, Harry could see a huge, oval craft, its pulsating blue and green lights casting an otherworldly glow on the silent landscape. Corkscrewing down at incredible speed, it appeared out of control. The trucks stopped at the crest of a low rise. From a safe distance they watched helplessly as the craft plunged to the ground and exploded on impact. A moment later, Harry heard a loud hissing sound like that of water being poured on hot coals.

"No live ones tonight, men," Bill said. "Let's let the Blues do their thing. I don't wanna be anywhere near that ship fer awhile."

The perimeter crew was very quiet. Harry had hoped his first incident might be different, one with a safe landing. He had heard rumors that there had been a rash of fatal crashes lately, and he wondered if there was any particular reason. He'd been under the assumption that Four Corners was a safe location where extraterrestrial scientists were welcomed at the end of their long journeys. Harry was both frustrated and saddened that these galactic pioneers, traveling incomprehensible distances without incident, should come to grief during the last few feet of their journey. *What was it about Earth that caused them to crash? Magnetic fields? High gravity? Surely, their technology should be able to handle all that.*

After about 15 minutes, the headlights of the Blue Team trucks signaled they were leaving the incident site. "Okay, let's see how many leftovers we can find," Bill said, climbing down from the cab of the truck. "Nadien, you and I'll go over'n stand guard at the crash. The rest of ya guys fan out with yer counters and bags. The treasure hunt begins."

Ever since his first day of class at Crawford, Harry had wondered how he would react at this moment. Stepping down from the cab of the truck, he was overcome with conflicted emotions. Awe followed by amazement at being only a few feet from the hissing, popping remnants of a ship from another world. And overwhelming sadness for the incinerated occupants. He relived their last moments with them, once they knew that death on this alien world was inevitable. *What did they believe about God and life after death?* he wondered.

Suddenly he realized he hadn't given any thought to their appearance. Or that he might be repulsed or frightened out of his wits when he saw them. *They're living beings, and I just want to see them walk out of their craft alive.*

"Goin' through the stages, Harry?" Bill asked. "Don't worry, son. Every damn one of us has bin there, emotions goin' every which way." Placing his hand lightly on Harry's shoulder, he continued, "It's hard to handle at first, but ya'll be all right. Maybe the next one'll come down safe. Ya'll feel better when ya see one of them little guys step outside."

Harry was thankful Bill had sent the rest of the crew away to pick up whatever they could find of the craft. Judging from the violence of impact, it would be a long night.

The next alert came exactly three weeks later. The siren screamed, and the radar crew chief sounded frantic over the loudspeaker system. "Malfunction of the radar warning system! Ship on the ground in grid five!"

Harry remembered from Crawford that this could happen when a craft materialized from a dimension not detected by conventional radar. As the team rushed out to the waiting vehicles, they all seemed to sense that something unusual was about to happen. The air itself felt charged with excitement and electricity. Even the siren had sounded different.

The landing site was close to the crash of three weeks earlier. Harry wondered what was so special about that particular spot. It just looked like a flat stretch of sagebrush and hardpan to him. *Maybe that's what they require for a safe landing, but it hadn't worked last time.*

Stopping their vehicles just over the rise in the landscape, the crews stared at the silent ship. The nearly full moon illuminated the desert, but couldn't compete with the craft's intense, pulsing strobe light. The craft was oval-shaped with a single row of windows midway around its center. It hovered in absolute silence, only a few feet above the ground, seemingly preparing to settle onto the desert floor.

In the lead truck, the Blue Team chief studied the craft through light-enhancing binoculars and radioed, "No sign of movement either inside or outside. We're going in. Bill, cover my six."

Both crews approached cautiously, parking their trucks a short distance away, and climbing down. The pulsating light reminded Harry of the strobe lights in nightclubs. The Blue Team members walked in single file to within a hundred feet of the craft, then stopped and watched as it slowly settled down on the ground. Moments before touchdown, three tripod-like legs emerged silently from the underside of the craft. Directly in front of the Blue Team the outline of an opening appeared in the otherwise featureless silver-gray hull. The PST members edged up close behind the Blues.

Still there was no sound, no sign of movement inside the lighted windows, and no change in the shimmering light that glowed from the surface of the craft. A moment later, a hatch opened silently and lowered itself to the ground, forming a ramp. Light streamed from the craft's interior.

Harry's chest ached. Then he remembered that in the excitement he'd forgotten to breathe. Whatever or whoever was in the ship was about to emerge. Harry looked at Bill, then at the rest of the crew. Each appeared nervous and tense. No one dared move. The Blue Team leader stood about ten feet from the opening, staring into the interior of the ship. Harry could hear a faint rustling sound, like dry leaves on a sidewalk.

A shape appeared in the doorway. Pausing for a few seconds, the being looked at each Blue team member and then the members of the PST crew. When the being gazed directly at him, Harry felt a warm, full sensation inside his head. Reflecting on it later, it had seemed to be a rather pleasurable feeling.

Is the extraterrestrial probing me for telepathic communication, Harry wondered. *Now what do I do? This wasn't covered at Crawford.*

The Blue leader followed the extraterrestrial's gaze, which remained on Harry, and said, "It's okay to tell him what happened to the other ship, Harry. They usually pick one person to communicate with. This time it happens to be you. Just let him know how you feel about what took place, the details as you remember them, and your feelings. Don't say it out loud. Concentrate real hard, and visualize it clearly. Let our visitor pick it up from your mind."

Harry closed his eyes and recalled seeing the doomed craft spiraling down, out of control, experiencing the same rush of emotions he'd felt three weeks earlier when gazing at the smoldering wreckage. He recalled his overwhelming sense of sadness at the loss of the occupants' lives.

The being moved somewhat stiffly and mechanically down the hatch and onto the ground. Harry felt an impulse to move closer, and figured that the being had sent the thought. He took short, cautiously deliberate steps forward until he was near enough to reach out and touch the frail-looking being. Close up, it didn't exactly match any of the extraterrestrials shown in the classroom materials. This one was about 4'6", with long, spindly arms and legs that seemed quite out of proportion for its small, thin body. Its skin was pale greenish-yellow, and its eyes were huge, dark, and oddly-slanted, eyes that focused unwaveringly on him. Where its mouth should have been there was only a tiny horizontal slit. It had no lips, and its chin tapered markedly until it receded into its thin neck. *But with telepathy, who needs to speak,* Harry reasoned.

A silvery gray, form-fitting, one-piece suit extended down its legs and over its feet. An insignia patch on the chest of the uniform showed a triangle with three horizontal lines running through one side, exactly as in the book.

As the alien continued looking directly into Harry's eyes, he again felt warmth spreading inside his brain. It wasn't an unpleasant sensation, just unfamiliar. The warmth turned to thoughts from the visitor without any effort on his part. "Do not be afraid. We come in peace. I wish to express gratitude for the compassion you have all shown for my comrades who perished in the crash."

Harry wanted to reach out and touch the alien, but he wasn't sure if he should. Feeling strangely compelled to make a physical expression of compassion, he didn't know if it would be appropriate. Becoming more confused and stressed, he was unsure about what to do next. This whole concept of mental communication was still so new to him.

"Put yer hand out real slow, Harry. If he puts his out, go ahead and touch it. Be careful, and watch fer his reaction," Bill whispered from somewhere behind him.

Harry removed his heavy gloves and, as if reading his mind, the extraterrestrial reached slowly for Harry's right hand, brushing it gently. Harry noticed there were only four fingers on each hand, but no thumb. The fingers reminded him of insect feelers, long and prehensile. Surprisingly, the skin was cool and pleasant to the touch.

Harry's gaze was drawn back towards the alien's eyes. Melting into their blackness, he knew the alien was expressing gratitude not just to him, but to the entire crew. Then, turning and walking slowly and stiffly back up the ramp, the alien disappeared inside the ship. The hatch closed silently behind him.

Both teams stood rooted to the ground, but when they heard a soft "whoosh" from somewhere beneath the craft, they instinctively moved back a few steps. The craft rose, hovered above them for a few seconds, then shot upwards to become one of the thousands of stars in the clear desert sky. Three holes in the ground from the tripod landing gear, and the tracks of the team members leading up to them were the only physical evidence indicating that something extraordinary had happened.

Harry stared into the night sky. *Why did you communicate specifically with me? I don't get it, but thank you,* he thought.

As the rest of the team headed back toward their vehicles, he stayed behind, trying to regain his composure. Bill walked up behind him and put a hand on his shoulder. "Still goin' through the stages, Harry? Like I told ya, this time was better. Yer instructor was right. Ya do have a real special feeling for the little guys. I hope ya liked it, because they'll be lookin' ya up again. Ya can count on it! Oh, and I'm goin' to accelerate yer transfer to Blue Team. Pretty soon, ya'll be on the front line, where yer sensitivity to our visitors'll come in real handy."

Chapter 13

Harry Assumes Command of Four Corners — 1966

While going through some old papers stuffed away in his desk, Harry came across a bill for four new tires from Bradie's Tire Shop in Las Vegas. How well he remembered the day nearly five years earlier when he'd first driven his old bald-tired Chevy into this out-of-the-way place that didn't officially exist.

The bill triggered the memory of how, after three months straight at Four Corners, he'd been given a three-day pass. The lure of the bright lights and big city of Las Vegas just 150 miles due south had beckoned seductively to him. On arrival, he'd noticed that his tires were now completely bald, so he'd withdrawn a large chunk of his automatically deposited paycheck and purchased four new tires. The idea of driving on lonely desert roads and maybe having to walk fifty miles in the blazing sun to the nearest gas station if he had a flat was a great motivator. Anyway, he had the money and not much to spend it on. With that chore taken care of, he hit the casinos, mixing with the crowds, generally having a good time, even stopping at the Kitty Kat Ranch on the way back for a little female companionship.

Yet no matter how many times during the last five years he'd gone to Vegas and partaken of its pleasures, there always came a time when playing the slots or sitting at a bar would lose its glitter and excitement. The crowds would blend into a mass of dull anonymity, nothing distinguishing one person from another; their voices mixing with the noise of the clinking slots, forming a cacophony of nothingness. Then he would find himself longing for the peace and quiet of the desert. The very isolation that many of the Four Corners crew found intolerable was his comfort. The desolation of the Nevada desert became a blanket of protection, covering him and his new family.

Once, looking around a casino, he'd wondered, *How could any man-made lights begin to compare with the incredible display of lights that I'm treated to almost every night? What a pleasure it is to sit on that lonely knoll near the gate at twilight, watching as the planets, stars, and galaxies slowly, quietly, make their presence known. What can beat the thrill of seeing a streak of light, followed by the wail of the siren? Winning a few hundred dollars pales in comparison to the silver ships dropping like magic from the night sky.*

It was always the same. In the midst of the glitz of Las Vegas, he would find himself homesick for Four Corners, a feeling that would consume him until he got in his car and returned to the base. *Gotta admit it, Four Corners is home. I love it, and I've never been able to leave it for long. Oh, to be back out in the desert, where I can relax and let its vastness envelope me and let the smell of sagebrush take hold of me, leading me to a place where I can release my mind to travel into the openness of eternity!*

Tossing the old invoice back into his desk, Harry realized the military had responded to his devotion by promoting him much more quickly than if he'd been on regular duty. Promotions or not, he wanted to stay here for the remainder of his career.

Smiling, he recalled his first feeble attempts at thought-transference communication. Later on he'd relaxed more and improved rapidly from then on. Only twice had the gift failed him. Both times the big Greys had landed uneventfully, setting up an invisible force field encircling both them and their craft. The force field had prevented the team members from approaching closer than about fifteen feet and the Greys had seemed unwilling to communicate with Harry or anyone else. They hadn't stayed on the ground long either time. They were not pleasant in any respect and no one could figure out why they'd even come. If their intent had been intimidation, it had worked well. Everyone on the Blue Team had been relieved when they'd gone.

Harry found the physical appearance of this species particularly menacing. Their eyes had a riveting, sinister look, almond-shaped at the center, angling sharply up at a forty-five degree angle, with yellowish-green slits accented sharply against the rest of their dark blue-black eyes. He'd seen reptiles with eyes like that, and these big Greys looked at least as deadly as a crocodile or a cobra.

Although their heads sort of resembled human heads, their noses were large and beaked, protruding as did their squared-off jaws. Each had an exaggerated bump at the back of the skull. Their ears, if they had any, were never visible, as they always wore one-piece metallic-like flight suits with an attached head covering similar to a helmet. Tight-fitting boots were attached to the suit. These guys were six to eight inches taller than their smaller, friendlier, and more frequently visiting cousins. All the visitors had one thing in common, however—the triangular insignia on their uniforms and craft that marked them as belonging to the Intergalactic Council.

Harry remembered the day his life had taken an abrupt right-angle turn. About two years into his Four Corners assignment, Bill had asked him to take a walk with him, and once, the two were out of earshot of the buildings, had confided, "Harry, ya seem to have a real sensitivity for communicatin' with our visitors, wouldn't ya say?"

Harry had nodded, wondering where this was going. Bill had continued, "There's a lot more goin' on at Four Corners than ya know. Ya can't talk to the others about this. Ya with me on this?"

Again, Harry nodded, consumed with curiosity. Suddenly, Bill dropped the good old boy persona and became deadly serious. "Harry, Four Corners is more than just a recovery operation. It's also a kind of embassy for extraterrestrials. We have a joint team of humans and the small Greys working deep underground on several projects, some of which are extremely complex. And with some of the more difficult concepts, our scientists run into communication problems. Now you seem to have a valuable quirk of a mind that lets you send and receive with our visitors. I'm assigning you to work with the team as an interpreter, or ambassador, if you will. As a cover, this special assignment will be in addition to your regular Blue Team duties, so you'll be working long hours. You up for that?"

Harry's mind spiraled in several directions at once. *Extraterrestrials actually working in a secret facility under the very ground they were standing on? And on long-term assignment? And I'm to be an interpreter for them. My God!*

"Am I to take your silence for agreement?" Bill asked, enjoying watching the young airman struggling to embrace the bombshell he'd just dropped.

"Yes, sir. You bet, sir. When do I start?" Harry had blurted out, to Bill's amusement.

"Well, that's good, because they asked for you specifically. Apparently, they routinely probe the minds of the staff around here, and seem to think you'll be ideal for the job. As for starting, no time like the present. Let's go to my office. To prepare you for your first assignment, there's something you need to see."

Bill Walker had shown him a copy of a treaty made some years previously between the United States government and a group of extraterrestrials. Harry recalled something about it from his orientation class. "Yeah, as I remember, and from what I've read since, Bill, the government gave permission to abduct and perform experiments on humans and animals in exchange for certain advanced technology. Also, the government would operate a cover-up and discrediting program to quash any publicity the abductions generated. However, the treaty did specify a quota of abductions, but ATIC suspects that the aliens have blatantly ignored that quota limit over the years. The treaty didn't specify exactly which group of extraterrestrials, but I have a gut feeling that it's the big Greys."

"Reckon yer right there," Bill replied, reverting back to his good old boy persona. "It's them big Grey buggers, all right."

Harry continued. "So tensions between humans and the big Greys have escalated over the years. According to the reports, ranchers are finding more and more dead cattle with various parts of their anatomy neatly removed, primarily the rectum, vagina, penis and testicles, ears, lips, and mouth. And there's never any sign of bleeding from the precise incisions that seem to be made with some kind of heated knife-like instrument. Sometimes the cuts have pinking shears edges and look as if they've been made with a cookie cutter. Christ, what type of instrument makes those cuts? And do you think the animals are alive for the procedure?"

"Don't know, but I hope ta God they aren't. Go on. Yer a regular fund of knowledge on this stuff."

"ATIC suspects that the bizarre surgeries are conducted on board the ships, and then the animals are put back in the field, dead, when they are finished. Officially, the government does its best to downplay the whole thing, but it's becoming a real problem."

"Problem's the word all right. If yer up to it, we need ya to meet with some of our visitors, the small Greys, and delicately ask if they're involved or whether it's the big Greys. Okay?"

"I'll do my best, Bill. When do we start?"

"This afternoon'll be fine. Why not go back out there and get some fresh air? Ya need time ta absorb what I've jest told ya. Meet me back here at 1400 and I'll take ya down there."

Harry had no stomach for lunch as he nervously awaited whatever the afternoon would bring. Promptly at 1400 or 2:00 P.M. he knocked on Colonel Walker's office door. Bill appeared and led him out of the barracks building to a nondescript barn that Harry had never visited. Inside, Bill punched a code into an elevator control panel and the door silently swished open. Ushering Harry inside, Bill hit the button for level 4 and the elevator began its rapid descent. Harry had no idea of the actual distance traveled when the door opened to reveal two heavily armed MPs waiting in a small lobby.

"We need ta change elevators fer the lower levels," Bill told Harry, as he held his palm to a small glass panel. "Access is strictly controlled below level four."

Another elevator door opened and they entered. Bill punched the button for level 7 and the elevator dropped. The doors opened onto a long corridor and Bill led the way past several doors, stopping at a heavy steel door. He held his palm to another panel and a green light lit up. The door slid silently open and they entered. Another door opened to reveal a comfortable living room, and Harry's jaw dropped. Lounging on sofas were three small Greys.

"Sit down, Harry, and make yerself comfortable. They've been expecting ya."

Harry sat, his mind was flooded with warm greetings. He responded with thoughts of how pleased he was to meet the visitors and that he hoped they were in good health. Bill left and, for the next few minutes, Harry and the three extraterrestrials tuned into each other's thought patterns.

As his ability to converse and answer questions in a nonverbal manner improved, Harry felt ready to ask the questions that had brought him here. "Do any from your planet still participate in the animal experiments?"

He rapidly received clear thoughts in return. "No, we are no longer involved in that type of research. We have discovered that DNA and blood products from cattle are remarkably similar to those of humans and hybrids, and can be used interchangeably as needed. We have stockpiled a large reserve supply of tissue samples that might be needed in any future experiments. More importantly, we have perfected a cloning procedure to assure that the supply is perpetual. However, we are presently involved with human abductions, conducting experiments in crossbreeding extraterrestrials and humans, using DNA from tissue we have cloned from both humans and animals in the past, in order to maximize the results we desire."

They went on to tell Harry, "The big Greys who originated on the farthest planet in the constellation Zeta Reticulum are still carrying out research studies in interspecies reproduction and are stepping up their program of animal abductions and mutilations. They appear obsessed with the challenge of hybridizing humans, animals, and extraterrestrials."

Harry asked, "Why is no blood ever found at the mutilation incisions?"

"That is because the animal is lifted from the ground by a vortex of highly charged light particles to a waiting spacecraft hovering high above. There it undergoes surgical excision of the desired body parts using an instrument capable of extremely high degrees of heat. It instantly cauterizes and seals off bleeding on either side of a precise microsurgical incision made between the rows of cells. Then the animal is returned to Earth by a light vortex similar to the one that transported it to the ship."

The door opened and Bill returned to find the four in silent communication. Harry arose, bowed slightly to the three, and thanked them for their insights. His mind was again flooded with warmth and an urge to return and talk more at his convenience.

As Bill led the way out of the underground center and into the first elevator, Harry relayed what the aliens had said about the species conducting the abductions and experiments.

"Jest confirms what I thought about them big Grey buggers, Nadien," Bill said. "Mean damn bastards. No telling what kind of stuff they're doin' ta the humans they take, crossin' 'em with them cows. God knows what'll come of it."

Harry agreed with Bill. "Yeah, I think the big Greys are far more dangerous than we'd originally thought. They show obvious contempt for the terms of the treaty, as well as for communication with us, too. I don't think they ever had any intention of cooperating with anything or anyone. The smaller Greys, like those three, on the other hand, are much friendlier. I got nothing from their thoughts about any imminent threat. And they did their best to communicate and cooperate, although they may be good at hiding their true intentions."

"Well, Harry, now that ya've got full MAJIC clearance, ya'll be in great demand. We get a lot of geneticists, biophysicists, astrophysicists, and medical people down here and they often run into trouble in dealing with complex concepts. Words are useless, and most of our people haven't got the hang of telepathy, jest can't get onto it. Their minds are already too full of formulas and equations."

"I'd be honored to act as interpreter. I really enjoyed interacting with those three."

"I know ya did," Bill said. "I had another sensitive monitoring yer progress, and she said ya did real good. Better than her, in fact, so ya've got the job. Now, let's get yer palm print on record so ya can come down here any time."

As they exited the first elevator, Bill said to the MPs, "Kin ya'll fix Captain Nadien here up with a security profile?"

"I'm not a captain, Bill. You know I'm still a lieutenant."

"Not any more, Captain. I'll give ya yer bars when ya get topside. Not that ya'll get a chance to wear 'em here," Bill grinned and left.

"This way, sir," one of the MPs said, opening a door off the lobby. Harry followed the MP, still stunned at his promotion.

"Just put your hand on this plate, sir, and the system will do the rest," the MP said, and Harry complied. "The four-digit code for the elevator topside is changed weekly and I'll put you on the list of people to be notified by voice of the new code every Sunday. For obvious reasons, it's never written down. Hope you've got a good memory. This week, it's 2243."

Harry thanked the MP, and headed for the elevator to the surface. Once there, he took a long walk around the old buildings and through the sagebrush, as the reality of what had just happened began to flood in on him.

About six months after his assignment to the extraterrestrial group, one of the ETs they called Chisky, because that was how his name would sound if it could be spoken, had expressed to Harry his keen interest in learning to communicate orally because he felt it would enable him to interpret more easily between humans and his fellow exchange scientists. It was much more difficult to teach humans to telepath and required more time. Harry had relayed this to Bill, and ATIC had quickly arranged for a team of linguistic specialists to work with Chisky and a couple of others to devise a communication protocol. It was a challenge because routine physical examinations revealed that many of the smaller Greys had no vocal cords, although in rare instances they did have some that were vestigial. Additionally, their oral and nasal cavities were far too small to form sounds. These entities were therefore unable to speak, no matter how great their desire. Chisky's physical examination revealed that, although his vocal cords and his oral cavity were small, there was a good possibility that he might learn to speak, at least to some extent.

In rapid sequence, Chisky progressed from mental telepathy with Harry to spoken words. Harry was astounded at how quickly Chisky learned to speak. At first his voice was high-pitched and mechanical-sounding, but with speech therapy, the squeaky pitch gradually dropped a few tones. The ATIC team was overjoyed at the success of their first attempt at teaching an extraterrestrial to speak.

From that moment, Chisky and the rest of his fellow alien scientists more easily shared their knowledge and expertise in the fields of space travel, intergalactic politics, astrophysics, and medicine. Chisky served as both interpreter and go-between, but Harry was still a pivotal member of the team and sat in on all the sessions in case Chisky ran into trouble with a concept for which he hadn't yet learned the vocabulary.

Since the entire operation at Four Corners carried a MAJIC security classification, only those few government and NASA scientists with a similarly high clearance were allowed to participate. The government still held the opinion that the public and most of the military was not ready for such controversial information. Many civilian researchers who could have benefited from this exchange were denied admittance. In fact, they were completely unaware that it even existed.

Harry spent countless hours in turmoil reflecting on the impact of the government's denial and its mass-deception programs. Millions of people worldwide were being allowed to die of ailments such as cancer and autoimmune diseases that the extraordinary alien medical knowledge could have cured, all because the government was unwilling to admit that the information had come from extraterrestrial sources whose existence was officially denied. He'd come to the conclusion that the problem wasn't so much that alien life forms and unidentified flying objects were real and that the public wasn't yet ready to hear it; the real problem was that, in admitting the truth about ETs and UFOs, the government would have to confess to fifty years of disinformation, outright lies, and cover-ups. When the American people realized the monumental scale of deception, trust in the government would quickly vanish, and those in power would be removed. That was the real reason behind the continued cover-up.

The government would find it extremely embarrassing to admit that extraterrestrials had been here for decades with its full permission and collaboration. There was really no way that lies of this magnitude could be admitted to, at least at the present time, and maybe never, so the secrecy just rolled on year after year. The government took the attitude that keeping the secret was far less complicated, and silenced those who dared to tell the truth. Harry thought of a variation on the old saying, *Oh, what a tangled web we weave...*, only to catch ourselves. Although he hated to admit it, he was part of the problem, not the solution.

Lately it seemed to Harry that he'd become Bill's right-hand man, helping him with a great deal of the unit paperwork, sitting in on personnel acquisition interviews, terminations, and transfers. He even assisted in the counseling sessions with team members when they got too stressed out. He sensed that Bill was gradually easing himself out. Every member of the detachment would hate to see him go, but they all knew his time to retirement was getting short. He hoped the next CO they got at Four Corners would be half as good as Bill. He'd sure as hell be a tough act to follow.

One afternoon Bill called Harry into his office and closed the door. Taking two cold beers out of the small refrigerator wedged between two file cabinets, he popped the top on each and held one out to Harry. Leaning back in his chair, Bill took a long pull on his beer and rested both feet comfortably on the desktop.

"Nadien, I'm handin' ya the reins now. Yer in charge of the detachment startin' the first of June."

Harry was astounded and sat stiffly in his chair for a moment, waiting for an appropriate reply to pop into his mind. When none came, he took a small sip of beer and sat back in his chair, hoping to give the outward impression of being comfortable. Inwardly his thoughts were racing, searching frantically for the right words to say. *I know exactly what Bill means about wanting to get out of the day-to-day stress and responsibility of running this place, but I hate the thought of him leaving. Christ, I don't feel ready to be the new boss. Hell, I don't even know if I want to be the boss. I'd known for some time that Bill was planning to retire soon, but I had absolutely no inkling that he'd pick me to take over. Running this outfit will be the biggest challenge yet.*

"You really think I'm the right one for the job, Bill? The three unit leaders are more qualified than I am, and they're majors, too. How will they feel? I'm just a captain. And what about ATIC, what do they say?" Harry stopped talking. He had been caught off guard and was afraid his flood of questions betrayed this fact.

"Don't worry about a thing, Nadien. Effective immediately, yer promoted to major. I bin talkin' to headquarters lately, and they said with yer performance reports, and my recommendation, yer in. Yer the new boss, so git used to it. The rest of the guys'll accept ya. It don't matter if they like it or not. They'll go by what I say and what ATIC says. This ain't like any other Air Force unit. Ya can't just bring anyone in here as CO. Ya gotta grow the CO on the job, like you an' everyone else here."

"What are you going to do, Bill? You're still a young man."

"It's time fer me to see if Gracie can still remember what the hell I look like, see if I kin still ride them green colts any more. I've put my twenty in, an' it's time to get back to a normal life, if ya know what I mean."

With that pronouncement, Bill sat back, uncrossed his feet, and set them down on the floor, his body language indicating the case was closed as far he was concerned.

For the next two weeks, Harry immersed himself in learning the detailed workings of his new job. *This will be the biggest challenge I've ever faced. But I'll give it my best shot, be a success no matter what it takes. Of course, I'll continue the informality that Bill has instituted. Life here's so stressful that the only way we can survive emotionally is to relax the regulations whenever possible. Bill started it, and I'll simply carry on the tradition.*

Colonel Bill Walker retired from the Air Force at the age of thirty-nine. For ATIC, that was considered old. He'd spent the better part of his career at detachments similar to Four Corners, tiny little places that weren't on any map; places where there were no telltale clues evident above ground to give any indication that anything was or ever had been there. His official military record would make no mention of his assignment. To the rest of the world, he'd spent twenty years as an obscure supply officer with an honorable discharge.

Bill loved his work, feeling he had the best job the military had to offer, but he was ready to put the stress of this life behind him. His wife, Gracie, whom he saw once a year when he went home on leave, had kept their little horse ranch going up in the highline country of Montana. He was eager for the more easygoing way of life waiting there for him, to be in a place where the big excitement of the day would be the birth of a new foal. Maybe if things got tight, he'd turn his place into a dude ranch, and get paid for doing what he'd already be doing for free. He could think about that later.

Bill was one of a handful of people assigned to ATIC who was married at the time he enlisted, a time when that was still allowed. He and Gracie had gotten married the month before he joined the Air Force and, though his status was openly frowned upon by MAJIC and ATIC, there was nothing they could do about it as long as he kept the nature of his work to himself. He never told Gracie what his job entailed, or even where he was physically stationed. His letters to her, and hers back to him, were all passed through Masters Air Force Base, and that was where she presumed he was located. He never told her anything to the contrary, and she never asked.

When Bill announced that the new CO would be Harry, one of their own, the team members had cheered, pleased that some new broom from another detachment would not come in and start sweeping clean. Few other officers could have understood how things worked here. So even though Harry wasn't the most senior major there, the news that he would be the new CO was met with relief.

Chapter 14

Rescue — 1969

Other than the emptiness caused by Bill's leaving, nothing changed much at Four Corners. Team members came and went, rotating on an 18-month tour of duty. Almost all were relieved when their tour was over, never quite getting used to the isolation of the base.

There were a few crashes, but most craft landed safely, apparently having improved their control systems to deal with Earth's gravity, our radar systems, and the ever-fluctuating magnetic field in the area. The visitors came and went as guests of NASA and the government, working in the underground laboratory alongside the human scientists. Harry still found time to engage the visitors in telepathic conversations, although two especially sensitive young female officers now did much of the grunt work.

Chisky was one of the few aliens who remained, participating in the ongoing research projects. He'd arrived in one of the safe landings several years earlier, and made an occasional trip back to Zeta I, but he never remained there long. Chisky now considered Earth the most favorable location for conducting his experiments in cloning and cell propagation. He provided ATIC with blueprints of the laboratory equipment necessary for his research, and ATIC made sure he received equipment fabricated to his exact specifications. They were especially gratified by his interest in the Humanization Project that had just been proposed by MAJIC.

Through the years, Harry and Chisky had become close friends. They met for about an hour each evening, once the day's duties were over. Only an arriving craft could break the tradition. They were an unlikely pair sitting across from each other in their lounge chairs seven floors underground, conversing back and forth —a burly six-foot officer in fatigues, and a frail, four-foot extraterrestrial, clad in his ever-predictable silver jumpsuit. Chisky never tired of learning about the complexities of humans, and of life on Earth, and he eagerly probed Harry's mind to glean human history. Harry was equally eager to absorb everything he could learn about extraterrestrial life.

Discussing the physiology of the myriad of intelligent life forms each had come in contact with, they were both thankful that most seemed to have a bipedal humanoid appearance. They were easier to relate to than the insect or plant types, or even the sentient plasma clouds.

One evening Chisky explained, "Many races of extraterrestrials have, over time, lost their reproductive abilities, and now rely almost exclusively on the creation of new beings by cloning them from the existing population. The cloning programs always emphasized superior intelligence, at the expense of emotional and physical development. Only when it was too late to remedy did they notice that their physical strength and stamina were declining dramatically and that the population was becoming progressively more frail. Replicative failure during cloning only furthered the physical frailness, and infant mortality soon became a problem."

"Some species," he continued, "have physically deteriorated to the point that interbreeding with a healthy dynamic and compatible species is the only way to achieve sufficient strength and vigor to survive. Since humans and these species all share the same genetic heritage going back millions of years when Earth was first seeded with life, humans are the ideal species to interbreed with. We combine human ova or sperm collected from abductees with its extraterrestrial counterpart for in vitro fertilization. Then we implant it inside a human surrogate mother. Two to three months later, we remove the fetus during another abduction and incubate it in a propagating solution."

"And how do the human mothers feel about this?" Harry asked. "Do they see it as an invasion of their bodies?"

"It depends on how it is done," Chisky replied. "In some cases, the mother is fully aware during the procedure and the memory is blocked later. We prefer to work with fully consenting women, whom we keep fully informed at every step. We found very early on that the mother's fear is transmitted to the fetus, and that produces undesirable lifelong emotional scars."

"So are surrogate mothers always used?" Harry asked.

"Not always," Chisky explained. "Another method of increasing the physical vigor of the various civilizations is to extract DNA from human subjects, combine it with DNA taken from the extraterrestrials and then incubate the tiny hybrid embryos in containers, nourished by a nutrient-rich propagating solution in the same manner as those created with conventional sperm and ova."

"And how were you chosen for this work, Chisky?"

"As a hybrid myself, the successful result of the interspecies breeding program on Zeta I, my own planet, and as their leading geneticist, I was the logical choice to head the research program in interspecies propagation on Earth."

Harry was about to ask another question, when the earsplitting sound of the siren shattered his thoughts. Jumping up, he ran for the elevators and just made the lead truck, jumping inside one of the open doors as it pulled out.

As the small convoy of vehicles raced to the site, a huge flash illuminated the night sky, indicating another crash. He knew that an explosion of that magnitude, seen from such a distance, meant no survivors. The best they could hope for was that someone may have been thrown clear on impact.

Nearing the site, he saw the ship with its interior partially exposed. The impact had ripped a massive gash in its side. Twisted metal and sagebrush melted together, and the craft shimmered in the heat haze. Even with their protective suits and headgear, it was impossible to approach closer than a hundred feet. As soon as things cooled down, they'd check it out, down to the smallest piece. That was standard procedure. If enough of the craft remained intact, and the antigravity unit had still been working at the time of impact, there was always a possibility that a crew member had survived the impact. Tonight a good-sized portion of an inner compartment appeared to remain relatively intact.

Through his light-enhancing glasses, Harry saw three badly charred bodies on the ground about fifty feet from the craft, apparently thrown clear on impact. They were recognizable as bodies only because of the few scraps that remained of their metallic suits. "No reason to rush in, guys. No survivors here. Again," Harry said, shaking his head sadly. "This part always upsets me, and I'll never get used to it."

Suddenly, fire broke out inside the craft and threatened to destroy what was left of the ship. Just then Harry thought he saw a movement through a small window in the undamaged portion. "Hold on, fellas. I might be wrong. Wait here while I go in and check this out."

Pulling his headgear down tight and securing it in place, Harry moved cautiously toward the craft. About a hundred feet from the wreckage, he began to feel the soles of his boots heating up. Continuing to walk slowly forward he thought, *I'm sure I saw something moving in there, and I'm damn well going to find out what it was. Maybe someone's still alive in there. Damn the heat. If we wait for things to cool down, whoever's in there doesn't stand a chance.*

The intact section of the craft rested flat on the ground, landing gear either still retracted or blown off on impact. Sweat poured off his skin inside his suit as he reached the craft. Looking through the hatch, he saw flames beginning to consume the incandescent interior. Just to the right of the opening he saw a door, intact, which he assumed must lead to an inner compartment. Just about the place where he'd seen the movement.

Stepping inside the ship, he cautiously approached the door. Touching what he guessed was a control panel, the door slid open. Not six feet from where he stood, a tiny body lay motionless on the floor, trapped under a fallen equipment panel. Possibly because the being was so much smaller than any of the others he had encountered before, he felt it was a female. The small Greys were pretty androgynous, and he usually never thought much about their gender, but somehow this one was different. *She looks like Chisky, only smaller,* he thought.

Bending over her small form, he was drawn to her eyes. Huge and rounded at the inner corners, angling up at an unusual slant around onto her temples, they were like Chisky's eyes, yet they were somehow slightly different, a riveting shade of light green. Trapped in an expressionless face, her eyes told him she was alive and terrified. Trapped under the panel, all she could do was stare up at him with those enormous avocado-green eyes.

Quickly pulling the panel clear of her frail body, he noticed the sleeve of her silver bodysuit was torn. He lifted the soft, metallic material gently away from her arm and inspected the yellowish-green skin beneath it. A pale reddish substance was beginning to congeal on her arm.

He'd never seen anything like this before. The others that had been wounded had nearly always exuded a sort of thin, colorless liquid that the lab had identified as a chlorophyll-based compound, or occasionally something similar to leukocytes. Always the liquid had been clear and colorless, but this was definitely a light shade of red. Then he remembered that Chisky's scratches would bleed the same light pinkish-colored liquid, too. That would explain why she looked so different from all the others. That's why her eyes were like Chisky's, and why he'd felt an instant bonding with her. *I'd bet a month's pay that she's a human hybrid. God, could this be one of the Humanization Project members that Chisky told me would be coming?*

Suddenly he felt a familiar warmth in his head. She's trying to communicate with me, he thought. Information flooded his mind. "We came here to assist Chisky in the Humanization Project and have been selected to become part of it. There were four of us, and I am aware that the others have perished. I am uninjured except for the small laceration on my forearm. I am already healing that with a special breathing technique used by my people which causes bleeding to stop and tissue to restore itself almost instantly."

"They'll be lookin' ya up again," he could hear Bill's voice echoing over the years. He hadn't understood the full meaning of those words then, but something in his heart told him he soon would.

"Major, you okay? Better get out. The fire's getting worse," a voice called.

Suddenly, Harry realized how hot he'd become in his suit. Stooping, he gently gathered the little female in his arms, turned, and stepped back out of the craft. The medical recovery team had pulled its vehicle up as close as they dared on the still-hot ground. Any closer and the tires would melt. Placing the alien on the gurney, he helped them load her into the ambulance. Then he did something that surprised him as much as it did the ambulance crew. He climbed inside with the medics and sat down on the narrow jump seat beside the tiny passenger. It was the first time he'd ever accompanied a crash victim to the medical facility.

He pulled off his gloves and held one of her tiny hands in his, telling himself, *I'll only stay until she's safely in the hands of the nursing staff. Then I'll go back to the office and write up the incident report. God, I need sleep, but my mind is way too busy for that right now. I need to think about what it means to be specifically looked up by the extraterrestrials, and why do I have special feelings for this tiny alien female? Why did she completely captivate my senses the instant I looked into her eyes? None of this makes sense. Sure, I care about all the visitors, but this is more. It's almost personal. No, it is personal. But why? And how?*

But he didn't go back to the office. Instead he went inside with her, walking beside the gurney, holding her tiny hand as the recovery crew wheeled it to the dilapidated barn structure. Then, MAJIC clearance medics took it into the two elevators down to level 8 that housed the medical facility. Harry sensed that the female wished him to stay with her, so he accompanied her through the various physical examinations, and the many tests that were routinely performed on all crash survivors.

Chisky and a colleague arrived and immediately went to work devising a form of nourishment compatible with her physiology. The two base nurses, Fran and Wanda, carefully removed her tattered jumpsuit and sponged her thin body with lukewarm water and a soft cloth. Dressing her in the smallest size scrub suit they could find, then rolling the pant legs up several times, it was still much too large.

"It'll have to do for now," Wanda told Harry. "Fran and I can shop for some children's clothes in Vegas during the weekend. Her flight suit's just good for cleaning rags."

"How is she?" Harry asked, still puzzled at his level of concern.

"She's asleep, so there's nothing much to be done until the morning."

Harry walked out into the corridor just as Chisky returned from checking the lab results and sat down next to him. "I believe she is from my star system, possibly even my planet. One thing I am very sure of, though, is that she is a hybrid, but just what proportion and what derivation is uncertain. Her blood is similar to mine, but it contains human DNA markers. My colleague and I have formulated a liquid with which to nourish her for the present, and we have begun developing a solid substance for her to eat, also. She will be unable, however, to eat or drink anything other than these formulations. Nothing else at all."

Harry nodded, then Chisky added, "Other species do not have nuclear families as you do on Earth, but to the extent that we do, the three who died were her family. She is now alone. With the proper care and nurturing, she could become quite humanized, more so than any hybrid I have seen. It is indeed a challenge for you to consider."

Smiling the small, faint smile he had mastered, he got up and left, leaving Harry in stunned silence. He knew exactly what Chisky meant. *I'm going to do it,* he decided, and realized that he'd made up his mind the moment he'd first laid eyes on her. *Yes, it will be a challenge, the biggest one I've ever faced, even greater than running a place that isn't supposed to exist. I'm going to do my level best to help her. I owe her that for making the trip. Hell, I owe it to myself.*

As he walked out into the cool night air, he breathed deeply and looked up at the stars hanging in the clear desert sky. Chisky had shown him star maps and he was able to identify her home, the Zeta constellation. *It'll be unusual,* he thought, *and maybe crazy, but yes, I will take personal responsibility for her. She can have the two empty rooms next to my office. All they need is paint, carpet, and furniture. It'll be perfect for her. In the morning, I'll check with ATIC headquarters for permission. I'm sure they'll agree once I tell them that she'll be the first young hybrid, and the first female, to participate. As far as I know, there are no other hybrids in the experiment. The rest of the participants are aliens with no degree of humanness. Chisky is the only other hybrid working with us, and his mission is solely to participate in the Information Exchange Program.*

Christ, I don't know how to take care of her. There's only so much I can do for her. She's definitely going to need a woman's touch for a proper upbringing. I'll need help from Fran and Wanda. I need to ask them if they'd be willing to help me raise her. In fact, I'd better do that now, he decided, returning to the underground facility. Harry arrived at the exam room just as its door opened, and three figures emerged, Fran and Wanda supporting the tiny, fragile female between them. She moved stiffly, with a shuffling gait, but she was walking. It was a strange sight, a little being no more than three feet tall, dressed in a green scrub suit many sizes too large. Her skin appeared to be a faint yellowish-green and the slightly darker shade of her huge green eyes contrasted starkly with its paleness. Her nose was tiny and had almost no bridge, and her mouth was a small slit with thin, straight lips. Her spindly arms and legs appeared awkward and much too long for the frail little body.

"We want to keep her, Harry," Fran said. "Of course, that's if we can find a place for her to live. There's no space here at the lab, and our rooms in the barracks are way too small, but there's that extra space over in the barn, next to your office. We've been talking about it, and we're willing to get it ready, if you say it's okay. We could help you take care of her, too."

"That's exactly what I've been thinking. I could never do it all by myself. I was going to ask you two how you felt about helping me out. First though, before we do anything or make any plans at all, we've got to get approval from ATIC. But I think this'll fit right in with the Humanization Project. I'll call them first thing in the morning and see what they say."

He looked at the small figure and tried to explain with his thoughts what he wanted to do for her. He wasn't sure he'd gotten through to her until he again felt the familiar warmth suffuse his head. He realized then that she understood and had listened in on the whole conversation. "I would like to accept your offer. I want to stay," he heard in his mind.

"One more thing, Harry," Wanda said. "We've named her Raechel. It's a pretty name, and we think it fits her just right. That is, if you like it."

"What I like isn't the point," Harry said, and directed a thought to the visitor. He felt the warm glow once more and heard the words, "I like that very much. It is a pretty name. Thank you."

"Okay, Raechel it is. Where will she spend the night?"

"We're both going to stay here in the observation ward with her tonight. Chisky and his buddy are making up something for her to drink until the lab is done formulating solid food so we can safely feed her. Then tomorrow we'll get those rooms fixed up for her. If ATIC approves, that is."

And even if ATIC doesn't approve, Harry thought to himself. *The matter's settled, at least in my mind.*

"Good night, Raechel. I'll see you in the morning," he telepathed and smiled.

"Goodnight," he heard back, smiled again and left.

Harry skipped breakfast and called headquarters. His boss was extremely enthusiastic about his proposal, especially the prospect of using a young hybrid for the Humanization Project, and he promised to run the idea by the ATIC top brass.

An hour later, the phone rang and Harry had his answer. "ATIC says go for it, Harry. They have only one stipulation. For legal purposes, you must adopt her as your daughter. If you will, I'll have all the necessary paperwork in your hands by 1600. Oh, by the way, Harry, the courier will also be bringing a couple of colonel's birds for that uniform I know you never wear."

Harry said, "Thanks, general, and sure, send the paperwork over," and hung up the telephone, his head spinning. *Did I just get promoted to colonel and officially adopt an extraterrestrial female as my daughter? My God, if I legally adopt her, I'll be responsible for her for the rest of my life. Hers, too. What the hell have I gotten myself into?*

Christ, I've got to tell somebody, but who? Bill Walker! He'll understand and won't think I'm insane. He reached Bill at his ranch in Sweetgrass and told him about the latest turn of events. Bill hadn't changed at all, except maybe to become a little more laid back, and he didn't seem the least bit surprised at Harry's news. He sounded very happy and relaxed and it was good to hear his voice again.

"Told ya they were gonna look ya up again. Sent ya a nice present this time, they shore did. Listen, soon as ya get a few days off, bring yer little gal up to the ranch. Anybody who kin ride a spaceship clear to Four Corners and survive a crash-landing oughta be a helluva bronc rider. Gracie and I'd love to see ya both."

Harry felt as though he were an actor in some kind of bizarre play without a script, playing out his role under the guidance of an unseen director. *My God, in less than 24 hours, I've managed to res-*

cue and adopt a daughter named Raechel—an extraterrestrial. No, part extraterrestrial and part human, he corrected himself.

All I asked ATIC for was permission to let her stay at the detachment for a while outside the underground extraterrestrial quarters. I hadn't planned it to be a permanent thing. Why the hell are they insisting on legal adoption? I wish I understood the reasoning behind it, but the general didn't seem willing to explain. Acted like he'd been expecting my call, though. Weird. Then all of a sudden I'm promoted to a colonel with no time in grade. The more I think about it, the more totally insane it seems.

Suddenly he felt overwhelmed by the responsibility that faced him. *I have absolutely no idea how to raise a human child, much less a human/extraterrestrial hybrid. That could take quite a bit of doing,* he figured, *but I suppose I'll manage somehow. I can learn. And I have three good helpers in Chisky, Wanda, and Fran. Both women have just reenlisted, so they'll be around for at least four or five more years. That should be plenty of time to get Raechel started on learning the ways of humans, females in particular. It'll all work out. It has to. There's no going back now.*

Harry sighed as he leaned over the desk and cradled his head in his hands. "Annie, what have I done? Are you engineering this? Is this your way of giving me a reason to live? I wish you were here to help me, to love me and love Raechel, too."

Chapter 15

A New Type of Communication — 1969

Pouring himself a fresh cup of hot coffee from the carafe in front of him, Harry finished the sweet roll he'd taken earlier. He checked his watch. *There's enough time before lunch to walk over to the medical facility and see how Raechel's doing. There are so many things I want to say to her,* he thought, as he walked to the medical building. *I'll tell her she doesn't have to be frightened anymore, that she doesn't have to worry about a thing. I'll tell her I'll take care of her from now on. Will she even understand the concept of father and daughter? Most importantly, though, she needs to understand that she's safe, and that I and everyone else at Four Corners want her to remain here.*

As Harry approached the lab, he saw Wanda coming towards him. Dressed in her off-duty outfit of jeans, blouse, and sneakers, she was headed for the shed where she kept her Jeep parked. "I'm going into Vegas, Harry. Last night Fran and I checked out the rooms that Raechel is going to use. We made a list of what we'll need to fix up them up. I'll get wallpaper, curtains, things for the bathroom and bedroom; and some clothes that will fit. That scrub suit looks awful on her."

Wanda paused to catch her breath, and before Harry could get a word in, she continued, "Fran's on duty today and she'll keep an eye on Raechel until I get back. I think we're starting to pick up a few of her thoughts, but we're not sure our answers are getting through to her. We're not used to talking that way.

Glad you're here, since you're the expert on that stuff. Gotta go, Harry. See you later," she called as she hurried to her vehicle.

The room where Raechel had spent her first night at Four Corners contained four cots along one wall, and an old chrome kitchen table and four chairs placed around it along the opposite wall. As Harry stood in the doorway, he saw Raechel seated at the table with her back to the door. She sensed his presence, stood and turned toward him. She started moving in his direction with her awkward, jerky gait. Harry stopped and waited. Approaching to within a couple of feet from him, she stopped and gazed intently into his eyes.

The familiar warmth surged through his head, followed by several thoughts, one after another. "I am grateful for being rescued from the crashed spacecraft. I feel safe with you, and Fran and Wanda. Chisky came to visit me earlier this morning. He told me the DNA testing had determined the exact proportions of my genetic makeup. I would be pleased to remain here and participate in the Humanization Project if you approve."

The inside of Harry's head then immediately began to feel cooler, signaling that Raechel had finished communicating for the moment. Her huge green eyes remained fixed on his face as she awaited his reply.

Harry debated with himself. *Should I express myself as I would to a young child, or to an adolescent, or to an adult? How old is she, anyway? Judging from her size, she could be nine or fifteen. Or maybe she was twenty-five and has reached full growth. Hell, I can't even judge the ages of humans. Maybe where she comes from, there's no such thing as age as we know it. Maybe just different stages of physical development, small, medium, and larger. The thought transference from her can only be described as universal, not age-specific at all.*

A sudden thought popped into his head and he said excitedly, "I think I've got it, Fran. Raechel just told me. Where she comes from, they just are. Their minds are fully developed right from the beginning. The body starts out small, then grows bigger and finally stops when it gets to whatever size it's supposed to be. But the mind never changes. It's so simple, so uncomplicated that I'm surprised I haven't thought of it before. God, they're so damned far ahead of us, we must seem like idiots to them. I've never been able to figure out why the hell they'd waste their time on us."

Harry felt a light touch on his sleeve. Looking down, he saw Raechel looking up at him, her eyes locked on his. Ashamed that he'd been ignoring her, lost in his thoughts again, he sat down at the table and motioned to her to sit in the chair across from Fran. Before he could begin telling her all the things he wanted her to know, he felt the inside of his head once again suffuse with warmth, and he realized that Raechel had been picking up his thoughts from the minute he'd entered the room. "No, earlier," she corrected. "When you talked to the important human on the communication device," she said into his mind.

"Oh, you mean when I phoned the general."

She nodded and telepathed, "Do not be concerned about how to communicate with me. Simply hold whatever you wish to say to me in your mind, and I will take it from there."

What a relief, Harry thought as he realized that he had had a temporary block with Raechel because she looked so human. *How incredibly simple! No worrying about whether or not I'm saying it just right. She'll understand whatever thoughts I hold to send her. He sheepishly remembered being concerned about the language barrier. What if she can't understand English? How will she understand my thoughts?*

"Thoughts are a universal language," Raechel said to Harry. "There is only one language of thinking. Stop worrying. Simply think what it is that you wish to tell me."

"Of course, you're right," he sent back. "Language doesn't exist where thoughts are concerned. It's still amazing to me that someone who doesn't speak English can communicate with me in such a simple fashion."

He swallowed hard, put both hands on the table in front of him, and held the thought, "I am taking full responsibility for your welfare while you're on Earth. I will take good care of you. Either Fran or Wanda will be with you most of the time so you will never be lonely or frightened. And you also have Chisky and his colleagues for company.

We're just a father and daughter chatting over the kitchen table. My daughter and I. Wow, my daughter! My daughter, Raechel Nadien. I, Harry Nadien, have a daughter, Raechel!

Raechel locked gaze with him and he felt her confusion. He signaled back, "I'll explain later."

"I want to know about this place," she telepathed.

He tried to hold the thought of Four Corners as a spaceport and embassy for the visiting nonterrestrials, and that his job was to assist the visitors from distant places who survived the long journeys.

He added, "Because you are partially human, I would like to teach you to live as a human, if you agree. Would you participate in the Humanization Project in that capacity?"

He stopped projecting thoughts for a moment, took a deep breath and looked at her, hoping his thoughts hadn't come across too quickly and too garbled for her to understand.

Raechel's face had remained expressionless during his thought transference. Harry assumed that she, like nearly all the other extraterrestrials he'd seen, was essentially unable to move her facial muscles, and he was surprised when the corners of her thin, small mouth began to move upward slightly.

Harry continued his silent conversation with her, explaining about the new living quarters that Fran and Wanda were going to convert into a comfortable, pleasant home for her. He told her that Chisky had taken responsibility for creating a substance she would use as food. He hesitated, unsure whether she understood what he'd told her, or if she even understood the meanings of "office" and "living quarters." It turned out that he'd been worrying over nothing, again, for the warmth returned.

"Yes, I understand. I will cooperate as best I can. But there is a great deal concerning humans and many aspects of how you live that I do not understand at all. I will require a great deal of help in learning all the things I need to know."

Harry held the thought, "I have one final question for you, not that it really matters, but I'm curious. How old are you?"

"In the human concept of age, I am intermediate. I cannot define it further. But if it is important to assign an age to me, I will leave it to you."

Harry turned to Fran. "I asked her how old she was and she called herself 'intermediate.' If that equated to about fifteen years old, that would allow her sufficient time to complete whatever education she'll get while she remains here and be an appropriate age to enter college when I retire in about five years. That is, if she wants to go to college, when the time comes."

"How will you educate her?" Fran asked. "She won't relate to the Dick and Jane books we all learned to read from."

"You're right. The next time I talk with ATIC, I'll ask if they can suggest something appropriate to whatever her knowledge might already include. They've done a remarkable job with the adult extraterrestrials.

Glancing at his watch, he saw it was 1530. "Hey, I gotta run. The NRO helicopter carrying the courier and the adoption papers should be here in half an hour. Just time enough to get over to my office and close up my report to ATIC so I can send it back with the courier. I'll put something in the report about needing help with her education."

Harry knew his report would come under the intense scrutiny of the entire MAJIC group, the Aquarius Project, and everyone else involved in collecting information concerning extraterrestrials. His report and those in the future concerning Raechel's progress would most likely end up on the desk of the President of the United States. Every single thing he and Raechel did from this day forward would be a matter of extreme interest to the government. He'd been entrusted with the responsibility of raising a hybrid extraterrestrial in a totally human environment. It was an experiment that, as far as he knew, no one had undertaken before.

Raechel reached timidly across the corner of the table and-touched Harry's hand with her long, spindly fingers. They felt cool and dry. With his other hand, he covered her small, thin hand for a long moment. Her skin had an unusual texture, reminding him of something familiar. Mushrooms. That's it. Her skin feels like the velvety surface of a mushroom. She had initiated the touch. *We're holding each other's hands,* he marveled, *and it feels good.*

"Raechel had better stay here one more night, Harry," Fran said. "As soon as Wanda gets back, she'll take over for me and keep her company. Then we'll have a painting party and bring in some old furniture from the barracks and the storage shed. By tomorrow, the whole place will be all prettied up and ready for her to move in."

The warmth in Harry's mind signaled communication from Raechel. "I understand you must leave now. After you leave, I will speak to Fran."

"Get ready Fran," Harry joked. "You're about to have a lesson in nonverbal communication. It'll be easy. Just relax and let Raechel take the lead."

Fran was already transfixed by Raechel's eyes, oblivious to anything or anyone in the room. The expression of sheer amazement on her face told him that lesson number one was under way.

As soon as all the members of the detachment were seated in the dining hall for dinner, Harry stood up and cleared his throat loudly to get their attention. "As of 1600 hours today, I officially became a father. Some of you already knew that I was going to check with ATIC for permission to keep the survivor of yesterday's crash here for a while. Well, the only way they'd agree to let her stay is if I adopt her and raise her as my daughter."

Harry waited for the hum of conversation to die down and, clearing his throat again, he continued. "I signed the paperwork this afternoon."

He paused for a moment and looked around the table at the astonished faces. "That's all I've got for now. By the way, her name is Raechel. Raechel Nadien."

He sat down. After a moment's stunned silence, every person in the room stood up, cheered, and applauded. Harry felt embarrassed at the display of emotion, even more so when one of his men shouted, "Three cheers for Colonel Nadien."

"Anything we can do to help, let us know, Harry."

"You gotta lotta guts, boss, adoptin' an extraterrestrial. We're behind you a hundred percent."

"Where're you going to keep her? You need help fixing up a place, let us know."

It was clear he had the support of every person in the room. Harry didn't feel quite so confident, though. His misgivings began to take over. *What if it doesn't work out? What if we can't keep her alive? We've never been able to sustain an extraterrestrial for long. They just don't possess the same digestive systems and alimentary tracts as humans. They require a complicated, synthesized chlorophyll-based liquid that they can assimilate through their skin. This is awkward and inconvenient. Although all the extraterrestrials in the program cooperate enthusiastically, their health invariably begins to deteriorate and they usually ended up returning home. But Raechel is a hybrid. She has some human genes. She'll survive better.*

Chisky had assured him, "Her physiological makeup is fairly close to mine, approximately one-third to one-half human, close enough that I am confident I have formulated a life-sustaining diet for her. I think this will suffice," he said, handing Harry a vial of colorless liquid. "This is just temporary. My colleagues and I will develop more substantial nourishment for her body. Using the basic formula we devised for adult extraterrestrials and hybrids, we will modify it to include additional nutrients for Raechel because she is still growing."

With the problem of Raechel's food solved in his mind, another worry surfaced. Something he hadn't thought about. *As long as we remain at Four Corners, we can tailor her environment specifically to her needs. But in a few years, I'll be retiring and then what will happen? Could she adapt to life away from here? Could she function being away from Fran and Wanda, Chisky and the others?*

Chapter 16

Raechel's New Family — 1969

That night, every person not assigned to critical duty turned out for the room-painting party beginning at 1900, and the work was finished by 0400 the next morning. When Harry entered the dining hall for breakfast at 0500, he found the whole crew assembled, eagerly waiting to see what his reaction would be to their efforts.

Following Wanda through the door into the two rooms that had been dingy and unfinished the previous day, he saw instead a fresh, clean, attractively furnished suite. It was difficult to believe that such a complete transformation had been accomplished overnight.

"Don't get any ideas, Harry," Wanda said, pride and paint splotches covering her face. "We're not going to give your office a makeover. This is special, just for Raechel."

The woodwork was a glossy white, and the bedroom walls were papered in a delicate floral print on a pale pink background. A matching pale-rose bedspread covered the bed, an old government-issue olive-drab iron affair that now sported a coat of gleaming white enamel. An ancient dresser, its top covered with a crisp linen scarf, gleamed sparkling white in the corner. Harry was amazed. Every surface, every object, had been scrubbed and/or painted.

Opening the closet door, he saw several new outfits hanging inside. Two shoeboxes were on the floor. He didn't look inside the dresser drawers, but he supposed they would probably contain underclothing. Wanda had done an unbelievable amount of shopping in the short time she'd been gone. He was deeply touched at the display of love for his new daughter.

Inside the small bathroom, towels and washcloths hung between the sink and shower. The new smell of the plastic shower curtain mingled with a more fragrant odor of flower-scented soap on the sink. Although it had been a long time, it reminded him of Annie. He was sure it was the perfume she had worn. He couldn't help but wonder whether Raechel had ever used scented soap wherever she came from. She had agreed to try living as a human, and it might not take her very long at all to fall into human ways, teenage girl ways. But that was Fran and Wanda's department. It was completely out of his field of expertise.

He walked into the second room, which the crew had turned into a combination living and study room. Bright new slipcovers decorated an old dayroom couch he recognized as coming from the barracks. A newly painted desk and an old set of bookshelves from the storage shed stood near the couch.

Fran, Wanda, and whoever else had coordinated all of this had put a great deal of effort into creating a nice place for Raechel. He'd been completely unable to visualize anything even remotely close to this. Raechel should be very comfortable here, and he could hardly wait to show her where she'd be living.

Entering the dining area, he was surprised to see not only the crew, but Wanda and Fran, with Raechel between them. "Listen up, you guys," Harry said. "Thank you, thank you for doing this for us. There's just no way I could have done it by myself."

He choked the words out, struggling to hold back the tears that welled up in his eyes. Ron, the burly guard who'd been the first person Harry had encountered at the gate the day he reported for duty, broke the embarrassed silence. "Hell, boss, we're like family here. It's the least we could do for you and Raechel. I was just getting off duty when Wanda came through, heading for town. So I went along and helped her with the shopping. There wasn't any time to come back and get a pass, but we were really on official government business, getting supplies an' all. Sure hope it was okay for me to take off like that." Harry nodded.

Fran spoke up. "Raechel's got something to tell you, Harry. She and Wanda talked about it last night. Well, not really talked, but you know what I mean. She told Ron, too, just now while you were in there, looking at everything."

Raechel took a step towards Harry and stopped. Again Harry felt the warm sensation inside his head, and the word "family" became clear in his mind. "You...are...all...my... family," she told the gathering, and many of them, especially Ron, teared up at the words of the brave, orphaned extraterrestrial, marooned millions of miles away from home.

It dawned on Harry as he remembered that Ron, like the other guards, had been recruited by ATIC specifically because he was an orphan, and had no family. Harry had been puzzled by Ron's embarrassment because he'd never worried before about going off-base without a pass, technically being AWOL. But he realized that the idea of finally belonging to a family, even an unconventional one like this, would mean a great deal to him.

Harry remembered something he'd read once that some families are made up of members who are totally related only by the love and respect they hold for one another. He understood now exactly what that meant. This little band of people at Four Corners was far closer to him than his own family had ever been. And ironically, it had taken the arrival of this small alien female to bond this diverse group into one of the main things ATIC frowned on ... a family.

Oh, Raechel, he thought, *life is going to be interesting around you.*

Chapter 17

Communication with Humans — 1969

"Thank you for coming so quickly," Harry said as Suzanne Brent stepped out of the ATIC helicopter. "I requested a linguistics expert only yesterday."

"This project is very important, and teaching Raechel to speak will be a major step forward," Suzanne said, holding out her hand. "Shall we get started?"

Harry was impressed. This competent-looking, businesslike woman had come highly recommended, having already taught several extraterrestrials to speak. The medical team had ascertained that Raechel had enough vocal cord tissue to speak, and testing revealed she had an extremely high IQ—enough to handle linguistics. With intensive speech therapy, she should be an outstanding participant in the Humanization Project.

Even though Suzanne had trained several of the visitors to speak, she'd never had an opportunity to teach any of them to read. There simply hadn't been a need. The others had all been mature, already expert in their various fields of research, and involved in projects where the only materials they needed to read were symbols and computer language.

Within a few days of Suzanne's arrival, Raechel was able to vocalize a few words, filling in with thought projection when she struggled for the correct wording. Two weeks later, she could communicate using speech alone.

After Suzanne had tested Raechel, Harry arranged for her to consult with Chisky. "Raechel can speak," she began, "in that she knows the words and can construct complex sentences, but I'm having trouble teaching her inflections. She just can't seem to put emotion into her speech patterns. Her voice remains somewhat stiff and mechanical in tone. Can you explain to me why your race determined that speech and emotions were nonessential?"

"Emotion was eliminated centuries ago when we, the galactic community, observed it to be a primary source of diverse social problems," Chisky replied. "We saw how uncontrolled emotion and passionate speech resulted in devastating wars on Earth as well as on other planets. Therefore it was deemed a dangerous and undesirable component of our personality. Genetic engineering of hybrids is relatively new for us, and the degree of emotion any one hybrid might display is carefully monitored. If problems arise as a result of too strong an emotional component, we reduce the amount of human DNA to eliminate this undesirable trait in any future generations of hybrids. If someone displays too much emotion, he is closely monitored. We cannot risk this undesirable trait running rampant among us."

In the end, Suzanne, Harry, and Chisky agreed that the important thing was for Raechel to concentrate on simply vocalizing the words. It would be up to the listener to mentally provide any necessary inflection. Suzanne conveyed their feelings to Raechel, and from then on there was less stress, and the lessons went much more quickly and smoothly. Raechel would now be able to verbalize and everyone would be able to understand her.

Suzanne had never before put together a reading curriculum for a hybrid. She had asked ATIC to furnish her with reading primers, and they arrived the next day. However, when she unpacked the box, she exclaimed, "These are useless. How stupid. Dick and Jane and their dog Spot. What were the idiots thinking? No offense, Dick and Jane, but you're not exactly appropriate for someone whose IQ is off the scale. What the hell am I supposed to do?" she said, tossing the books back in their packing box.

What can I use that she would relate to? Damn, she thought. *Raechel's so eager to get started, and so am I! We'd have been better off if they'd sent some books on astronomy and quantum physics. At least she could identify with those subjects.*

Calming down and collecting her thoughts, Suzanne decided to make up some stories for Raechel. She could type them out on a typewriter, and illustrations would make the lessons so much more interesting. She could barely draw a straight line, much less a picture.

Suzanne was puzzling over the problem when Ron stopped by for his regular visit with Raechel after coming off gate duty. Raechel told him in her mechanical, squeaky voice, "I am very eager to learn to read. The books ATIC sent are not right somehow. Suzanne is planning to make me some special books."

Suzanne added, "I don't know what they were thinking about. Sending Dick and Jane books, for God's sake! I can write the stories we need, but I can't illustrate them, and they just won't be as effective without pictures."

"Not to worry, Suze. Before I joined the Air Force, I was a commercial artist, mainly comic book stuff. I still like to doodle around just for fun. So either you give me the stories and I'll put something together to go with them, or I can draw a series of pictures and you can weave a story around them. I'll get right on it this evening."

"Oh, Ron, that'll be great! If you can do some drawings first, that would be so much better. We won't need many, though. She's so darned intelligent, she'll be way past this stage in a week or so," Suzanne said excitedly. "Wait 'til I tell her!"

"There is no need to tell me," interjected Raechel, "I can understand everything I hear. And I pick up the thoughts behind the words, too. It is just reading the words on a page that presents a problem for me."

The next afternoon, Ron proudly showed Raechel his first batch of drawings. "Do you know the objects I've sketched?"

She identified the components of each spacecraft he'd drawn and their function, information that was totally new to Ron. He'd also drawn some constellations and she told him her name of each star and its planets. When he later checked with his buddies in the astrophysics lab, he was surprised that much of what Raechel had told him wasn't in any of the astronomy books.

Suzanne was overjoyed when Ron handed her a stack of drawings. "Perfect! These are really great. Now it's time to find out what kind of a writer I am."

After Raechel had gone to bed for the night, Suzanne began typing stories around the spacecraft, extraterrestrials, planets, and galaxies in Ron's drawings. There were enough sketches for three stories of several pages each. By the time she'd finished the last one, she was stiff from sitting in one position for so long.

Time for some tea, she thought. She stood up and looked at the clock. *0115. Wow, I've been sitting there for nearly four hours. Thank God, it's finished, at least the first batch. We'll start the lessons in the morning. I hope she likes what I wrote. Thank goodness for Ron's help.*

Chisky stopped in every day for an hour or so to help Raechel with her speech exercises. Together they practiced shaping sounds and putting words together, "Look... out... the... ship... is... out... of...

control. We... are... going... to... crash...," Chisky said in his monotone squeaky voice.

In her monotone but even higher and squeakier voice, Raechel repeated the words.

The blind leading the blind, Suzanne thought, smiling. Neither will ever achieve the level of skill they're striving for, and their speech will never sound quite human, but they're working hard at it. Raechel seems to learn much more quickly from Chisky than she does from me. Maybe it's the added telepathic link between them.

Chisky's speech also improved remarkably as a result of the daily practice sessions. Suzanne began to take a real liking to this strange little fellow who showed such an interest in Raechel. People on the base had told her that he'd done so much for Raechel already, working nonstop in the lab until he'd perfected formulas for the food and drink she subsisted on. And now he was volunteering to help her learn to speak.

As the days rolled into weeks, all the hard work began to pay off. Gradually the pitch of Raechel's high, squeaky voice lowered as she became more accustomed to speech and learned how to breathe in new patterns. Her voice began to sound a little more human, although the mechanical quality would probably never disappear entirely, and she couldn't get the hang of contractions. Suzanne knew this was a constant source of concern for Raechel who longed for her voice to sound like that of her teacher.

Chisky was constantly interested in Raechel's progress, encouraging her to follow Suzanne's instructions to the letter, and insisting she practice with him daily. Both he and Suzanne eventually abandoned the prospect of Raechel verbalizing with any amount of expression in her voice. Raechel was making such phenomenal progress in every other area of the Humanization Project that her lack of vocal inflection was relatively insignificant. Both agreed that the most important thing was for Raechel to be able to make herself understood.

Raechel's reading skills advanced rapidly, as she quickly correlated thoughts, spoken and written words. Every evening Ron brought a new batch of sketches, and Suzanne wrote a new story for Raechel to read the next day. Soon Raechel was making up stories of her own to go with the drawings. Suzanne would record these stories on a tape recorder and Ron would bring them to life with his sketches. Suzanne typed them up so that Raechel could practice reading her own stories. Together they created books about the future and for the future, so that no other hybrids would have to go through the trials that Raechel was going through in learning to read.

One evening, Suzanne confided to Harry, "Raechel is making such rapid progress that soon she'll be able to do just fine without me. That means my assignment at Four Corners will be over and I'll be returning to ATIC. Leaving will be very difficult, however. Against everything they taught in indoctrination courses, I must admit, I've become attached to Raechel and Chisky."

"Headquarters just doesn't realize what it's like out here," Harry said.

"Before I left ATIC," she went on, "my boss told me, 'Do not, under any circumstances, become attached, because these extraterrestrials are just that. Extraterrestrials. Aliens. Becoming emotionally involved on any level with them will eventually compromise your professional skills, your judgment, and your emotional health.' That's bullshit. Personal involvement just means that we go the extra mile for them. And these two are very special, much more so than any of the other extraterrestrials I've taught."

"I know what you mean," Harry replied. "Maybe it's because they're both hybrids."

Suzanne agreed, "Yes, the human aspect of their personalities is very compelling, overriding their more alien characteristics. Their curiosity and eagerness to learn, their sharing of knowledge, the energy they put into mastering their lessons, and their spirit have won my respect, and a place in my heart. I tell you, Harry, I'll miss them when I leave."

Chapter 18

Leaving Four Corners — 1972

Harry had known this day was inevitable, but that didn't make it any easier. Reading his transfer papers for the tenth time, he figured someone or something must have pushed them through faster than normal. But you don't argue with the Air Force.

Jeez, when I walked into that recruiting office all those years ago, I never believed my life could have taken all the turns it has, putting me in charge of this group that's become the family I longed for my entire life. Got to admit, though, the isolation and stress of constantly dealing with the "unknown" has lost its appeal lately. The endless paperwork, incident reports required of each landing, and the daily progress reports on dozens of projects have become tedious and mundane. Whether the craft lands safely or crashes, whether the crew lives or dies, stays or leaves, the reports are pretty much the same. Only the date changes.

I'll miss them all, both terrestrial and otherwise. Their physical diversity has never mattered to me, the way it bothers some people here. Living and sharing life is the bond that fuses us into a cohesive unit. The only thing that does bother me is the crashes. With all their sophisticated technology, why do they still crash? Is some unknown branch of our government using the very technology they've gleaned from the aliens to destroy them? God, I hope not, but I have my doubts. What a waste for them to travel so far only to fail in the last moments. And we're denied the information they've come so far to share. They're like a long-lost family.

"Still goin' through the stages, Nadien?" He could still hear Bill's question on the night of his first experience with the extraterrestrials. "Yes, Bill, I'm still going through the stages. Only you didn't tell me that it never stops."

Once again, he felt like a teenager leaving the safety of his family nest. The isolation of Four Corners insulated him from the rigors of everyday military protocols. Of course, he'd had periodic doses of "regulation" when he'd attended officer training and technical classes. Expectations and regrets, relief and concerns, alternately fought for dominance in his consciousness. Now he had family responsibilities. Raechel was nearly ready to try integrating into society. She had no choice. As the first real participant and test subject of the Humanization Project, it was time for her to attempt life in the real world. *And that,* Harry figured, *is why my transfer has come through early. The brass is eager to see what will happen.*

He read his orders again. Liaison between Air Force Security and ATIC. Yeah, pushing papers in some office. But, becoming a desk jockey will provide stability, and allow me to spend time helping Raechel face the traumas of socialization. I need to be with her, to ease her transition, answer her questions, and comfort her pain. So I guess I'm ready to pull over into the slow lane for a while.

On weekends, I'll take her fishing. We'll go exploring in the foothills of the Sierra Nevada, retracing the steps of the old forty-niner gold-miners and pioneers. We'll be pioneers of a sort, too. Searching for a home and a place in society together. I still wonder if I've taken on too much, but now I can't imagine life without her.

It's ironic, he thought, *that my new duty will put me in charge of Air Force public affairs for extraterrestrial matters. My job will be to squelch information regarding the alien presence here on earth and all the time I've got a daughter who's half extraterrestrial herself. I'll have to fabricate press releases for the media, making up stories the public will accept ... at least most of them will accept. There'll always be the conspiracy theorists who seem to know. My job will be to use ridicule to downplay anything they may have seen or heard. Venus, swamp gas, weather balloons, mass hallucination. Take your pick.*

I can play the game however ATIC wants me to for the next few years. I'll just coast up to my pension, putting in my time until I'm a civilian. Then I'll be free of the absolute control that ATIC's had over my life, free from the duplicity, the false front I've had to maintain for years. I'll be able to do whatever the hell I want to from then on. They'll have no hold on me. Just a few more years.

Harry's thoughts turned to Raechel. *I've got to admit it, during the last three years, Fran and Wanda have done a marvelous job of helping me bring her up, teaching her the ways of a young girl. Not that they were any more successful than any other parent, but they've done their best.* He smiled when he thought of Raechel's greatest stumbling block. She'd never gotten the hang of selecting clothes whose colors matched. I even had her eyes checked and her color vision's far more acute than a human's. She simply has no idea of which colors go together. *Thank God Fran and Wanda came up with the idea of one-piece jumpsuits.*

Raechel steadfastly refused to give up the torn jumpsuit she'd been wearing when her craft had crashed. *It's like a security blanket for her, a link with her past,* Harry thought, remembering the time when he'd checked to see if she was asleep, but had found her outside, looking out into the vast expanse of the night sky, holding the tattered jumpsuit close to her chest.

Raechel had thrived on the special diet that Chisky had formulated for her, adding another two feet to her stature. Of course this made trips into Vegas a necessity.

He remembered the accounts given by Fran and Wanda of their shopping trips. Raechel would wear wraparound sunglasses and a wide-brimmed hat so there was no chance of inquisitive strangers staring at her huge eyes and thin, wispy hair. They'd discovered one particular shop that carried a large selection of jumpsuits, and had come back with several in different colors, as well as some white and beige sandals that went with everything. Raechel looked forward to these outings away from Four Corners, and was beginning to feel more at ease around strangers. But either Fran or Wanda was always at her side to keep any potential curious onlookers at a distance.

For lunch, they'd pick out a fast-food restaurant with outside tables in the shade and pick an out-of-the-way table. One would stay with Raechel while the other went inside for hamburgers and sodas. Then the three of them would sit comfortably in the shade, the nurses eating their hamburgers and Raechel sipping her "green stuff." Raechel loved watching the customers come and go, and was intrigued with the thoughts they carried around in their heads. Nobody ever suspected a thing. Just two women and a young girl having lunch.

Once he'd received his marching orders, Harry had begun telling Raechel about what life would be like in California. "We're going to live in a home, just like the ones Wanda and Fran showed you on your trips to Vegas. It'll be like your two rooms, only larger and more of them. There will be people living next door, but in our home there will just be the two of us. No more crowded living in a barracks. We'll have grass and trees and flowers in our yard."

ATIC made attending college a condition of her participation in the Humanization Project, and, before Suzanne had left, she'd told Raechel, "You'll be a natural in any of the sciences, especially physics, astronomy, and mathematics. If you do decide to go to college, though, you might want to consider living with another student for the socialization skills you'll gain. Living closely with a human female, someone close to your age, will be a great opportunity to learn about life on Earth from another point of view."

"I think I would enjoy that, Suzanne. Thank you," Raechel had replied.

As soon as Chisky had heard they'd be leaving soon, he'd wholeheartedly encouraged Raechel to learn everything she could while she had the opportunity. He reminded her, "Harry will help you select an appropriate college and will always be close by to help if you have any problems. I will always keep in touch with you. Communication between us is not limited by distance."

Raechel told the nurses, "I am willing to attend college, but I am concerned about my appearance. I know I look much different than humans. What can I do to look more human?"

Wanda suggested, "Well, you could wear a scarf tied around your head, one of those long, pretty ones like the fashion models wear in the magazines. On our next shopping trip, we'll buy some silk prints that coordinate with your solid-colored jumpsuits. That way you'll have no problem matching them to your outfits. Wear the dark, wraparound sunglasses whenever you're in public. Lots of people wear dark glasses all the time because their eyes are sensitive to sunlight, nobody will think it at all unusual."

"Looks like you've run out of excuses, Raechel," Fran joked. "I'm going to miss you. You've become like a little sister to me. But it's time to go out on your own." She was close to tears. "You'll do just fine, sweetie. Harry'll take good care of you," she said tearfully, hugging Raechel.

Harry and Raechel had all their possessions packed and loaded into the car. Taking one last walk around his office and the two rooms that had been her home, they stopped by the lab to say goodbye to Chisky.

Wanda and Fran came topside to say their good-byes, and Fran gave Raechel a watch as a going-away present—an old Timex she'd had for several years but still ran well. She'd already had a new strap put on it to fit Raechel's tiny wrist, and as she helped Raechel put it on, she said, "Every time you look at it, it will remind you of how hard you struggled to learn the concept of time in human terms."

Raechel thanked her, and, as they drove away, she waved good-bye to the nurses and pointed proudly to the watch, leaving them with the thought, "It is time for me to leave."

At the main gate, Raechel got out of the car to hug Ron. Harry smiled at the odd sight of the burly six-foot MP in fatigues hugging the tiny girl in a jumpsuit. As the MP's eyes filled, then spilled tears, Harry thought back to his first day at Four Corners when he'd been intimidated by the very same guards and their "hounds from hell."

"Water under the bridge and a long time ago, Harry," he said to himself. "A lifetime ago."

Chapter 19

Raechel is College Bound — 1972

After a complete overhaul by the mechanics in the motor pool, Harry's old, almost antique Chevy seemed filled with enthusiasm for the trip. Driving north to pick up the new Interstate, Harry passed the little town famous for its bad coffee, and wondered if they still served the same noxious beverage. Eagerness, anticipation and excitement crackled like electricity between father and daughter.

Raechel loved repeating the names of the towns they passed through, such as Ely and Austin, but had a real problem with Eureka. Her favorite was Reno, where Harry pulled off the road and found a quiet motel for the night. Taking two rooms, he got Raechel installed in one, and showed her how to operate the remote control so that she could watch TV while he went to buy take-out food. Returning with Chinese, they watched an "I Love Lucy" rerun, parts of which Harry had to explain to Raechel as she sipped on her liquid nourishment. Chisky had made up two weeks' worth of meals for her and promised to ship replenishments to Harry's new assignment at Masters AFB.

The following day they tackled the Sierras, and as they crested Donner Pass, the two modern-day pioneers could barely contain their excitement. Raechel was in awe of the scenery, and actually sounded almost excited as she pointed across the Truckee valley at a passenger train winding through the mountains.

As they dropped down towards Sacramento, Harry said, "Once I've checked in at the base, I'll call some of the colleges to see if you can get late registration. As soon as you decide which one you prefer, we'll look into getting you a roommate."

"I can hardly wait to meet people my own age. They will not be too different from you, or Fran, or Wanda, will they? What will my roommate be like? Do you think we will be friends? Will we be like sisters and do things together?"

The volume of her questions revealed Raechel's enthusiasm concerning this new turn of events in their lives, something that pleased Harry.

As soon as they were settled in the officers' quarters at Masters, Harry visited the Relocation Assistance Office and learned of two junior colleges in the immediate area. Harry called the Admissions Office at each and was pleased to hear that they both were still accepting new students. Both had openings and would accept Raechel's home-study certificate from the military in lieu of a high school diploma. Each offered an excellent series of courses in physics, astronomy, and many other subjects that interested Raechel. Both were located on an attractive campus. Lost River was smaller but on the base side of town, while the larger college was on the opposite side. Harry said, "Since you're the one who'll be attending, it's up to you to make the final choice. How about checking them out this afternoon?"

Driving through each campus, Raechel was much more impressed with Lost River than the other college. Harry liked it better, too, and it was closer, but he kept quiet, not wanting to influence Raechel one way or the other. She especially loved the beautifully landscaped campus, every walkway lined with flowers and shrubs. "It is so different from the desert, Harry," she said. "I would enjoy living here."

Parking in a visitor's spot just inside the main entrance, they followed the signs to the Admissions Office, just a short walk away. Eager and a little apprehensive, Raechel felt the old uncertainty about being accepted socially by her peers. But, taking a deep breath, she recalled that it had taken only a few hours for her to be accepted by everyone back at Four Corners. Certainly that had been a greater challenge than this would be. Wanda had reassured her, "Colleges are where young people can establish their identities. And sometimes these identities manifest in strange behavior, and even stranger dress. Don't worry. You'll be accepted here... as long as you wear your disguise. There'll be nothing to suggest that you're any different from the rest of the new students on campus."

"I am ready, Harry," she said as she took his arm, and together they entered the Administration Building.

Chapter 20

Roommates — 1972

Struggling out of bed early Sunday morning, Marisa stumbled into her kitchen and started the coffee brewing. The aroma of fresh coffee filled her new apartment as she dressed. She'd just poured herself a cup of the brew when the doorbell rang. *That's got to be Raechel and Harry,* she thought. *I figured they'd be early, but not this early.*

Marisa opened the door and exchanged greetings with Raechel and Harry. "There's fresh coffee if you'd like some. We could take it out on the deck."

Harry said, "I'd love a cup. Thanks," and helped himself. Raechel said, "Thank you, but I do not drink coffee."

Once they were sitting on the patio chairs, Harry said, "Sorry to be so early, Marisa. Hope we didn't wake you. Raechel was anxious to get over here and get her stuff in. She's so excited, she couldn't sleep… or let me sleep either. To tell you the truth, it's fine with me. As soon as the car's unloaded, I'm going fishing. We've been living in the desert for the last few years, and the nearest fishing was hundreds of miles away. It's the one thing I really missed. If I catch any, I'll bring them by for you. I'll even clean them. I see you've got a barbecue, so I'll have them ready to cook. Raechel is on a special diet and can't eat fish or anything like that, but you might enjoy some fresh trout or a bass."

Finishing his coffee, Harry rinsed his cup and set it down in the sink. Then he went down the two flights of stairs to the parking lot and returned carrying two large cartons. After a few more trips, Harry had hauled up all the cardboard boxes, one of which Raechel brought into the kitchen. "Marisa, this is the special food I mentioned to you before," she said as she opened the refrigerator door. "It comes in little white boxes that need to be kept cold. If it is all right with you, I will store most of them in the freezer. It keeps better if it stays frozen until just before I eat it. I just defrost a box at a time."

Marisa picked up one of the boxes, figuring it weighed about the same as a box of frozen peas. From its blurry image, it appeared to be plain white with no distinguishing markings. "Sure, go ahead. I have to rely on my memory about what I put in there, so I try to keep my frozen food to a minimum."

Harry set a large box on the floor. "This is Raechel's drinking water," he said. "I'm setting these jugs beside the refrigerator next to the wall so they'll be out of the way."

Taking the jugs out of the box one by one, he lined them up in a neat row. "In case you're wondering, Marisa, Raechel doesn't have some kind of weird disease or anything like that. It's just that her digestive system is a little different from other people's, and she needs this special stuff to eat and drink. She can't have regular food or water. Nothing but what's in the boxes and jugs."

"Well," Marisa said, "because of my diabetes, I can't eat anything with sugar in it, so that rules out most junk food. I'm used to being careful about what I eat," she added, consumed with curiosity over Raechel's special food. *Why don't those boxes have any labels? And the water bottles, too? First chance I get, I'll check them out with my magnifying glass. I hate to snoop, but I've got to know.*

"Guess that's everything, Raechel," Harry said. "If you need me for any reason, call this number at the officers' quarters at the base and leave a message for me. If it's an emergency, they can contact me immediately. But don't have an emergency today. I've got a date with some fish."

Kissing Raechel's forehead lightly, and saying goodbye to Marisa, he ran down the stairs, two steps at a time.

"I like your dad, Raechel," Marisa said wistfully. "He seems nice."

"Oh, we have a great deal of fun together. He has promised to take me fishing on one of his trips. I think I would enjoy that."

"I'm not sure how much use I'll be with your unpacking, but I'm willing to help if you need me," Marisa offered.

"Thank you. Shall we begin?" Raechel replied and both girls went into Raechel's room, looking forward to becoming better acquainted, each secretly hoping the other would be the sister she never had.

Chapter 21

Helen's First Visit to Marisa's Apartment — 1972

Working in her garden did wonders for both Helen and the garden. Her favorite thing to do after work was to change into a T-shirt and jeans, slip on an old pair of sneakers, and attack the weeds. She loved being among the beautiful flowers, bathed in the freshness of their perfume. The monotony of pulling weeds freed her mind and released the cares of the day. She played a game with herself. For every weed she pulled, she visualized uprooting a bitter memory. Tossing the weeds into her compost pile became the symbolic dumping of her cares. By late evening she was physically exhausted, but mentally cleansed and rejuvenated.

After showering she made a cup of tea to help her sleep and slipped into bed. As she fell asleep at 10:30, she wondered if Jon would try his usual stupid trick tonight. Although he wasn't directly harassing her anymore, he still found ways to annoy her, such as revving the motor of his pickup for a couple of minutes when he got home from the Drop Inn. This would awaken her, and cause enough irritation to keep her awake for a while. Many times she was tired when her alarm went off. But other than childish passive-aggressive games, he pretty much left her alone. He remembered the rules. If he left her alone, she'd help him get the job. He hated the power that gave her, but that was the deal.

At 2:00 A.M. she was rudely awakened right on schedule by Jon racing his engine outside her window. "You bastard," she muttered, and rolled over.

At 5:00 A.M. the alarm jolted her out of a deep sleep, and she rolled out of bed, trudged into the kitchen, and hit the coffee-maker switch. Leaving the house by 6:00 avoided the long lines that formed at the base's main gate, and earned her a good parking place right next to the Procurement Office instead of having to park half a mile away. That also meant she had time to enjoy a leisurely cup of coffee before the office filled up. She savored the peaceful transition from the insanity of home to the orderly business of the base. Leaving early also made sure she didn't cross paths with Jon, not that he was aware that six in the morning even existed.

Mulling over her life and wondering about Marisa, she was startled by the raw jangle of the phone. Her heart leaped into her mouth. Would this be her? She knew her daughter would never call her at home, but still, it had been three weeks.

"Procurement," she announced.

"Hi, Mom, it's me. Is this a good time?"

"Marisa, are you okay? I've been thinking about you every minute since you left and was anxious for your call. I'm so glad you got away safely. It's so good to hear your voice, but you sound tired."

"Yeah, I'm okay, but it's been difficult. The apartments around me are so noisy, I really have to concentrate to study. And it's difficult to sleep in all this racket. But I think I'll get used to it before long. At least the noise is not inside my apartment."

"How is your new place?"

"I really like it, Mom. It's small but it's furnished, and has everything I need, including a laundry room two doors away."

"Is it a safe area, Marisa?"

"Of course, Mom. Bobby walks me home after classes every afternoon and then we go over our homework. He even keeps a close watch on my cupboards and refrigerator to see if I'm getting low on groceries. Then he takes me shopping. I'm really getting along pretty well, considering this is my first time away from home. I'm going to be on my own for about a week. Class break is coming up and he's taking a few extra days to go to the coast with his parents."

"It sounds great. I'd love to see your apartment some time," Helen said, angling for an invitation.

"Sure. Come by some night after work. It's near campus, so it's not really out of your way. I'd love to have you see it. And I want to see you, too. I've missed you so much."

"I've missed you, too, dear. So has Bo," Helen said, all cares and pain of the three weeks vanishing. This is exactly what she'd been hoping to hear. "How about Friday afternoon at five? If you'd like, we could go get a pizza or I can pick one up on the way over. Maybe that would be better, then we can sit back, relax and talk while we eat."

"That'd be great, Mom. I'd rather do that than go out somewhere. I hate to ask you, but I need a few groceries. I was wondering if you could stop and pick them up. Bobby won't be back until late Sunday night, and I can't wait until then. I have a hard time getting around on the bus, especially when I'm carrying things. I don't need too much. I'll pay you when you get here."

"Just tell me what you need, and I'll make a list," Helen said. "Maybe we better make that closer to six Friday night. That way, I'll have plenty of time to get the groceries and the pizza. So what's your address? And your phone number too, just in case I get lost. You know how I am at following directions."

Jotting down the few things Marisa said she needed and her address, she tucked the note in her purse along with other important notes and the few extra fives and tens that she was putting away for her own move to freedom.

The whistle in the office building blew, signaling it was time to begin work. Hearing it over the phone, Marisa said, "Mom, I've got to get to class. Miss you and love you. See you Friday."

Savoring every word of the call, Helen felt that Marisa sounded much happier at the end of the conversation than she had at the start. And she seemed excited at the prospect of their upcoming visit together.

The week dragged. It seemed to be ten days long, with twenty-hour workdays. On Friday afternoon, Helen took off work a few minutes early to avoid the traffic jam when everybody rushed out of the front gate at the same time. Getting caught in that mess was no fun, and she wasn't about to let anything eat into her precious time with Marisa.

Inside the supermarket, she gathered the items Marisa had asked her to get, noticing that they were mostly staples that could be used to cook a meal from scratch. It was cheaper than the prepared mixes and, besides, Marisa had always loved to cook. She added a second can of coffee, several more cans of soup, and another box of cereal.

She knew Marisa's only income was the small monthly disability check she received since she'd been declared legally blind, and that didn't go very far. Knowing she could barely afford the few items she'd asked for, these extra things would be her treat, a housewarming gift.

In the produce department she chose a variety of fruits and vegetables, since she knew they were essential parts of Marisa's diabetic diet. In the meat department, she added chicken, two rib steaks, and a couple pounds of stew meat to the ground beef on the list. When she got to Marisa's apartment, she'd divide the meat up into individual portions to store in the freezer for later use. From the dairy case, she grabbed a half-gallon of milk, a pint of cottage cheese, some jack cheese, and a pound of margarine. With her mothering instincts satiated, she headed to the checkout.

While waiting at the pizza place, she asked the delivery person for detailed instructions to Marisa's apartment, figuring that he'd know the campus. Then, carrying the cardboard pizza box that was so hot it almost burned her fingers, she placed it on the back seat of her car. To her relief, she found the apartment without making any wrong turns and parked in a visitor space.

Juggling her purse, three bags of groceries, and the pizza, she carried everything up the steps and set the bags down. She wanted both arms free when Marisa opened the door.

As soon as she touched the doorbell, Marisa opened the door, a big smile on her face. Helen took her daughter in her arms and held her tight. "Marisa, it's so good to see you again. I'm so glad you're okay! I missed you, baby."

"I missed you too, Mom. It's been such a long time. And I miss Bo, too. Come on in and I'll give you the grand tour. I'm kind of proud of it."

Picking up the groceries, Helen followed her daughter inside. It was a lovely little apartment, clean and neat, still smelling of fresh paint. She set the bags down on the counter and reached for a tissue. Marisa was wiping her eyes, too. Helen had no idea how much she'd missed her daughter until this moment. They both began to talk at the same time, elated to see each other, and with so much to say.

Marisa began taking the groceries out of the bags. "Mom, what's all this stuff? I only needed a few things. Is some of this yours? Look on the receipt and figure how much I owe you," Marisa said, sounding concerned.

"Oh, just a few extra things to get you started in your new place. I don't want you to pay me for any of it. It's my treat," Helen replied. "And so is the pizza. I'm putting it in the oven to keep warm while we put the food away," she added as she turned on the oven and slid the box onto the top rack.

"So how are things going for you? How's school? I want to hear about everything," Helen said, starting to divide the meat into portions, and packaging it in the freezer bags she'd also bought. She labeled each package in big letters.

Opening the refrigerator to put the fresh fruit away, she noticed some neatly stacked white boxes on the shelves. It was a brand she'd never seen before, labeled simply with a triangle and three horizontal lines but no printing. Must be a generic brand, she thought, as she shoved them aside to make room for the fruit.

"What's in those little white boxes?" she asked.

"I don't know. They belong to my roommate. Her name's Raechel. I've no idea what she looks like, but from the way she talks, she's spent a lot of time in another country. She went out with her dad tonight, but I hope you'll get to meet her one day. Then you can tell me what you think about her appearance."

"Yes, I hope so, too. Now let me hand you the cans."

Helen told her what each can contained, and Marisa arranged them carefully on the cupboard shelves, so that she would remember what went where. The aroma of hot pizza emanating from the oven was tantalizing.

While Helen cut the pizza, Marisa poured the iced sun tea. Between the two of them, they ate the entire pizza, while they caught up on each other's lives.

Finishing her last bite, Marisa said, "Thanks, Mom, that was so good. I haven't had any treats since I moved in here. I really appreciate you bringing it. The groceries will be a big help, too. I had to spend most of my money for deposits on the utilities and phone, and there wasn't much left."

Helen saw her daughter's eyes fill with tears. "In fact, I wasn't sure how I was going to manage until the end of the month."

"We could make this a regular thing if you like, say every other Friday. But not two weeks from now. I've got to go with Jon for that sheriff's deputy job interview," she said, hating to even mention his name. "I'll see to it that I make a good impression on those good ole boys so he'll get the damned job and move up there. Then I'll really have something to celebrate. We could do a little shopping at the mall and then stop at Sisto's for a steak."

"That's sounds like fun. It's a date."

Suddenly they both yawned at the same time. "Wow, that pizza made me sleepy, Mom."

Helen looked at her watch. "As much as I hate to leave, it's time to go home."

"Thanks so much for coming over. I've missed talking to you. Come back whenever you have time. I'll call you at work next week and let you know how things are going. And thanks again for all the extra treats you brought."

Helen gathered her daughter tightly in her arms and hugged her. It was a hug that said all that needed saying. "I love you… I love you… I love you."

Chapter 22

Helen's Plans Work Out — 1972

"Report to the administration building at nine o'clock Wednesday morning to take the test for a buyer's position in the Procurement Division." *At last,* Helen thought, as she read the instructions from Personnel for the third time, her heart soaring. *After all my studying, I know I'll pass. I just know it. And I'll place well enough to get that job. The raise will almost double my paycheck, then I can start looking for an apartment. My test on Wednesday, and Jon's interview next week. It's all coming together. I'll be okay, Marisa will be okay, and even Jon will be okay. Thank you, thank you, thank you.*

With five other nervous candidates, she waited in Room 101 in the administration building. The test supervisor entered and ushered them into another room with rows of desks, on six of which lay the test papers, face down.

"You have exactly one hour. When you're finished, hand your answer sheet to me and wait outside. I'll score them and let you know the results within a few minutes. It's now 9:15. You may begin."

Scanning the first few questions, Helen was pleased that she'd spent so much time studying the Procurement manuals. Most of the questions required answers taken straight from the books, word for word. She raced through the questions, finishing just after ten. She handed her test paper to the supervisor, who said, "If you can come back in about ten minutes, I'll score your test while the others finish. There's still about fifteen minutes left to go."

Walking outside, she took deep gulps of the fresh morning air, filling herself with the promise of freedom. The air inside the test room had been stuffy, reeking of stale tobacco smoke despite the strict no-smoking policy. *It's probably been years since the place has been aired out*, she thought.

She made one complete circuit around the building, and returned to the testing room, knowing her future was riding on what she would find out in a few seconds. *I know I made the pass/fail threshold, but is my score high enough to beat out the other five?*

The supervisor handed her a slip of paper with her score written on it, saying, "You did very well — 94 — so your name's pretty sure to be one of the top three. Congratulations."

"Thank you, thank you. You have no idea how much this means to me," she said, clutching the precious passport to freedom, holding back tears of happiness and relief.

As she left the building, she thought, *I wonder if the other five need that job as much as I do. I hope not. I'd hate to think that any of them is that desperate. A promotion's nice, and the extra money that goes with it, but to me it's a matter of life and death. 94. My new lucky number. Now I'll be able to support myself and have a chance for a decent life. Without this, either I'd have killed Jon, or he'd have killed me. God, you really do help those who help themselves. But please don't leave me on my own just yet. I still might need a little more help. I'm not out of the woods entirely.*

"Helen," said the voice on the phone. "You've been selected for one of the positions as buyer. Your current boss has agreed to release you a week early so you can begin your new duties next Monday. All I need to know is whether you still want the job. Then I can send the paperwork on through to personnel."

"Yes, I would still like the job," she replied, almost afraid to believe the voice on the other end of the line was real. P*erhaps this is all a dream and suddenly I'll wake to the sound of Jon revving his engine and realize that none of this really happened.*

It became more real when her boss stopped by her desk and said, "Congratulations, Helen. I know how much getting that job means to you."

While thanking her boss, she thought, *You have no idea just how much.* "Thanks for letting me go on such short notice. I'm caught up on the filing and there are no pending invoices," she told her boss, thinking, *thank God for that because who knows where I'd file things in my state of mind. I can barely concentrate on anything. Oh, so many changes, and all of them good.*

Letting herself into her home after work, she noticed an opened letter on the table. The return address indicated it concerned Jon's upcoming job interview. Knowing he'd left it there for her to read, she picked it up. Breathing a sigh of relief as she read the note, "Due to scheduling conflicts, we are asking you to come to your interview one week earlier than previously scheduled. We hope this will be convenient for you."

Slipping the note back in its envelope, she thought, *That's this coming Saturday. Great. We can leave in the morning. It's only a two-hour drive. By Saturday evening, I'll be well on my way to a new life. I won't say anything to Jon about my promotion. He probably isn't interested, anyway. Becoming a cop is the only thing on his mind these days, that and messing around at the bar. The less he knows about what goes on in my life, the better. Even after they hire him, which I'm pretty sure they will, he'll still have to stay in my good graces until he actually moves. One wrong move, one wrong word, and I'll have him fired before his first day.*

Helen had never seen Jon as nervous as he was on Saturday morning. "Don't worry, Jon. You're smart enough to give the answers those good ole boy cops will want to hear. And I'm sure I can convince them that I'm exactly the kind of wife they hope their new deputy will have."

He'd better get the job, she thought. *He'd damn well better not screw up now. If he doesn't get it, I know he'll find a way to blame me, regardless of the real reason. There'll be hell to pay. Whatever I've had to endure in the past would be nothing compared to what my life would be then.*

Taking one final look at herself in the full-length mirror, she decided she looked good. Conservative and demure. A docile little wife entirely devoted to her husband and his career. Honored to be a cop's wife. *I'll knock the socks off those good ole boys.*

The ride to the interview was two hours of silence. More accurately, two hours of rock and roll music, which she hated, and which Jon knew she hated. *At least it saves talking to him,* she thought. *Not that we have anything to talk about anymore.*

Pulling into town, they drove by the courthouse where the interview would be held. They'd made good time and had almost an hour to kill before the interview. "Got time for lunch if you feel like it, Helen. I saw a little Chinese restaurant down the street. We can park here and walk over. My treat," Jon said, almost pleasantly.

Now that they'd arrived, and hadn't had a fight on the way, she was relaxed enough to realize she was famished. Neither of them had had the stomach for breakfast.

They ate in silence, each waiting for their separate futures to happen. Finally, Jon announced, "Time to go."

He paid the check and they walked the short distance back to City Hall. He went in first, while she sat on the long bench outside the building under the welcome shade of an enormous oak tree.

What a boring little town, she thought. *Hardly anyone on the streets. The men down at the local bars watching TV while their wives clean and cook. Dutiful little wives, doing what they're expected to do, pleasing their men. Why do they even need a damned police force if it's always this quiet?*

"Helen," a voice called. It was Jon, and she turned to see him with a man whose badge told the world he was the police chief, despite a wrinkled navy blue uniform shirt tucked into faded Levi's that stopped about two inches above dirty white sneakers. His belt buckle faced downward, losing the battle against a huge beer gut. "Howdy, ma'am. The boys inside would like to talk to you for a few minutes. We've pretty much made up our minds after talking to your better half here, but we want to make sure the little woman will be happy living here. It ain't exactly big city life."

Grimacing, she thought, *What else could I expect from a police chief who wears dirty sneakers and high water Levi's to a hiring interview? He looks like an unmade bed, and not an especially clean one at that.*

Smiling pleasantly at the chief, she said in her sweetest voice, "Sure, chief. I'd be happy to."

The chief escorted her into the interview room, and took his place behind the long, narrow mahogany table. She noted that the other three were noticeably neater in appearance than their chief.

Without introducing the others to her, the chief began, "Helen, I gotta admit, we were wonderin' if you could make the adjustment to life up here."

"Oh, I won't find it at all difficult. I was born and raised in the country, and always hoped I'd be able to return to a rural community someday. The cities are so noisy and dirty nowadays. No, I definitely won't miss the crowds in the stores and all the traffic. It gets worse every day. Especially the crime. Now that's something you gentlemen know all about, I guess," she added, putting on her sweetest smile.

One of the other men cleared his throat. "I was wondering what you would do besides keeping house for your man."

"My hobbies? Oh, I like to sew, and garden, and I love to read."

"We know you're giving up a job with the government. There aren't too many opportunities for work here. Would that be a problem?"

"You mean would I be planning to look for a job? Oh, no, I'm going to stay home and take care of the house and have meals ready for Jon whenever he gets off shift. If I had a job, it might conflict with his schedule, and I know he'll have rotating shifts. The way I see it, keeping house is a full-time job right there. Oh, maybe I can do some volunteer work, perhaps at the library or the hospital, something that would fit around Jon's schedule. After all, his career does come first."

Silently to herself, *Been there, done that. No, thank you.*

Their red, sweaty faces relaxed. They nodded and winked slyly at each other, pleased that here was a wife happy to really stand behind her man. Just what they'd been hoping to find. *Goddamn, this was one fine woman!*

The four men excused themselves politely and stepped to the rear of the room to discuss their decision. When they returned, the chief called Jon back in. "I'm pleased to tell you that we've unanimously decided that you have all the qualifications we were looking for. Also, the little lady here has also passed with flying colors. How soon can you start?"

Breathing a huge sigh of relief, Helen congratulated herself. *I've done it, pulled it off in spades! I told them what they wanted to hear. They have no idea that they just hired a corrupt, alcoholic, womanizing wife-beater. Oh yes, life's gonna be peachy-keen here in Billy-Bob land once Jon moves here.*

As they shook her hand she noticed their palms, like their faces, were plump, beefy, and sweaty, and made her feel dirty. She wanted to wash her hands right then, but knew she'd have to wait until all the stupid backslapping and congratulations were over with.

She smiled demurely, thinking, *you look like four fat toads asking your ridiculous questions. How do you guys even get to run anything, much less a town? But I am so very, very grateful for your stupidity.*

When all the congratulating bullshit was over, the other three left and the chief took Jon aside, not even far enough away to be private, to discuss the perks of the job. She could hear every word he said.

"Now, there are a couple of things you need to know before you start. Real important things. First, about the town drunks, the locals. Don't bother arresting 'em. Just give 'em a ride home or a bed in the drunk tank to sleep it off. No sense going through a bunch of unnecessary paperwork. They're all pretty good ole boys who just don't know when they've had enough. We'll give you a list of names to help you out until you get acquainted and know their faces.

"There are two town drunks who get special attention, though. The city attorney and the judge. You gotta handle them with extra discretion and make sure the public doesn't get wind of what's going on. Or just how drunk they get most nights. Take their car keys and drive 'em home. Be real quiet about it. No sense stirring up a fuss. They make big cash contributions to the department every month or so, which we divide up among us. It's a small town, and one hand washes the other, if you get my drift."

"Perfectly, sir," Jon said, eager to show that he was one of the boys.

"Now, the second thing is a little more touchy, and you'll have to figure out how to handle it as best you can. The county coroner's son is one of the main drug dealers in the area, and you'll find that looking the other way is better than winning at roulette. Fringe benefits, we call it. This is a real money-maker for all of us, so don't make waves, ya understand?"

Jon nodded vigorously, and the chief continued, "And one last thing. Anytime you bust a new dealer in town, we keep enough of the stash for evidence and divvy up the rest equally among the city police, the highway patrol, and any other agency in on the bust. It's handy stuff to have around for parties out on the river. Or you can sell your share and make a nice chunk of change. Why, several cops have made enough to buy small ranches when they retire and live happily ever after. Now some busybody citizens may wonder how cops manage to save enough on our salaries to buy ranches, racehorses, boats, and fancy cars. We just say we got lucky in Reno. For the most part, though, people here don't ask too many questions if they know what's good for 'em."

Walking them out, the chief said to Jon, "We'll see you in a week's time. We've got an apartment all ready for you. The little woman can follow once she's taken care of the packing. Y'all drive safe, ya hear?"

After washing her hands and face, Helen went outside and got in the car. *Well,* she thought, settling back in the passenger seat, *in less than a week, Jon will be moving out and, in two weeks, I'll be in my own apartment, forever free.*

Chapter 23

Suspicions are Aroused — 1972

Having a roommate wasn't quite what Marisa had hoped it would be. There was hardly any interaction between the two of them, although from the very first day Marisa felt an inexplicable bond of closeness to Raechel, somehow sensing that her roommate felt the same. While Raechel always seemed open to conversation, her fund of teenage knowledge was nearly nonexistent, and "girl talk" was virtually impossible. For the first few days, Raechel had stayed in her room, except when she attended class. Marisa figured she must be homesick, shy, or needed to get her things arranged in her room. Then Raechel started taking long walks, saying she was supposed to be getting lots of exercise to keep her muscle tone built up. Finally, after about a month, Raechel started spending more time in the living room, and talking with Marisa. Actually it was the other way around, Marisa did most of the talking.

One evening, Marisa asked "So, Raechel, who's your favorite singing group?"

"I do not have one. What is your favorite singing group?"

"Oh, I like Simon and Garfunkle, their 'Bridge Over Troubled Water.' Which song of theirs do you like the most?"

"I do not believe I have ever heard them."

I can't believe it, Marisa thought. *Just how remote is this place she and her father call Four Corners? Even in the desert, they must have a television or at least a radio.*

"Well, if you don't listen to music, what television shows do you like?"

"I rarely watch television, and do not much care for it," Raechel replied. "I spend most of my time reading, especially books on astronomy and cosmology."

Marisa joked, "Okay, you're the bookworm type. Bet you make time for boys, though."

"Not really. I have never had a date. I do not know any males of my age."

Okay, Marisa thought. So *she doesn't seem to be the least bit interested in boys, either. Geez, I wish I could see what she looks like. There must be some explanation for her weird behavior. Maybe she avoids meeting people because she's really ugly. But that doesn't explain why she's completely unaware and not interested in anything. It's like she's from another planet or something.*

"Well, what about girlfriends? Surely you have those."

"The only other females I have ever met before I met you were my instructor who was sent to the base to teach me to read, and the two nurses who helped take care of me."

That doesn't sound right, Marisa thought. *If she's 18 now and was on the base for three years, she'd have been maybe 15 when she arrived at the base. So why did she start learning to read then? Why not by age five like anyone else? Where was she until she was 15? And why did she have people taking care of her when she was a teenager? And why doesn't she share anything about her life before she got to Four Corners, and why hadn't she heard of World War II? It's beginning to sound more bizarre all the time.*

"What sports do you like to play, Raechel?" she asked, hoping to hit on some common thread they could share.

"I am not familiar with the term 'sports.' Could you explain it to me please?"

"Well, you know. Physical activity, like bowling or roller-skating or horseback riding. Or team sports like softball or basketball."

"No, I have done none of those things. I am not much of an outdoors person. Being sensitive to sunlight, I must stay indoors as much as possible."

Marisa puzzled, *I wish I could figure out whether she just doesn't want to talk to me or if she really doesn't know anything about these things. If only I could see her face, I might be able to learn more. Her weird manner of speaking doesn't tell me anything either. I just can't believe that anyone could have led such an insulated existence.* Frustrated, she shrugged her shoulders thinking, *She's an odd one all right. I guess she really is from another planet. She's way out there anyway.*

There was no way Marisa could have seen the hurt expression on Raechel's face as she read that last thought.

I still can't figure out what could have happened in Raechel's past to cause this obvious lack of experience. Maybe she had an accident when she was 15 and suffered amnesia. That would explain her ignorance about everything up until then. Or maybe some terrible trauma wiped out her memory, so she had to start over, learning to read and speak from scratch. Her intelligence is off the scale, and her manners are impeccable. The only mystery is her life before she and Harry went to that Four Corners place.

And why does she call her father Harry, and not dad or pop? Maybe he's her adopted dad or stepdad. I could never call Jon "Dad." Something else. Why is her voice so mechanical? She enunciates each word de-lib-er-ate-ly, halting ever so slightly between syllables, like she's speaking to the rhythm of a metronome. And her vocabulary is too extensive for someone our age, like she's spent all her life around really smart adults, scientists maybe. If only I could get a good look at her. Maybe I can arrange for Bobby to meet her, and then he could tell me what she looks like.

As it happened, the next afternoon she and Bobby were working on a test, and Raechel came in and went straight to her room without acknowledging either of them, even when Bobby called, "Hi, Raechel. How ya doin'?"

"That Raechel's an odd one, isn't she?" Bobby commented quietly.

"She hardly ever speaks and when she does, it's as though she doesn't quite understand what I say," Marisa whispered back.

"How come she always wears those dark glasses, even in the house? And something on her head, too?" Bobby asked.

"She told me her eyes and skin are very sensitive to sunlight. That's all I know. But you're right. There's no sunshine here in the house. Maybe she just likes hats. She's real different from anybody I've ever known, but she's easy to get along with. We never argue, and she's been really nice to me. She even helps me pick out which clothes to wear, although she hasn't got a clue about which colors go together. Sometimes they really clash. I've ended up wearing such outrageous things to school that people ask me why I'm dressed so oddly. Even you've mentioned it a time or two. Of course, I have a good reason, but she doesn't. Next time mom comes over, I'm going to ask her to put some tops and bottoms that match on the same hanger. It's the only way I know to dress decently and not have to ask Raechel to help."

Privately, Marisa hoped, *maybe I won't have to ask for nearly as much help if my eyesight keeps on improving the way it has been the last month or so. It fluctuates almost daily, fairly good some days, worse on others, but overall, it seems to be getting better. I hope it's not just a temporary improvement. Soon I might be able to see well enough to get around the apartment without running into things. Maybe my vision will get good enough to see exactly what she looks like. That might give me some insight as to why she acts the way she does. I've already seen enough to know that she's got wispy, reddish hair that's a little sparse. Kind of reddish blonde, a shade I've never seen before. And she's got attractive features with high, slanted cheekbones. I'm sure she's a pretty girl, so that rules out hiding because she's ugly.*

"You know, Bobby, once, when our schedules allowed us to eat dinner together, I asked her for a taste of the weird green stuff she eats. She refused, saying it would make me sick. I think it would, it almost makes me sick just to smell it. It feels like finely chopped spinach, only it has a mushy feel. It reminds me of a TV dinner that's been re-warmed so many times that it's just unappetizing slush.

"And she has it delivered. Whenever she's about to run out, a new supply of the boxes magically appears outside the front door. I never hear them being delivered. It's really uncanny how anyone would know when she's running out. She never telephones anyone to ask for a delivery. At least not from here. When I asked her who delivers her food, she said they were just some people who worked with Harry, but that she didn't remember their names. That sounds fishy, if you ask me."

"Yeah, it does sound odd."

"One morning, Raechel had an early class and left an hour before I did. So I grabbed my magnifying glass and examined one of her food boxes. The only marking is a small red triangle with three horizontal black lines running through it. I've never seen a logo like that before, but it's probably some kind of a trademark."

"What about the water bottles?" Bobby asked.

"Just the same tiny red triangle with the lines running through it. Of course, that's logical, because they both arrive at the same time, so they obviously come from the same place. Those little red triangles have really piqued my curiosity. I'm determined to find out where her food comes from, and who delivers it."

"Does she have any other visitors?"

"Well, for the first month, only Harry, her dad. Then, one morning she stayed home, telling me her first two classes had been canceled, so she was going to clean her room, read, and maybe go for a walk. Huh, why don't mine ever get canceled? You remember that morning when I forgot the test answers that had to be handed in?"

"Yeah, you said you'd go back and get them, and that I should go on to class and take notes if you missed anything important," Bobby said, and then asked, "Is your eyesight improving, by any chance?"

"It's better on some days than others. That was just a good day," she replied, trying to downplay the improvement. "Anyway, I was just about to reach for the doorknob when I heard voices inside. It sounded like two men and Raechel talking. I knew it wasn't the television because she never watches the thing. I went in and walked through the living room to my bedroom. I glanced into the kitchen and saw Raechel sitting at the table with two men dressed in dark suits. They both wore a black fedora with a brim. The one sitting on the far side of the table, facing Raechel, had a black attaché case open in front of him on the table, and he had some papers in his hand. The other man had his back to me and I couldn't see his face. I didn't want Raechel to see me looking too closely. My instincts told me that something wasn't quite right about that meeting. The men didn't seem to be threatening, and Raechel didn't seem at all frightened. I think they may be gangsters.

"'Who's your company, Raechel?' I asked, since none of them, including Raechel, offered any kind of a greeting. Each man quickly pulled his hat brim a little lower over his eyes like it was a twin reflex action. It didn't seem like a real friendly gesture, but I couldn't be sure. Neither man acknowledged my presence, just acted as if I weren't there.

"Raechel said, 'Oh, these men work with Harry. They come to check up on me every week or two. We are almost finished.'

"Raechel seemed completely at ease with the two strangers, so I decided to wait and ask her more about it later that afternoon. I went into my room, picked up the test answers, and hurried out of the apartment. On my way out, I noticed an unfamiliar large, black car parked in a visitor's space. There was something odd about it and, at first, I couldn't put my finger on what it was. Then I remembered seeing a car like it in an old World War II movie I saw back when my vision was okay. Like a German officer's staff car. A big black Mercedes. I wondered if it belonged to Raechel's visitors. I'm sure it doesn't belong to anyone who lives here. When I walked by I knelt down and looked at the license plate. It was black and completely blank except for a small red triangle with three horizontal black lines running through it."

"Just like on Raechel's food boxes," Bobby said, pensively. "Go on."

"Well, it was the strangest delivery vehicle I've ever seen, and even stranger looking delivery men. I wanted to wait and see if it was theirs, but I had to hurry to class."

"Did you ever see them again?" Bobby asked.

"Yes. The next time the men in black, as I call them, came was about two weeks later on a Saturday morning. The doorbell rang just after nine o'clock, and when I answered, it was the same two men. The taller of the two told me they needed to talk to Raechel privately for a few minutes. The tone of his voice implied that he was accustomed to having his orders followed with no questions asked. They both brushed rudely past me and walked toward the kitchen. They didn't even wait to be invited."

"'This will not take long, Marisa,' they said. 'Could you go into your room and close the door while we are here?' Just then, Raechel came out of her room and said, 'I am sorry, but this has to be very private.' Her voice, which is usually rather high and mechanical as you know, was lower in pitch and she sounded almost apologetic. So I said, 'No problem. I need to straighten up my room anyway. Just let me know when the coast is clear.' Those two scared me a bit. I got the impression that they might be very dangerous if I didn't comply with their wishes. But it's my apartment too."

"So did you get to see their faces this time?"

"Yes, when I opened the door, and I felt even more apprehensive than the first time I saw them. Their faces were white and pasty, which contrasted sharply with the dark sunglasses they wore. They looked like a pair of ugly Mafia types who'd just gotten out of jail. They seemed really ominous. Almost dangerous. I just wanted out of there, so I went back into the kitchen and said, 'Raechel, I've changed my mind about staying in my room. It's so nice out, I think I'll go down and sit by the pool. Then when your visitors leave, come down and get me.'"

"Why did you say that?"

"To reassure all of them. To make them believe I'm the helpless little blind girl I'm supposed to be. Before I went to the pool, I walked out to the parking lot and saw the same big, black limo parked in the same visitor's space as before."

"Did you go to the pool?"

"Yes, and I had the place to myself because it was still early. That was fine by me. I didn't feel like making small talk. I needed a few minutes alone to let these latest events sink in. It's getting frustrating, wondering what exactly is going on with Raechel. I just wish I could see better, everything is so fuzzy and unclear."

"With Raechel's odd appearance and so much weird stuff going on, it's kind of lucky that you miss so much because of your poor vision," Bobby observed.

A sudden thought hit Marisa. "Hey, wait a minute. Suppose it's not luck. Suppose it's no accident that we're roommates. Maybe

Harry deliberately chose me precisely because I can't see much. Maybe I've simply been too naïve to realize what's really happening."

"You've lost me. What do you mean?"

"Well, think about all the unusual circumstances surrounding Raechel that I've just accepted at face value. The special diet, the wraparound sunglasses, always wearing some kind of a head covering even indoors, her odd mechanical-sounding voice, her inability to coordinate colors, being completely unaware and out of touch with things that any normal teenager would be familiar with no matter where on Earth she'd lived. And now the weird men in black who drive a foreign model car with blank license plates and come to check up on her every couple of weeks. Suddenly it all makes perfect sense. Why on Earth didn't I figure it out sooner?"

"Sorry, Marisa, but I still have no idea what you're talking about."

"Forget it. I need some time to think this all through. Just don't say anything to anyone, okay?"

"You got it. I wouldn't know what to say, anyway. Listen, I gotta go. Same time tomorrow?"

"Yeah. And thanks for being such a good friend and listening to me rattle on."

"Any time. Ciao," Bobby said, getting up.

Marisa went out to the patio and plopped down on her lounge. *For the time being,* she thought, *the best thing I can do is just observe what's going on for a little longer, before I dare mention this to anyone. Watch and listen.*

Then she let her mind go blank and just enjoyed the sun caressing her skin with its golden rays, and the breeze ruffling her hair.

Chapter 24

Helen Meets Raechel Up Close and Personal — 1972

Excited, Marisa called her mother. "Mom, I need to see you very soon. I have a couple of surprises for you. Can you stop by on your way home tonight?"

"Of course I can, dear. You make it sound mysterious. What's going on?"

"Not over the phone, Mom. I'll tell all tonight."

The minute Helen stepped inside the apartment, Marisa's words spilled out in a rush, "Guess what, Mom! I can see! Sort of. I still have to use the magnifying glass to read, but I can see fuzzy shapes well enough for me to get around campus and take the bus around town by myself, and do things here in the house. It's such a relief to not have to depend on Bobby like I did before!"

An elated Helen hugged her daughter. "I'm so happy for you. I hadn't dared hope for this big a miracle. Maybe the picture of Jesus you always hang over your bed has more power than I thought. Or the fact that you've always believed so strongly that He'll take care of you."

"Isn't it great, Mom?"

Helen nodded, resolving, *I'll say a prayer of thanks tonight for what He's done for Marisa. I'll tell Him how sorry I am that I ever doubted His power. He's helped both of us get back on our feet, and now He's given Marisa back part of her vision. Maybe if the two of us continue to pray and believe in Him, our lives will straighten out and go the way they're supposed to.*

Marisa started pouring cold tea into the tall iced glasses. Helen jumped up, saying, "Here, let me help."

"Sit down, Mom. I can manage. Oh, I made some oatmeal cookies today, too."

Handing a glass and plate to her mother, she continued, "It's the first time I've baked in a long time. It's great to be able to cook again now that I can read the recipes. I didn't realize how much I'd missed doing things like that."

"And now my clothes are going to match, too. Raechel was putting together some terrible color combinations for me. She means well, but I don't think she has any sense of what goes with what. She wears one-piece jumpsuits all the time, so it's not a problem for her. I was going to ask you to put some things that matched on hangers so I wouldn't have to ask her, but now I can do it myself."

Taking a bite of cookie, Helen commented, "This is really delicious. How wonderful that you can do things for yourself again. I know baking is one of your passions and what a blow it was when you had to stop. Hey, what are those big jugs of water for over by the refrigerator?"

"Those are Raechel's. You already saw the white boxes in the freezer. She says she's not allowed to eat or drink anything other than what's right here. Nothing, not even iced tea. And I know she sticks to that. She doesn't even want to taste anything I have. The stuff she eats looks like spinach baby food. You know, that real mushy stuff. I asked her for a taste of it once, and she said it would make me sick."

"That's strange."

"Oh, you haven't heard the half of it. New jugs of water and boxes of food mysteriously appear outside the apartment door just as she's about to run out, but I've never seen or heard the person who brings them. Of course, now that I can see a little better, maybe I can discover who it is," she said, smiling at her mother.

Helen looked around the apartment. "This is a real home, Marisa, and not just a place to live. It feels comfortable. Oh, I've got some news, too. Jon got that deputy job. He started this past Monday, so he's gone once and for all. And now for the really good news! I got the buyer's job, which means I almost doubled my paycheck. I found a nice big duplex only a couple of blocks away from the house, and some friends helped move me in last Sunday. So I'm all set and so is Bo! He spends most of his time sitting in the window in the living room watching birds in the bushes in the front yard."

"That's fantastic, Mom. I've got to see it some time. Have you any idea how good it feels to be able to say that?"

Helen and her daughter hugged and they continued catching up on each other's lives. All too soon, Helen realized it was late and time for her to go. "I hope to meet this Raechel some day, especially since you make her sound so unusual," she said, having already formed a mental image of what the girl must look like, and wondering how close it would be to the real thing.

"I'm so glad that you're finally able to see a little, and can do some of the things you've missed doing for such a long time. I hate to leave but I still have to pick up a few groceries for myself, and poor Bo is completely out of cat food. I'll come again a week from Friday and we can go shopping. Neither of us will have to get up early the next morning."

As Helen and Marisa were sharing one last hug by the front door, they heard footsteps coming up the concrete stairs. "That sounds like Raechel," Marisa said, just as the door opened.

Helen knew immediately that it must be Raechel, because the girl was wearing huge wraparound sunglasses that seemed too large for her small, oddly shaped face. Her forehead was wide and high and her cheeks tapered sharply from high cheekbones to an almost nonexistent chin. Her nose was tiny and flat, with little or no bridge. There was something else about Raechel's face that disturbed Helen in a vague sort of way, but she was so excited about finally getting the opportunity to meet Raechel that she dismissed it from her mind for the moment.

As Raechel started to walk past them, Marisa said, "Hey, Raechel, I want you to meet my mom."

Raechel said, "I have been so eager to meet you. I hope we can have a chance to get better acquainted soon. For now, I must pick up something I forgot and get back to class."

Helen and Marisa stepped to one side as Raechel hurried past them on the way to her room. Returning almost immediately with a notebook, she started through the door, tripped on the doormat and started to fall. Instinctively, Helen reached out to catch her. Grabbing Raechel's arm with both hands, she helped her regain her balance. After a moment, Raechel regained her composure. "I am sorry for being so clumsy. Thank you for catching me. I hope to see you again soon."

As Raechel walked quickly down the walkway toward the stairs and out of sight, Helen's knees weakened and she felt the color drain from her face. A faint buzz began to sound in her ears, her head suddenly felt warm. Her mouth became dry and cottony when she tried to speak. She returned to the kitchen and sat down at the table.

"She's really odd," she said to Marisa. "When you were introducing her, I noticed a peculiar greenish-yellow tinge to her skin. I wonder if she's ill. And her voice sounds strange too, rather mechanical like you said. With my musical background I notice speech patterns more than most people. Something strange is going on here. I've had a buzzing sound in my head ever since I touched her. It's getting louder, too. It's the same sound I've heard so often before, every time I'm about to become involved in some kind of danger or trouble. I've no idea what kind of threat Raechel could be but, still, I've learned to never ignore the sound. It's always a sign that something extraordinary is about to occur that will involve me or someone close to me."

"I wonder what it could be, Mom."

"I don't know. There's something else about Raechel, too. It happened when I reached out and grabbed her arm to keep her from falling. Something I saw and felt. Sorry, I'm in absolutely no shape to drive home right now, not after that."

Marisa sat down across the table from her. "Mom, you're scaring me. What did you see?"

"This is not going to be easy to put into words, so bear with me. You said there was something different about Raechel. You were right. Raechel is definitely not what she seems to be, or for that matter, not who she's supposed to be."

Taking her daughter's hand for reassurance, Helen continued, "When Raechel tripped, I grabbed her arm to break her fall. Her sleeve slipped up and I grabbed her bare skin. It didn't feel right. When I was a little girl, my favorite doll, Beverly, had arms and legs made of a synthetic material that was supposed to feel real, and it almost did, but not quite. Raechel's skin felt just like Beverly's. Sort of cool and spongy, almost real, but not quite.

"But what really upset me was when those wraparound sunglasses slipped down, falling sideways on her face as she stumbled. Just for an instant, I stared into her eyes. No wonder she keeps them covered all the time. They were huge and shaped like a cat's eyes except the inner corners were more rounded, and the slanted outside corners reached around onto the sides of her temples.

"I tell you, Marisa, they were not human eyes. They had no white in them at all. They were a solid light green color, like the inside of an avocado. I didn't see any eyelids either, but I can't be sure. Her eyes are set at an odd angle in her face, too. They slant up towards her temples. Not like Oriental eyes, though. I've never seen eyes like that on a human being. To say that Raechel is a bit different is the understatement of the century."

"Could it be a birth defect, Mom? One of my classes covered some pretty rare birth-defect syndromes. Maybe a birth defect could have left her with skin that feels spongy and artificial, and huge cat eyes that wrap around the side of her head."

"That doesn't explain her odd speech. No, a voice inside me is telling me that there's a lot more to it than that. It's telling me that what I've just seen is not of this world. But that's ridiculous. What's a girl from outer space doing, as your roommate, and attending junior college? It doesn't make any sense. I tell you, she's not normal."

Helen stopped, feeling a little dazed and wondering if she were losing her mind. "I just don't know what to think."

Finally she stopped trying to speak and just sat. Marisa broke their silence, "Mom, this is the second surprise I had for you. I've had a lot going on here and, at first, I didn't see how I could ever explain it to you. But when Raechel tripped and you caught her, the whole thing sort of took care of itself. I'm sure she's wondering right now what your reaction is, afraid of what you'll think. And what you might do or say. If you've got time, I'll tell you what I know."

"I'm not going anywhere for a while."

Helen sat on the sofa, removed her sandals, and put her feet up on the coffee table. Leaning back on the sofa, she smiled weakly at Marisa. "Tell me everything you know about her."

"Earlier today, Raechel said to me, 'I perceive that your vision is beginning to return, and I think I may have to leave because you might be afraid of my appearance when you see what I really look like. I have talked to Harry about it and he thought the same thing. I enjoy our apartment and would like you to let me stay, although I would understand if you chose otherwise.'

"Then Harry called to say that, as soon as he gets off duty tomorrow, he'll come here to tell me the whole story of Raechel's background. He said that I deserve to know the truth, and that he never meant to mislead or lie to me. He also promised me that I'm in no danger, and that Raechel needs more help than I do right now."

"He makes it sound very mysterious. What did you say?"

"I told them both that I didn't want her to go. That she helped me so much when I was completely blind. And that she's still the same good person now that she was when I couldn't see what she looked like. She accepted me the way I was then, and now it's my turn to accept her the way she is. I told Harry that we've become really good friends, and that it really doesn't matter to me if she doesn't look like the rest of us."

Helen didn't reply. She was still trying to get her mind around something huge. And besides, she couldn't get her mouth to work right. She sat numbly, staring straight ahead, her thoughts in an earlier time, "You know what this reminds me of. The time you first went into the hospital and befriended the rat baby. Looks have never mattered to you. Acceptance of other people, regardless of their appearance, has always been your strongest trait."

Still, Helen wondered, perhaps Marisa and I have unwittingly stumbled into some kind of twilight zone. Those huge, avocado-green cat's eyes had seemed to bore straight through her, knowing and invading her mind. She knew they'd haunt her for the rest of her life. If she lived to be a hundred, she knew she would never forget *Raechel's Eyes*.

Chapter 25

The Truth About Raechel — 1972

"Harry, they know. Marisa and her mother know. Why did we think I could hide the way I look? What I am? I am tired of trying to pass myself off as a normal human. How could we ever imagine I would fit in? I manage all right in class, but I can never get close to anyone and really become their friend. I cannot be something I am not. I am not human. I am me. Why will people not accept me for what I am? Why do I have to do this?"

Raechel's words flooded Harry's mind and heart with the pain of being different, of being alone, of never being what was considered normal. Each question pierced his heart until he thought he could no longer stand it. His daughter was feeling the human emotions of hurt and rejection.

As he drove from the base to his daughter's apartment, his arms ached with the need to hold and comfort Raechel. Thoughts tumbled in his mind. *I tried so hard to make her human. She'd learned so well. God, I've never felt so helpless and miserable. I never envisioned this incredible pain as being part of the Humanization Project.*

At Four Corners, there was never any doubt as to what Raechel was. She was accepted for herself. Her looks didn't matter and where she was from wasn't a problem, just as our looks and where we lived didn't bother her. She is a sentient being, we are sentient beings. That was, is enough.

Damn. All these years I bought into ATIC's controlling attitudes. I kept their goddamn secrets, their "family" secrets, but that only served to divide, increase suspicion, and create prejudice with the "outside" world. At Four Corners, without the duplicity and lies, it had worked.

I can't bear to see her suffer. I'll do anything to ease her pain. Someone once said, "True relationships are never built on a foundation of lies." *Well, we'll try honesty for a change and damn the consequences.*

With his decision made, the nagging weight of doubt that had bothered him all these years lifted. He rang the doorbell and Raechel answered. Walking into the girls' apartment, Harry held his daughter briefly before sitting on an old overstuffed chair. Raechel went to her room without saying a word.

"Marisa, I want to thank you for seeing me today, in spite of what's happened," Harry began. "I'm sorry I didn't tell you everything before, but this is not an easy thing for me to talk about. Most people would be scared off if they knew the truth. They wouldn't even give Raechel a chance."

Harry sounded extremely concerned. "They probably wouldn't want anything to do with me, either. We thought that since you were blind, you would be the perfect roommate for Raechel."

Marisa interrupted Harry, and called out, "Raechel, would you like to be here with us?"

When Raechel declined, Marisa could understand how painful whatever was going to be revealed must be to her. She stayed in her bedroom, but left the door slightly ajar.

"Raechel became very distressed when your mother saw her face up close. She thinks you'll probably want her to leave because you'll be afraid of her, especially when you learn the truth about who she is. You're the first real friend she's ever had outside of me and the people at Four Corners. She really wants to be your friend.

"I'll start at the beginning, so it'll make as much sense to you as possible. This is the first time I've ever told the whole story to anybody. Anytime you want me to stop, just let me know. I'll answer any questions you may have."

Marisa leaned back against the couch cushions, one leg curled beneath her. She expected this to be a rather lengthy story and that was fine with her. She wanted to hear the whole thing. She needed to hear all the details.

"Take your time, Harry. Start at the beginning."

"For years I was assigned to a highly classified unit of the Air Force called ATIC, or Aerospace Technical Information Command," Harry began. "We investigated unidentified flying objects and extraterrestrial intelligence, as the government described it. We worked closely with Project Blue Book, which you may have heard of, but our security classification was several levels higher than theirs. Actually we worked under the cover of several other projects, the names of which are never made public—the so-called black projects that have the highest security possible."

"Several times a month, craft carrying extraterrestrials would land. Sometimes they would crash. Some alien visitors stayed only briefly; others stayed for months to work on joint projects. One of them was a hybrid named Chisky. Hybrids are genetic blends of two or more species, including human. Chisky worked with us on a project to acclimate hybrids to life on Earth. We called it the Humanization Project. One evening, a craft carrying four visitors crashed and three were killed on impact. The sole survivor was Raechel. She's maybe fifty-fifty human-extraterrestrial. Chisky formulated a special diet for her, and two of the nurses took really good care of her. From the moment I pulled her out of the burning wreckage, I knew she was special."

Harry stopped talking for a moment, studying Marisa, who hadn't moved a muscle since he'd begun his story. The expression on her face was one of amazement, not horror or fright. She exhibited no reaction that indicated fear or rejection.

"Any questions so far?"

"No, not yet. I can't even think of anything intelligent to ask. Go ahead, I want to hear the rest of your story. I had a hunch from the very beginning that Raechel was unusual. You know, her speech and the awkward way she moves. But boy, did I underestimate. I jokingly said I thought she must be from another planet, but I really didn't believe it. Then I thought you both were connected with gangsters. This is the most incredible story I've ever heard but I know it's all true. You wouldn't insult my intelligence by making up such a story and trying to pass it off as true. Besides, not more than twenty feet away is living proof that what you're telling me is the truth. It's odd. Part of me is saying that I should be frightened or upset or something, but I'm not. Please continue."

"The only way ATIC would let Raechel stay on the base and participate in the Humanization Project was if I adopted her as my daughter. Since she was a hybrid, part human, part alien, she was the perfect candidate to try to integrate into human society. She was fully telepathic but couldn't speak. A linguistics expert was sent in to teach her to speak, read and write English. She learned quickly, but never quite mastered the nuances of speech, as you know."

Marisa had to smile too, as things began to make sense, "No wonder she speaks so oddly. Considering all she's had to overcome, she's doing just great."

"Well, to cut a long story short, my assignment to Masters AFB here in town gave us the perfect opportunity to try and integrate Raechel into society. Because of her unusual appearance, you were a perfect roommate, but then you began to regain some of your sight. Then there was the incident with your mother. Because Raechel is still telepathic, she knew exactly what your mother was thinking. Basically that Raechel's cover had been blown. So rather than lie to you, or pull Raechel away from the only friend she has, I decided to come clean. I hope that you'll agree to let Raechel stay on. But I'll fully understand if you won't."

"Wait a minute, Harry," Marisa said. "I'll be right back."

She got up from the couch and went into Raechel's room. "It's all right, Raechel," she said, as she sat down on the bed beside her and put her arms around her roommate's thin shoulders. "Nobody is exactly like anyone else. I'm not like a lot of people because I don't see very well. You and I are different because we come from different worlds. That doesn't matter to me. We both need a friend, and that's what we are. Friends, only more so. You're like a sister to me. I don't want you to leave."

Bending forward, she gently wiped the tears from Raechel's cheeks with the back of her fingers. Raechel paused, then reached up and removed her sunglasses, gazing intently into Marisa's eyes. It was Marisa's first good, close look at the huge green eyes. "Don't worry, things will be just fine. You're staying here. It's okay to come out and join us if you want."

Marisa returned to the living room and sat back down. "Go ahead, Harry. Tell me the rest."

"Well, that's about it. ATIC expedited my transfer to Masters as our next step in the Humanization Project. I'm so grateful for the kindness and acceptance you've shown to Raechel. And for our good luck in finding you to be her roommate."

As soon as Harry said that, a nagging little thought at the back of his mind reminded him of something Bill Walker had told him a long time ago. "They'll be lookin' ya up again."

Is it just chance that these two girls have ended up as roommates? If so, why do Bill's words keep running through my mind?

Chapter 26

A Parting Gift for Marisa — 1972

One afternoon towards the end of the semester, Marisa opened the door of her apartment and felt a sensation of apprehension sweep over her. Something was terribly wrong. It was far too quiet and still inside the apartment. "Raechel, are you here?" she called.

Silence. Rushing to Raechel's room, she realized it was empty. Her desk and chair were gone, and all her books. In the kitchen, the special water jugs weren't by the refrigerator. No white boxes in the freezer. Not a thing to show she had ever been there.

In a panic, Marisa phoned the administration office at the college to see if Raechel had transferred. "I'm sorry. No one by that name is registered here."

Picking up the phone book, she shuffled the pages until she found the piece of paper on which Harry had written the number where he could be reached at work. She called, hanging up after the fifteenth ring.

She called her mother at work. "Mom, Raechel's disappeared and I'm worried. Could you see if you can reach her dad at Masters?"

Helen, sensing her daughter's alarm, contacted the civilian chief of security at the base. They had been friends over the years and he would probably do her a special favor. "Hey, Jim. My daughter's roommate has moved, and she wants to keep in contact with her. The roommate's father is Colonel Nadien at Masters. Could you look him up and find where he's been transferred to and how we can contact him?"

"Sure, Helen. I'll get back to you."

Within minutes, Helen's phone rang. "Helen, you must be mistaken. There's no one by that name at Masters. Never has been. You sure it was Masters? Check with your daughter again, she may have gotten the wrong name."

Helen called Marisa and explained what she'd just learned. "Look, I'll leave work early and come by to see if there's anything in the apartment that you might have missed."

"Okay, Mom. I'll talk to you later."

Heartbroken, Marisa hung up the phone and walked slowly back into Raechel's room. "She can't be gone. Not after all this. Not after everything that has happened. We've become such good friends. We enjoy our evening walks together. And sharing things and laughing about the college boys. We even double-dated and the guys never suspected a thing. No, she can't be gone."

Looking around the room one more time, Marisa noticed a small piece of paper taped to the dresser mirror. Removing it carefully, she read Raechel's half-written, half-printed message: "Dear Marisa, I will miss you very much, but I have left you a special gift to remember me by. Love, Raechel."

For a few seconds, Marisa puzzled over the cryptic message. *What special gift? I don't see anything here. Oh, my God! I can read without my magnifying glass! I can see without having to squint.* The message was now undeniably clear to Marisa as she gazed around the room. Raechel — her roommate with the large green eyes, had given her the gift of sight.

Part II

Introduction

As Helen told her story, questions kept coming to mind. Did she really have a daughter? Had the daughter been blind? Did she attend college, and did she have a roommate named Raechel? How did she know all this stuff? Why did she know it? Was she making it up? And finally, could enough information be found to verify her story?

Today Helen is semi-retired, living off Social Security and a part-time job. She is intelligent, quiet, and somewhat shy. Never, in the years I've known her has she deviated from her story, or seemed other than a normal middle-aged mother and grandmother.

Astounding as it sounded, I believed there was more to Helen's story and that perhaps hypnosis could help her remember.

Dr. June Steiner, a graduate of The Institute of Transpersonal Psychology and The American Institute of Hypnosis, agreed to do a regression with Helen.

Debunkers take great pleasure in extracting a sound byte from a regression, then pointing out that the hypnotherapist has, by asking what appears to be a leading question, led the person undergoing hypnosis. For example, someone reports a light in the sky. During hypnosis the hypnotist asks, "What did the UFO look like?" That's a leading question, introducing the suggestion that the object was a UFO.

It took several weeks to formulate the questions we wanted to ask Helen. Great care was taken by Dr. Steiner in allowing Helen to bring forward her experience without leading or influence by questions, tonality, or word choice, or by confirming, denying, or being surprised by what was said.

Dr. Steiner states concerning this case, "My interest in this case came when I was asked to assist in the hypnosis sessions and read Helen's story. She had extensive conscious memories, which I felt were a strong grounding for any further discoveries through hypnosis. My concern for Helen's well-being and care, and for the integrity of the inquiry, was foremost as we explored her experiences. In some instances, ideomotor responses were used to communicate directly with Helen's subconscious mind, bypassing the spoken word and conscious mind in order to obtain specific details."

Under hypnosis Helen was able to recall events that startled everyone involved, including her. We encountered deliberate suggestions by individuals and ETs to not remember or speak of events again, or of a time delay before remembering.

Dr. Steiner continues, "Many people experience screen memories, which is when they see an animal or other symbolic form rather than the ET form. This often happens because the person cannot see the actual form of the event because the mind does not believe it can be so.

"Helen saw different types of birds as screen memories and as contacts between hypnotic sessions. There were a number of unusual occurrences with pictures falling, two strange beings in a restaurant, and birds with unusual eyes. After each weekend she would experience one or more eagles that seemed to be in contact and symbolic of her experience during the sessions.

"Helen had very good recall of her experiences before the hypnosis sessions began. The sessions clarified much of that information and brought forward a great deal of additional memories. In places of fear, Helen was able to proceed and go deeper into the events and was able, eventually, to recall significant information about the relationships between her, Raechel and Marisa, and the hybrid experience. She had the capacity to recall and continue to tell her story without prodding and clearly answered questions, generally without hesitation, needing time and assurance only when the experience became unusually fearful. She also clearly substantiated earlier answers when faced with any planted questions that were occasionally used to see if she would contradict any part of her former answers."

To give the reader the full impact of what Helen experienced, a full transcript of the first regression is presented. It will establish in the reader's mind, as it did in Helen's heart, Dr. Steiner's careful and caring approach to hypnosis and hypnotherapy. It will also serve to show the difference between the television portrayals and real-life regressive hypnosis.

The investigation explored the darkest corners in the labyrinth of Helen's mind—where we saw a nice story with a happy ending slowly and inexorably metamorphose into something completely different.

An old English proverb states that, "The eyes are the windows of the soul." Raechel's eyes are the windows of humanity's soul. Looking through her eyes, we see the worst and best of humankind. Again and again, the research would reveal an answer, then the answer would reveal another secret.

Venturing to look deeper into Raechel's eyes in hopes of discovering the truth, we found ourselves unable to look away. At first Raechel's eyes were a mirror, reflecting a physical reality, our dreams, and hopes. Then she beckoned, promising more, asking us to look deeper. And again, as others had dared before, we hesitantly stepped into the world behind her eyes. We found ourselves caught behind the looking glass, at times frightened, sometimes laughing, often frustrated, and incredulous. Reality melded with unreality, normal with paranormal, revealing a new world we will never forget. In the end, we found her eyes were not just the windows to her soul; they embodied the past, present, and future of all souls.

> "Read every footnote, study the appendices, check the references, no one disappears completely. Somewhere there's a trace, a forgotten fingerprint, lying hidden in the shadows, waiting to be found."
>
> —former intelligence officer

Chapter 27

03/28/98: First Regression with Dr. June Steiner and Helen

June (J):[1] (Speaking to deeper mind). In this session, going deeper, will it be all right for Helen to remember information she has not yet consciously been aware of up until this time? Good. Wonderful. And during this session between Helen and June, I want you to know that if there's anything at all that Helen needs to take care of herself, that you can signal me at any time with your fingers or she can speak at any time to let me know what she needs, whether that be bodily needs or whether it be a fear or a need to speak something else, anything at all that Helen wants, needs, or that you want or need to protect Helen in any way, simply suggest to me through your fingers, and that will be taken care of. The very first concern here is for Helen's safety and Helen's comfort, knowing that this is a session that Helen has asked for, to go deeper into her own memory, to make sense out of what has happened to her, and to find some answers so that she can help integrate along with this. Is there something that Helen would like to say at this point in time?

Helen (H): (Sobbing) No.... I have to go through with this.... I have to do it. (Sobbing)

J: It may be difficult at times....

1. The hypnotic induction has been omitted.

H: Yes....

J: You will be safe and I want you to remember at all times that you made it past this place.

H: I know....

J: You're all right. And any experiences that are uncovered are in the past and they would not be coming forward now if you were not ready to hear this information.

H: I am ready.

J: What I'd like you to do at this point in time is go back to the time when Marisa first moved out of the house to begin to attend college. I want you to go back to the apartment that Marisa moved into with a roommate named Raechel, and let yourself go back to that first meeting with Raechel, and I want your deeper mind to go over the meeting first before you speak about it, and your deeper mind will recall everything that happened during that time. Your deeper mind will catch all of the inflections of voice, coloring, sounds, intuitions, actual movement and happenings, words that were spoken. Just let your deeper mind look for all those things which you consciously have remembered and all those things which up until now have not been consciously remembered. And I'm going to count to three, and on the count of three, I want you to be at that moment just before you first meet Raechel... ready to move into the experience of meeting Raechel and all of your awareness in that time.... One, two, three... Letting yourself be there now. Tell me what you're aware of.

H: I'm saying good-bye.... to, to Marisa, and she says... I wish you could stay a little while until Raechel comes, but I don't know how... I don't know when she'll be back... and I know you have to go... and just then we hear... we hear somebody come up... up the steps. She says I think... I think that might be her. Wait a minute... and, and so it is. It is. She comes... this girl... or whatever it is, comes to the door, and I... we were standing in the doorway, and so we step back... and she comes in and... and she starts to go right by us. She's in a hurry and Marisa says, "Well, wait a minute, Raechel.... This is my mother. I want you to meet her."

J: Helen, stay right where you are at this moment, and I want you to move even further into a deeper state where you are actually there and telling me what's happening in the moment—I am seeing Raechel.

H: I am seeing Raechel. I can't see her face very well... because... she has big glasses... all over her face... no, not all over her face, but her face is so small there's not much left below it... below the glasses... and... and she has... she has something on her head, a scarf... and then the scarf comes down, and it's tied underneath her chin. So I don't get a good look at her face... and she looks funny, she looks... she looks too thin, or too skinny, or... she doesn't look right. But she's in a hurry, and I can't... I don't want to stare at her but I really can't help it because she looks so funny.

J: How do you feel as you stare at her?

H: I feel awfully nervous... well, not nervous, I feel uneasy. I don't think I've seen anything like this before... she's not just a funny-looking person... she doesn't seem like a person.

J: What does she seem like?

H: I don't know... her arms are too long but I can't see them. She has long... she has a long... long sleeves on, but her arms hang down too far... or something... something isn't right... something's not right here (sobbing). But anyway I can't stare at her, that's not polite. But Marisa can't see me staring at her, so that's all right... but....

J: Just let yourself remember all the little details of what you did see. What do you remember her hands looking like?

H: They were too long. Her fingers were not right... they were fingers... but... they were supposed to look like fingers but... they looked artificial somehow... but I can't keep staring because she wants to go by... and... and Marisa is trying to introduce us and... I'm just staring... I'm not acting right... because I've never seen anything like this before... and I don't know what Raechel thinks... but I don't care really what she thinks. I'm so, I'm so upset... but I know I have to say I'm glad to meet you... and I'm not glad to meet her... I'm really not glad to meet her... because I'm afraid of her (sobs)... I'm afraid of her... (sobs)... and yet I know she's not going to do any harm....

J: How do you know that?

H: I feel it... and I think I'm... I think I'm overreacting or something and I don't know what's the matter with me. Marisa's not afraid of her, but... but yet I think it's not so much that I'm afraid but I don't what this is... it's not a real person... (sobs)...

J: So you're picking up on something...

H: (sobs) I just feel she's... she's not right.

J: You just trust that feeling and let yourself be all right with that feeling that's your deeper self responding to something that you know and feel. What happens next?

H: Well... we get through the introductions... and she says... I... am... so... happy... to... meet... you... I... have... heard... so... much... about... you... and I think, she doesn't even sound right. She says, she says something nice, but... but it's... the whole thing is... is wrong... this is not right... she doesn't sound right.

J: What does she sound like?

H: She sounds like a machine... like... like a mechanical voice... but yet it doesn't either... it's... it's... it's how she speaks that's so mechanical... it's not... her voice... ah... ah... I guess it was like a girl's voice... but every word was so... sounded just strange. I never heard anybody talk like that... So, anyway, I... she said that... and I said, I'm glad that I finally got to meet... No, I said I'm finally... I'm glad I finally got to see you, Raechel. And she said... I... must... hurry... which wasn't, that wasn't the right... she should have said, I'm in a hurry. I... must... hurry was not the right thing to say.

J: And as she says that, I want you to focus on her mouth and tell me how her mouth moves as she speaks.

H: I could hardly see it move. It's... it's like... when you try to talk with your, with your mouth closed or your teeth closed... like a ventriloquist.

J: Were you able to see her teeth?

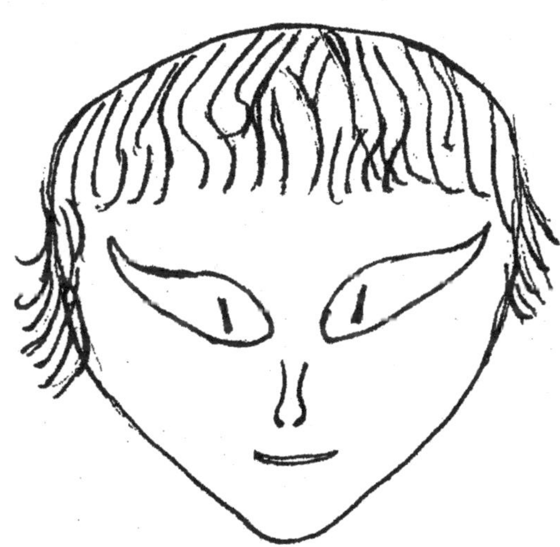

FIGURE 1. Drawing of Raechel as Helen remembers her from their initial meeting.

H: No… I didn't try to, but I don't know if she had any (whispering), but her mouth was so small… and then after I said that, she turned and went… she went towards her room, I guess, and I… Marisa and I started to talk about something, and just then Raechel came back… we heard her come back and I turned… to look at her… and we had to step back and this time… Marisa was next to the door… and I stepped on the opposite side of the doorway… to give Raechel room to walk through… and just as she got almost to us… there was a big wrinkle in the rug… and just as I saw it, I wanted to… to say watch out… you could, you could fall on that… you could trip on that. And I didn't have time to say it, and then she did trip on it… and she couldn't catch herself… well, she didn't try… she didn't try to catch herself… anyone else would… would reach out… if there's a person on each side… you reach out to save yourself… you don't want to fall, so you… you grab whatever is there. But she didn't do that. She just… she just fell forward. And I reached out… because I was afraid she'd get hurt… afraid she'd break her glasses… I don't know why I thought about that… but I did. And then anyway, I grabbed her arm, her left arm… with both hands… and… and… she sort of fell halfway down but then… then I kept her from going the rest of the way and I helped her to stand back up… and when she… when I pulled her back up… her glasses fell down… fell forward on her nose and they… they went sideways, but I didn't touch her head… I didn't… I didn't want to touch her head, but… but I couldn't because… because I had hold of her arm anyway. But her glasses slid down, and… and I got a look at… I looked at her eyes, and her eyes were… her eyes were not right… (sobbing)… her eyes weren't right… they were big and they were green….

J: Just keep looking at her and tell me what you see.

H: I was so scared for a minute... and I couldn't, I couldn't look away, I couldn't look away from her eyes... but she was more scared than I was when she looked at me... oh... I could see how frightened she was.

J: How could you tell she was frightened?

H: (whispering) She told me.

J: How did she tell you?

H: With her eyes... and I told her, it's all right, you're okay. I said that to her... and then I realized I still had hold of her arm... (crying)... and the skin wasn't right either... it wasn't right... it wasn't right... it was... it wasn't real... it... it didn't feel real. And she kept looking at me... and that time I didn't say anything. I didn't say anything.

J: What did the skin feel like? Feel it in your hands.

H: Oh... oh... it felt like mushrooms... just like cool... spongy.

J: When you say cool, how cool? Tell me, was it cold?

H: No, it wasn't... it wasn't cold. It was... I can't think... I can't think... it... it was... it... I can't think what it felt like.

J: It's all right. Just stay with the experience, and begin to tell me anything else that you are aware of about her body.

H: I should have let go of her arm, but I kept holding onto it. I... I shouldn't have touched it.

J: Why is that?

H: Because I don't think she wanted me to... But I didn't want her to get hurt.

J: I want you to go back again to the moment when you were looking into her eyes... and tell me approximately how big they were, what they looked like. Just be looking into them.

H: She didn't have any eyelids... her eyes took up the whole socket... or whatever it's called. I should know what it's called.

J: If you were comparing to a (word missing), what would be the approximate size of her eyes?

H: Uh... well... her eyes were probably the size of mine without any eyelids... the whole thing... the whole thing!... No, that's not right... (long pause)... they came up....

J: The ends came up and extended back like that?

H: Extended out like this... then they came down... the whole thing was all green... and a little thing in the middle...

J: What kind of a little thing in the middle?

H: It wasn't round. It wasn't round, it was up and down and black, and I felt as though I was just pulled into the black thing.

J: Pulled into it in what way?

H: Like that was where she told me that she was frightened.

J: So rather than be told it by a voice, it was as though you were somehow being communicated with by this black area of her eye? Is that what you're saying?

H: That's what I said.

J: Be there, looking into that black part of her eye. Tell me more about it.

H: Um... um... I can't...

J: When you say you can't, what does that mean?

H: Like she's going to see me again... that she wants to... she wants to tell me something, but she can't do it then... and I'm scared... and this is not the time for her to talk to me.

J: Well, Helen, we know that you didn't talk to her then. Would you be willing to look back in her eyes now and let her tell you what it was that she wasn't able to tell you then? You're safe, and you're here. Would you be willing to go back and re-look in her eyes and let her tell you?

H: Um... that she wants... she's supposed to be like other people... no, not like other people... she's supposed to be like people but she can't do it. She tries... she tries to do it, and it doesn't work out... She isn't the same. She doesn't... she doesn't look the same... and no matter what she does... she can't pull it off. And she's so frustrated and... and the reason that she can get along with Marisa... is that Marisa can't see. Not very well... so she doesn't see... Marisa doesn't see... how different Raechel is. All she knows is that Raechel helps her and she talks to her, and Marisa doesn't notice how funny she sounds. She says this to me... she says, I sound funny... and I try to talk like other... like the other people, and I cannot do it... and she said I do not know how long I can do this... The men tell me I have to... I do not have... I have to do it really soon or we are giving up... they are giving up... and I try as hard as I can... but I cannot do it. And she's really upset. And I... I don't talk to her... but I'm saying to her... I'm looking at her... right into those slits... and I'm telling her it's all right... it's okay... and I'm telling her, you know you're trying too hard, and people are afraid of you, too, and I was afraid of you, but I'm not now... and I said you know what, your eyes are so beautiful... your eyes are so beautiful. Because she didn't have her glasses... she didn't have her glasses on. She took them off... but this was another time. This was not, this was not when I first met her.

J: When was it?

H: A little later... um... I don't know. Two or three weeks... I don't know.

J: Where did it take place?

H: In the apartment... Marisa wasn't there... I don't know why... I don't know why I was... maybe I was waiting?... I don't know... maybe I was waiting to see Marisa, but she wasn't there. And that wasn't right that Raechel was there... I don't remember how I got into the apartment. I was in the kitchen... and I was standing by the window. She was there in the room, pretty close, four or five feet away, and she didn't have... she didn't have her scarf on either. And she was... she was really pretty.

J: What did she look like? What did her hair look like?

H: It was beautiful, red... red-blonde color. It was really thin and wispy and it was kind of... like it grew in different directions... I don't know how to explain it, but... but it was long enough... it was like it wasn't used to being combed or made to go in a direction... the right direction. It was pretty. But it was really thin and I could see why she had to wear... wanted to wear a scarf... because it didn't look quite right. But she wasn't worried about it. And I still thought it was really pretty.

J: What was she wearing?

H: Well... ah... (long pause)... it was kind of like a uniform but no, no, that's not right. It was, it was a jumpsuit... it was like a jumpsuit. But I don't know if had a top or bottom... I mean if it was separate. It... it was all one color.

J: Do you remember the color?

H: Blue... oh, a beautiful blue... like clouds, like sky-blue... and she had her sleeves rolled up... I don't know why she did that, because her arms were funny... her arms were so skinny.

J: How big around were they?

H: Oh... ah... like a little kid... like a little kid's arms... and they were so long, so long. And her hands looked... her hands looked funny, too. The fingers were just long, but they were like... like the fingers were all the same length... that's not right, either. It's not the way you should be... you're supposed to have different length... your fingers should look different. They shouldn't all look alike. But hers did. But before I looked at her arms, I looked at her face because I was looking at her eyes and thinking how beautiful, what a beautiful color they were. But then I noticed her skin, and... oh, God, that wasn't right, either. But I wasn't afraid, and I... I guess I should have been, but... but her skin was greenish, not... not bright green, but... but it wasn't pink. It's like there... there was no pink or color of a person's skin... it was greenish... and yellow... more green. And her arms were, too. I looked down then. That was when I looked at her arms first. I noticed she was the same color all over... what I could see. And then... then I noticed the fingers were... the fingers were all the same length.

J: What were the ends of her fingers like?

H: She didn't have any nails... and then, I started to feel a little sick... not very much, but I... and I tried to hide it... because I really wasn't afraid of her... but I knew she wasn't real, either... and I guess... I guess I got over that feeling because... I stayed a little longer and Marisa never did come... I don't know... I don't know how I got in the apartment.

J: I want you to go back for a moment to when you were conversing with your eyes and hers. And I want you to be looking in her eyes again, into the slits of her eyes, and tell me how long the slits were. Did they go a little ways, or top to bottom, what did they look like?

H: I never saw anything like that... I felt as if... I felt as if I was being pulled in, but... but I wasn't.

J: Let yourself be pulled in, whatever that means. Just let yourself be there. You'll be safe. And tell me everything that you're feeling, and anything that's happening. Just go into her eyes.

H: Um... (long pause)...

J: Deeper and deeper into her eyes.

H: Oh... I'm seeing lights... Oh...

J: It's all right.

H: Oh... oh, it's just like... just like... not like lightning, but it's where everything is all lit up... like flashes... Oh... but she says it's okay. She says she'll be... she's there... and it's okay, but I've never seen anything like it before... Oh... I don't feel, I don't feel that it's okay... and I tell her I... I don't want to go there... I don't want to go there... and she says no... she doesn't say it... but she tells me. Oh... and all I can see is the lights. I don't know what's happening. I don't know what is going on.

J: What color are the lights?

H: Blue and green... beautiful, beautiful shades of blue and green that I've never seen before... oh... and I don't know if I'm... I guess I'm still in the kitchen, but... but how can I be there and I can see... I can see these other things, and I feel it's like... like she wants me to go... to go wherever the lights are... but...

J: The kitchen is there.

H: The kitchen is there and I'm... and then, I am really afraid... Oh... oh, no... and then I step back and I grab the edge of the table, but I don't know why I do that... what good will that do?

J: I want you to move back a few moments before you step back and grab the table. I want you to go back to the blue and green lights, and I want you to know that the kitchen will be there when you come back out. But I want you to stay as long as you actually stayed in the presence of the blue and green lights and tell me everything that happened.

H: (Very long pause)... Oh... it's like I'm looking in a window. It's not a square window. It's longer than it is high... and there's blue light outside, but there's blue light in... there's blue light outside... and a different light in. And now Raechel's on the inside and she wants me to come through. And I tell her,

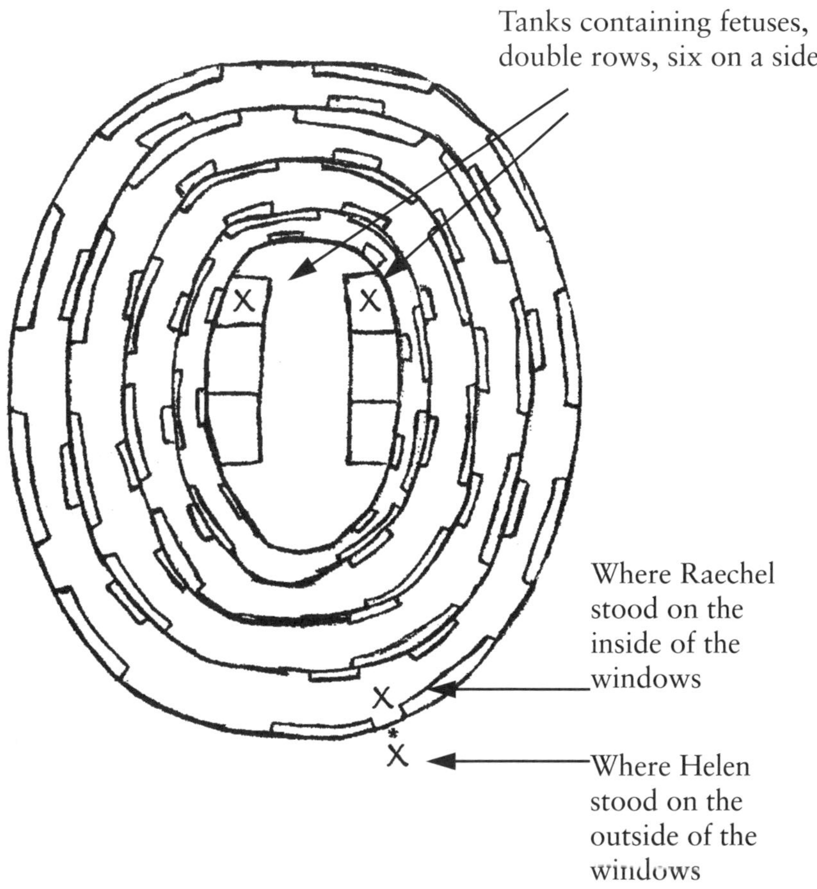

FIGURE 2. Drawing of the place Raechel took Helen during a visit to the girls' apartment. The * marks the spot where Raechel and Helen touched fingers, allowing Helen to pass through the windows and follow Raechel.

(laughs) "Well, I don't see a door." She said, "There does not need to be one." She said, "Just touch the window." Oh, God... oh... and I do touch the window on the outside, and then I'm on the inside of it... Oh....

J: How did it feel going through it?

H: Oh, it was so warm and felt good... but I was so afraid... and I felt so good, too... so warm... and then... uh... and then I saw more windows... it was like it was more hallways and more windows, and I told her I can't do this. I can't do this, Raechel. I have to... she said, well this is where I am going. I just wanted to, wanted to show you. But she said, I am not going now, and she said... but I did not want you to be afraid for me when I go... And I said well, I don't know, do you just live where there's windows, or what is this place?... and she said, well, I cannot tell you now, you have to go... you have to see the whole thing. But I cannot take you there now. I just want you to... I just want to let you know that it is warm and it is beautiful. And I said I have... I have to go back... I have to take care of Marisa. I have to take care of her... and then I was back outside the windows and my hand is on the table, and I'm thinking... where was I... what happened to me... what happened to me, and Raechel is still there where she was before, and she's still... she's still looking in my eyes, but... and everything's supposed to be the same, but it isn't. Um... nothing is the same.

J: What do you mean by that?

H: I know that she came from another... another place, but I know I went there too. But I don't want to go back there.

J: Helen, I'm going to count from one to three, and on the count of three, I want you to be aware if you have ever gone back with Raechel and gone through the other hallways and windows where she lives. One, two, three!

H: (Long pause)... (whispering)... I don't think so... I don't think I've gone... I'd like to. But I never saw Raechel after that day. But I think that's where she is.

J: Has Raechel ever contacted you in any other way since that day?

H: (whispering) I think so.

J: What do you mean?

H: I've seen the eyes. Not the whole eyes, just the slits.

J: When does that happen?

H: Birds...

J: Which birds are those?

H: Oh... eagles... the eagles.

J: Where were the eagles when you saw those slits?

H: At my house... but they weren't birds.... they were more... I don't know what they were. I thought they were eagles... but... the slits were like Raechel's eyes.

J: Then just be looking at those slits, and let yourself see the eagles in any other shape or dimension they may also occur in. And just tell me what you're aware of.

H: Hm... the Christmas bird... it was my Christmas bird.

J: And what was that?

H: It's... well, that's what I call it, but I don't know what it is. That had... its eyes were like the eagles', and they were like Raechel's. But it had funny feathers. The feathers were, (laughs) they were kind of like Raechel's hair... they went funny directions, but they, they were not pretty like Raechel. They were, they were pretty for a bird, I guess. But they were red and blue, and green... that wasn't right, either... that wasn't right, but the hair... it looked like her hair. And the eyes had slits, but it made me laugh and I was so sad.

J: It made you laugh and you were so sad?

H: When I had been so sad.

J: I want you to look at your Christmas bird, into its eyes, into the slits of the eyes, and tell me what you see or feel.

H: Oh... that she was... not she... it... I don't know if it was a he or a she... the bird... uh... said that... oh, God... it was always, it would always be close to me... and I don't know if I want that. But it said there was nothing I could do about it.

J: What else did it say?

H: That I wouldn't... that I'd never see it like that again. It would never look the same... and that every time I saw it, it would be different.

J: Did it say why?

H: Um... no... no, it didn't. I don't remember if it did. But... there has to be a reason... but I'm not afraid now.

J: Good.

H: I don't always laugh like I did at the Christmas bird, but... but I feel kind of comforted when I see the birds.

J: Comforted in what way?

H: Just at peace.

FIGURE 3. A drawing of the Christmas bird that alerted Helen and author Jean Bilodeaux that something strange was happening.

J: And so now is it all right if the Christmas bird comes back in other forms that you may see?

H: Um, hm... it's fine. But the cats are still upset... Oh, why... why if I'm not afraid... they are really scared. But I don't care how they feel.

J: Do you think perhaps you could help them to understand in some way?

H: Oh, yes.

J: Would you be willing to do that?

H: Um, hm.

J: And now, Helen, I'd like you to go back again to when you were with the two eagles and I want you to look into their eyes and I want you to tell me what you're experiencing.

H: Oh, oh... I see those lights again. Oh, the blue lights again... Oh, oh... but I'm not going any place... I'm not going. I can't. I can't. And Sarah[1] is so afraid... oh, and I tell her... no, they won't hurt you. But she says, they will, they're so big. And I say, be quiet. They're telling me something. Oh!!! Oh... oh, (very upset)... I don't want her to leave me alone out here.

J: What just happened now? What just happened? It's all right to talk about it.

H: The whole sky was all blue flashes... and that can't be... because the sky was all gray... oh... um...

J: Let yourself be in that place. Don't compare it to anything. Just let yourself be there and tell me what you see.

H: I don't see... anything but blue lights. But I'm not... um... I'm not where I was.

H: But she was a real person... she can't be this other thing. Oh.... oh, but she is... Oh... she always was... Oh... oh...

1. neighbor who witnessed the two eagles in a simultaneous sighting

There was nothing she could do about it... there's nothing I can do about it.

J: Tell me what you know. What is it that there's nothing she can do about it?

H: She can't change where she is now. She can't change what she always was.

J: What was she always?

H: (Long pause). She wasn't always human. But she looked like it, and she acted it.... So... that's why she and Raechel... that's why... that's why... Raechel came to meet her and to meet me. Oh... why wouldn't I know? But she says I wasn't supposed to... But I thought... and I remember... Oh... oh... and she's been... she tried to... I guess she's been trying to tell me, and I didn't understand.

J: And now you have a way to communicate with them both on an ongoing basis.

H: Oh, God.... Oh (very upset)... oh, oh, oh. Ah....

J: Tell me what you just became aware of.

H: Oh, God... that I had a child that wasn't what I thought it was.

J: When was that?

H: When I looked in the eagles' eyes... that was why Raechel... that's why when I looked in... when I looked... when I looked in Raechel's eyes I thought they were so beautiful. She was, maybe she started to tell me something then. Maybe she started to tell me the truth but it wasn't... maybe she felt... oh, I don't know what she thought.

J: Perhaps you weren't ready to hear it yet.

H: I don't... I don't feel very ready right now. I think that's it. But how... how could it be?

J: Is that something you would like to investigate right now or would you like to wait a few hours or days before you'd like to do that?

H: I think I need to know now.

J: All right. Helen, I want you to go even deeper. Feel yourself floating back even deeper. I'm going to count to three, and on the count of three you are going to be in a situation where you know how this all began. Know your part in it and know why. One, two, three.

H: (Very long pause). That can't... that's not right....

J: Just let the information come through and not judge it. What is it that you're aware of?

H: Oh... hm... but... but that was too long ago.

J: How long ago was that?

H: Oh, I was too young.

J: Too young for what?

H: Too young to have a baby.

J: How young were you?

H: Um... thirteen.

J: And what happened? Tell me what's happening right now as you're there.

H: Um... well... well, I don't know how I got there, but I remember, I remember the place because I used to go there all the time.

J: What place is that?

H: It was a little place I used to go to get away from everybody, everything. Just a little place in the woods... but I... I would spend the... a lot of time there... but I don't know what I did.

J: Were you alone?

H: I don't... I would go there alone but we used to talk about... but how could I talk if I was alone?... I... something's... it was a place where I could go and I could find out things.

J: Did you hear them or just know them, or....

H: I just... I just knew them. But how can... I don't understand how I can know... how can you know things if there's... if... well, how can you learn anything from yourself? I don't... I don't... I just knew things. But no one would listen. When I would tell them, they'd say, you're crazy.

J: What kinds of things did you tell them?

H: About the light.

J: What light was that?

H: It would be a blue light... pretty, beautiful light. But they said no, no, you're just crazy. So then I didn't talk about the light any more but I still went back.

J: And when you went back and saw the light, did you stay in the place to see the light?

H: Oh, yes. It was so pretty.

J: And when you were in the midst of the light, what else happened?

H: Oh... it feels warm. Like they really... cared... really cared about me.

J: Who is they?

H: I don't know... they weren't... well, they weren't people... well, not real people... but they would talk to me.

J: What did they look like?

H: They were about the same height as I was, but they were really thin. I used to take things for them to eat, but they would never eat them. Uh... they told me they didn't like apples and things like that.

J: Did they say what they did eat?

H: No. They said their food was different. But they wouldn't show me... because I wanted to see what it was like, and they said no, it's not good for you... but your food isn't good for us, either... and so after a while I didn't bring them any little treats... but they still kept... and I don't know how they knew

I would be there because it wasn't every day. Whenever I got there they would come... but I don't know how long they stayed.

J: Did you ever go anywhere with them? Or did you always stay there?

H: I think I stayed there. They asked me to...

J: They asked you...

H: They asked if I wanted to see where they... where they lived, they said, and... I don't know, I wasn't afraid of them, so I don't know why I didn't go. But I don't think I did... But...

J: I'm going to count from one to three, Helen, and if you ever went anywhere with them to see where they lived, on the count of three you'll be there. If not, you'll be in your place. One, two, three.

H: Um... I did not go with them. But they told me I was part of them.

J: What did they tell you about that?

H: That there was nothing I could do about it... but... they would see that... it was like oversee... they would oversee... they would watch me... they would watch me... like keeping track... and that I was too young to know.

J: Did they ever tell you that you might know later, or that you might not know?

H: They didn't... it was as if I was too young then to know, but when I got older I would understand. It was as if they would not be... exactly telling me, but some other way I would know. And I was confused, I didn't know what they meant... but it didn't seem that... I didn't think of questioning them.

J: Did you ever call them by name?

H: No.

J: And did they call you by name?

H: No, I don't think so... but I... after a while I would go back and they really never came again.

J: About how old were you when they stopped coming?

H: ... Maybe another year... uh... I don't know... fourteen... no matter how many times I went back, they were never there.

J: Helen, I want you to go back to the incident that happened when you were thirteen... that you said you were too young to have happen. And on the count of three, I want you to go directly to that incident, that event, and tell me what you are aware of. One, two, three.

H: They want to know if I would like to have a baby. And I said, of course not, I'm too young... and I thought... why are you talking to me like this... and they said, oh, we just wondered. We thought you might like to have a baby. And I said, I don't want a baby now... and they said, that's all right, that's okay, you don't have to have one now... later you'll have one... later you'll have one and it'll be... different.

J: Did you ask them what that meant?

H: Yes... oh... and they said... well, it will be... a baby that will look like... it will look like you, but inside it... it will think like us... and I... I didn't know what they meant... I didn't know what they meant.

J: And now, looking back, who were they describing?

H: Marisa... but it was a long time afterwards when I had her... I don't know how that... I'm not really sure how that happened... but it makes sense... but how could they do that to me and I don't know?... Shouldn't I know?

J: Let yourself go very deep now. And let yourself request knowing how and when that happened. On the count of three, let that information come forward. One, two, three.

H: Oh.... oh....

J: What's happening, Helen?

H: Oh… I'm just… I was just having a checkup… but… but it hurts… and I haven't been sick. Oh… but that blue light is there… but… oh… I don't need a checkup. But they say it's going to be all right… I'm fine, and everything will be just fine.

J: Who is they?

H: It's a doctor.

J: What does the doctor look like? Who is it?

H: I don't know him. I should know him. But I… I don't know him. I've, I've never seen him. I've never seen anybody. But that blue light is there and it's right in my eyes. I really can't see anybody very well. But they tell me it's, the checkup was fine and I'm okay and that… that everything is… everything is all right. But that's not my doctor. I don't even have a doctor. Ah… but… how would I get there? How did I get there? I'm… I'm not… I don't even know where I am…

J: Just let yourself slowly move back a few minutes at a time until you are just before the event and tell me what you are aware of.

H: (Long pause) Um… I had to stay home tonight… had to stay home… and somebody came by to see how I was. But I wasn't sick… I saw the lady before, and she always said hello to me, but I don't know where she lives. But she's… I see her… I see her different places. She always looks at me and she always says hello, but… but I just moved there. Nobody else says hello. So why does she?

J: What does she look like?

H: People say she looks like me… but she has dark hair, so she can't look like me. And she's tall… I don't know… I don't know… but she comes… she comes to see how I am… but how would she know where I live? I live upstairs over a bakery… how could she know that? Anyway, she says that what

I need is some fresh air. And I say I'm too tired, I just want... I don't want to go any place. I don't want to go any place with her, but I can't tell her that. I don't... I don't want to say that. She said, get your coat and come for a walk. So I get my coat and we go for a walk. And we go to a part of town that I... I had seen but... I think maybe one time... as though she said I have to stop here for a minute, I have to get something. I said I'll wait. No, she said, you need to come in. So I went in... and she took off her coat, and she had on... like a green scrub suit... like in an operating room. But then I thought, well, that's okay, we're in an operating room... looks like one. It looks like a doctor, another nurse, and I guess this lady's a nurse, and I see... they had a light turned on, it was the blue... a blue light. But this was a real light. This was not flashes, this was... it was like a... a light in an operating room... overhead light. And... I don't remember... I was on the table, and that's when the doctor said... everything is fine. Your checkup is fine. And I said, I don't want a checkup, I don't need one, I'm not sick. And he said, well, it's all over, and you're fine, you'll see, you'll be okay... and so I got off the table and they put my coat on... my coat, and the lady took me home... and I don't know... I guess I went to bed... I think I went to bed. Pretty soon my husband came home.... a lot later, because he had to travel a long way to get home that night. I never mentioned it to him... because it didn't make any sense to me, and he'd just yell... it would be better he didn't know... but there was nothing I could do.

J: Do you know what year that was, Helen?

H: Um... I don't know... ah... right, it was soon after I got married, I think... ah... 1951. It had to be because... yes, that's the year I got married... but I don't know who that lady was... why would she take me... but why didn't... I shouldn't have gone. But I couldn't help it. She tricked me, because she said we were going for a walk... and then we went in that place, and then it happened.

J: What do you think happened there?

H: I think... somehow... some kind of an implant... artificial insemination... I'm sure that's what it was.

J: In the next few hours or days, you'll have a clear memory of how it happened and where it happened, and when we ask you to go back into hypnosis, you'll easily go to that place and be able to remember everything that happened. And now, do you remember seeing that same woman ever again?

H: Yes...

J: When was that?

H: Oh... oh, I know that woman now... I know her.

J: She was... she was the lady... she was the lady who... she was a doctor... but she said, she talks different now... but I went to see her because I thought I was pregnant again and I was... I thought I had a miscarriage because I was bleeding all over. And I went to see her because she was the only person I could see right away. And she didn't say very much... and she took me... she took me into... she took me into... she said she was doing a D&C. She was going to stop my bleeding. She was going to fix my problem. And that... that is the same... that is the same lady that took me for the walk. I shouldn't have gone to see her, but I didn't know she was the same woman.

J: What was her name?

H: Her first name was Rosalind. I don't remember her last name.

J: And where were you when this happened? What town?

H: Johnsonville, New York.

J: Do you remember the year?

H: ... ah... ah... 1956 maybe... I can't remember her last name. She was a German lady. She spoke with a German accent. She was not very kind. She was really rough. I shouldn't have gone to see her. I don't know why I did.

J: Did you ever see her after that?

H: Yes.

J: For what reason?

H: She was a doctor at the hospital where I worked. So I didn't... I never talked to her. I would see her in the hallway... she was not a nice woman. Nobody liked her. So I don't know why I would go to her.

J: In the next few hours or days or weeks, you'll have a much better understanding of how you came to go to this woman for the treatment, and will be able to fully recall it at a conscious place. Is there anything else at this time that would be important for us to know about Raechel or Marisa in terms of their birth, you as a mother?

H: I don't think so. I don't know.

Chapter 28

03/28/98: Second Regression with Dr. June Steiner and Helen

June (J):[1] ....remember clearly everything that transpired in that meeting. And when you have that meeting clearly in mind, just raise your "yes" finger to let me know that you're there.... Now let yourself be there with the colonel, clearly aware of what's going on. And tell me exactly what's happening.

Helen (H): He's already there when I come in... and Marisa says, Raechel's father is here and he wants to meet you. And so I walk in... the living room where he's sitting on the couch, and he stands up and Marisa introduces us, but she doesn't say his first name.

J: How does she introduce you?

H: She says, this is Raechel's father... Colonel Nadien. And he stands up and reaches for my hand... and he says... I'm so glad to meet you, and... I can't remember his name, I can't remember his first name. But she didn't tell me... and I can't... it seems that he said... I'm Rich... I'm Rich Nadien... or something like that, but I didn't hear him very well and I didn't want to ask him to repeat it, but... so I guess his name would be Richard. But I'm not really sure.

1. This is a subsequent regression with some missing information—blank spot in the tape.

J: Just let your deeper mind for a moment go back in time to the other incidents where Marisa spoke to you of the colonel and used his name and just let your deeper mind swing over each conversation to see if his first name was used.

H: She always called him the colonel. And I only heard him say his name that one time, and I didn't… I really didn't get it. But I think it was Rich, so I guess it would have had to have been Richard, but I'm not sure.

J: All right, we'll just let that be fine, knowing that at any time in the next few hours or days or weeks, if a name other than Richard comes forward you'll keep it in your consciousness, will remember to write it down, and then we'll know if the name is different than Richard. For now, just let it be all right. And if during this session you should remember another name, you just bring it forward. Will that be all right?

H: Yes, that will be fine.

J: Can you tell me what it was that the colonel spoke to you about on that meeting?

H: Yes.

J: What was it?

H: He said that… since I had already probably become suspicious or had some… some doubts about Raechel's background, and I guess she had told him about… ah… the incident where I saw her face, that it was time I should know… should know the truth. And so he told me where he had… he had first seen Raechel when she was very small… and… she had looked into his eyes and he felt a bond of some sort… and she talked to him through… with her eyes and with her mind. And he didn't understand why he felt the way that he did about her because he had never felt that way about any of the other ones that he had ever seen. And… that's when he told me that he had decided to keep her and not send her back... because they needed a young one for the Project anyway.

J: What Project was that?

H: One that ATIC was... was trying to get started... no... they had started it... but for different reasons it wasn't... it wasn't working the way they had wanted it to. But with a young one, they thought maybe it would... and since he felt this special... he had a special feeling about her, that maybe that was one of the things that they had not had before, because the other ones were older and they didn't really seem to want to cooperate. But with a young one, maybe they could influence her enough so that they could learn from her and she could learn from them. So... he... he didn't know how he would do it, but he knew he would somehow or other. So when he got her back to the base... it all came together for him because everybody wanted to help. They all... I don't know why... but they all felt that they needed to do what they could. And she agreed. And then he found out... that he had to... he thought it would just be for a little while. But ATIC said no, you have to do it... you have to do it for a long time. So anyway, he went on and he told me about that... and about the problems that they'd had... they knew that they had to teach her to talk, and... she never... and she said she would try, but... but she never got very good at it, and that's why she always... she always sounded like a machine. But she was good enough so that she could pass most of the time and they helped her... he told how her appearance... they didn't know what they'd do about that... ah... it was fine on the base, but they couldn't live there forever. So, he told me about... how they had to figure out how to cover her up... so people wouldn't know what she was.

J: As he was telling you all about this, how were you feeling?

H: I was... I was sick inside... and yet, I was fascinated... to think such a thing could happen... and I knew he wasn't lying to me... even if he had been lying to me, I still saw her... I knew she wasn't from here. So I know he told me the truth.

J: Did he tell you any more about his job on the base?

H: When he got Raechel?

J: Um-hm.

H: Only that she was one of the few that looked halfway human. And that was another thing they looked for when they needed one that... that was closer to us... he said it was almost too much for him sometimes. He couldn't stand the sight of some of them... and, there were... lots that just didn't make it... and they tried to save them but they were burned or all broke up or something, and they couldn't do anything for them, and it wasn't the death that was so bad... it was just how these things would have looked if they had been all in one piece. So he said he welcomed Raechel coming... because he thought after the first day or so when he found that she could stay, that this was his out... so he didn't have to deal with the other stuff. But then... then he knew he had a problem because after... after a certain ... after she got so far... then he had to leave the base... and the goal was that he had to see how she would do among people. So they looked for just the right person... he didn't look, they looked... I don't know who. I didn't ask, I couldn't say anything.

J: As you watched and then listened to him talk, I want you to be very aware of his appearance, his body, his weight. Tell me everything you can remember about how he looked.

H: He was a really handsome man... and he had dark hair, dark brown... unusual blue eyes, not bright blue, but deep blue... and I don't know... I don't remember how tall he was, maybe... 5'10"... 6'... no... about that... probably about 180 pounds. He was a really well-built man. Very neat, in good shape. I didn't want to stare but he was a good-looking man.

J: About how old was he?

H: I don't know. I think he was in his early forties to middle forties... between... maybe forty-four, forty-five. I think, I don't know.

J: As you were talking with him, was Raechel there?

H: She was in her bedroom.

J: Do you know why she wasn't out talking with you?

H: She didn't want to hear it.

J: Did she say why she didn't want to hear it?

H: No.

J: I want you to focus back on the colonel again for me. As you listen to him talk, were you aware of any accents or unusual mannerisms as he talked?

H: No... he had a voice... may have been trying to have no accent... and seemed very much at ease... much more than I was... he just sat there and talked, but his voice did have no accent... and everybody has some accent, everybody should... unless you've been trained to have none.

J: And as he told you about the story concerning Raechel, is there anything he told you about what she needed to eat or how she needed to eat it, or...

H: Yes. He said she could never eat food like normal people... that's what he, like normal people do. He said he would keep her supplied with... with exactly what she should have, and he would see that it would always be there.

J: Did he say what that was?

H: Well... yes, he said, those big jugs in the kitchen on the floor, that's what she drinks.

J: Did he say what was in the jugs?

H: No, no, he didn't. It looked like water.

J: Was that liquid the only thing that she did eat?

H: No, she could... she could have the food that came in the little boxes... the little white boxes.

J: Did you ever see that food?

H: No... but Marisa told me what it looked like.

J: What did it look like?

H: She... she called it that "awful green stuff." It looked like chopped-up spinach that... that was heated, reheated too many times... and she said she had asked Raechel one time for a taste of it and Raechel told her, no, don't ever touch it. It'll make you sick. She really didn't want it anyway because it looked so awful.

J: And in this conversation with the colonel, did it take place before Raechel fell?

H: No, it took place after.

J: How long after?

H: Maybe in one or two months... not sure.

J: And how long was it after the conversation that Raechel left the apartment for good?

H: Probably another month or two... I don't remember exactly.

J: During that time, did you ever see the boxes or the jugs closely?

H: Yes.

J: Tell me what they looked like.

H: I didn't... I never touched them... but when I saw the jugs there were six of them in the kitchen and they were big like... five-gallon... like five-gallon jugs, I think. They were not small. They were like big, tall... distilled water jugs. I guess that's what they looked like and I wanted to remember... well, how could she lift those? Because they must be really heavy... but I never mentioned it because I guess it wasn't a problem... there were always six, two rows of three.

J: Were there any markings on the bottles?

H: Yes, but I didn't see them.

J: How do you know there were markings on the bottles?

H: Because Marisa, during one of the times when her sight was a little better and Raechel was gone, she checked the bottom of one and it had a triangle on it... with lines through it... and then....

J: How many lines?

H: Three. And then I saw the boxes in the freezer, and I didn't touch those, either. But they had the markings on, too. Little markings.

FIGURE 4. Triangular emblem seen on Raechel's food and water containers, on the license plate of the car driven by the men visiting Raechel at her apartment, and on a truck outside the underground base.

J: And those markings that were on the bottles and boxes, did you ever see that same marking anywhere else?

H: Yes.

J: Where is that?

H: The license plate on that funny car that those men drove.

J: Which men were those?

H: They were the men that came... they were friends of the colonel and they came... every two or three weeks to see... to see how Raechel was doing and... and I... I saw the car one time... and then I saw... it didn't belong to people that lived there. Those people had old cars, and this was so strange. It didn't look like any car I had ever been close to. I had seen pictures like that, but there weren't any cars like that around.

J: Where had you seen pictures?

H: In old movies, or in books, history books.

J: So it was not a new car.

H: No. It looked new. It was shiny... really beautiful, but I know it wasn't new. It wasn't American, either.

J: And that marking was on the car.

H: It was on the license plate.

FIGURE 5. A photo of a car that is similar to the one that visited Raechel's and Marisa's apartment.

J: Was there ever any other place that you saw that marking?

H: I don't think so. I don't remember.

J: I'm going to count from one to three and as I do, I want you to continue going deeper and deeper, looking anywhere in your awareness of ever having seen that marking anywhere else. And on the count of three, if you have any other knowledge of that marking it will come forward to you at that time. One, two, three.

H: (whispering) No, I've never seen that before. But Marisa had seen it.

J: Where had Marisa seen it?

H: She'd seen the car, too, at a different time.

J: Did she notice anything about the car that was different or more than you have already told me?

H: Not much. She knew it wasn't right, but she couldn't see it very well... somehow she knew it wasn't... it wasn't right... wasn't supposed to be there.

J: Can you tell me what else was on the license plate besides that marking?

H: Nothing. Nothing. It was black.

J: And the marking was in what color?

H: In red.

J: Was that also true of the boxes?

H: Yes... just the same, only smaller.

J: And the three men that used to bring those boxes and bottles and drove that car, what can you tell me about them?

H: I don't know if they brought the boxes and bottles. They never saw anybody... but I think they did. But they didn't bring them in the apartment, they always, whoever brought them just left them outside.

J: Outside where?

H: Outside the door. But it would be like they had just left it when the girls opened the door... the men were... funny-looking.

J: In what way?

H: They didn't look very healthy to me... they weren't thin or anything but their faces were really white... they looked... they just looked unhealthy like... like somebody that never got out in the sun, and I thought... this is California... these men... they don't look right for living here, but maybe they work inside most of the time. I didn't think much about it, except that they... something didn't look right, but they were mean... real... just... they looked like they wouldn't care if they killed you. That was the impression I got. And they nearly knocked me down the stairs as I was going up, and they were coming down, and there were three. Nobody stepped aside. I had to back down to the landing. If I hadn't of, they'd have knocked me down. I didn't like that.

J: I want you to be at that moment when they almost knocked you down, and tell me what you were feeling inside.

H: I was angry... for one thing... and I was scared. They looked threatening but they didn't say anything. But I knew they were the ones that had been coming to the apartment... I just knew. They were dressed so funny. They looked... their suits didn't fit right, and they had black suits that... they were too tight or something... they looked... the men looked like they had been dressed up to play a role or something and couldn't get suits to fit them right. They just did... nothing... the tops were too tight and they looked like they were old-fashioned or something. They just looked out of character. They didn't... they looked like they should have been in the thirties or something and they... well, it was like they were in costume. But I guess they weren't because Marisa said that's how they looked the times that she'd seen them. So I guess that's how they always looked but they didn't look right. And they were rude to her, too.

J: As they passed you on the stairs or any other time that you might have come in contact with them, did you ever hear their voices?

H: No, I never heard them.

J: Did you ever notice anything about them in terms of perfume or smells or anything else that might be something you were aware of?

H: Perfume... they smelled musty. They smelled... they smelled like their suits had been in an old... old closet that had been locked up and things smell funny. They don't smell fresh. But they only... they went by me pretty fast, but I guess that's why I was able to smell that.

J: And was there anything else that Marisa told you or Raechel told you about these men that you don't already know from your own seeing them?

H: Um... well, Raechel... Raechel told Marisa that they wouldn't harm anyone, they wouldn't harm her. They came to check on her progress... and they were friends of her father's... they worked with her father.

J: So they worked on the base or where did they work?

H: She didn't... Marisa didn't ask. I guess... I guess they worked on the base, but maybe not... because they didn't have uniforms.

J: Did she ever call them by name?

H: No, she didn't... she didn't call them by name... but Marisa asked her the names and she told me.

J: What were their names?

H: One was Auran... and one was Asaterek... and... oh... I can't remember...I can't remember the other one. I know it, but I can't think of it.

J: It's all right, just let it be for right now. It will come back to you.

H: Oh, yes... I know it... when they talked to Marisa, they told her... they asked her to leave... one time... so she did. She didn't think she should have to leave her own apartment, but she thought it was the best thing to do... so that was the time she went downstairs and... she got a look at the car. Because by then she could see better than... than Raechel thought she could. That's when she saw the license plate.

J: Were any of these three men ever described or talked about by Raechel or her father to you?

H: No.

J: Were they ever described or talked about by Marisa as having been told by Raechel or her father?

H: I didn't understand that.

J: Did Marisa ever tell you about any one of these three men as having worked with or been with Raechel's father?

H: No. Raechel told Marisa that the men worked with her father.

J: But didn't tell you anything about any of the individual men?

H: No.

J: Is there anything else that you can remember at this time about the three men that you haven't already told me?

H: I don't remember from where I am now... but... another time I saw through a window, and one man looked like an old movie actor. It was the same man that I saw on the stairs, one of the men. He looked like George Raft. It was funny because... he doesn't look like that now, where I am.

J: What do you mean he doesn't look like that now?

H: Where I am on the stairs... that... but I saw him at a later time and I know it's the same man. And that is who he looked like.

J: How do you know it's the same man?

H: Well... maybe I don't know... but I think it was.

J: Was he with the other men?

H: No, he was by himself.

J: Where was he?

H: I was looking through a window… and he was on the other side but he didn't see me.

J: Where was the window?

H: It was just a window… I know a window has to be someplace, has to be in a wall.

J: I'm going to count from one to three. On the count of three, you're going to be at that window with the man on the other side, and you're going to know where it is that you are. One, two, three…. Tell me what you're aware of.

H: It's a car window… but he's all by himself. The other two are not there… or… I don't see the other two.

J: What kind of a car?

H: The big black one.

J: Have you ever seen this car before?

H: In the parking lot… of the apartment house.

J: And it's the same car that has the license plate with the mark on it?

H: Yes.

J: Where is this car right now?

H: (Long pause)… it's in the parking lot but in another place… but he's all by himself.

J: And what does he do when you look in the window at him?

H: He looks straight ahead but he sees me.

J: How close are you to the car?

H: Um… maybe ten… fifteen feet. But he can't see me… He's looking… he's looking in the other direction, but I think he sees me out of the corner of his eye.

J: Why do you think that?

H: I just feel it… but I don't know why he would watch… I don't know why he would be there by… himself.

J: I want you to look all around you and see if you can see the other two men anywhere.

H: No.

J: How long do you watch the man in the car?

H: Only a minute or so. Because... he's kind of scary. Because when I saw him the last time he was with the other two... and they... they just ... they tried to frighten me. And they did it. So I thought I'd better just keep walking.

J: Where were you going when you saw the man?

H: I was going up to the apartment.

J: And just continue on up to the apartment. Did anything happen between the time you left the car and got to the apartment? Did you see anybody?

H: No, I didn't see anybody but I got to the apartment and rang the bell and I guess no one was there... So I didn't have very much time to spend anyway, so I just... just came back down the stairs and left.

J: And was the car still there when you came down the stairs?

H: Yes.

J: And was the man still in the car?

H: Yes.

J: Was he still alone?

H: Yes. But I didn't see anybody else.

J: Did you ever see him or any of the other men or the car again?

H: No. I would remember that.

J: I want you to go back for a moment to when you were talking to the colonel. Let yourself go back, be in front of him, fully aware. And I want you to tell me if you ever saw the colonel again after this meeting.

H: I don't think so. I never saw him there. I don't think I ever saw him anyplace else.

J: When you spoke directly to Raechel at the time that you described to me when she told you about herself, when you saw her eyes clearly, and you looked at her hair, did she tell you anything new about the colonel that you didn't already know?

H: No....

J: Did she tell you how she felt about the colonel?

H: She loved him... and I didn't know what she meant because... I wondered if they knew what love was.

J: Why did you wonder that?

H: Because I knew she wasn't from here... But she said... she was supposed to learn to feel like we do. So I guess she could learn.

J: What kind of behavior did she display to Marisa?

H: Did Raechel display?

J: Um-hm.

H: Friends... not in the sense that other girlfriends do...

J: One, two three.

H: ...that it was difficult at all for Raechel... I don't know why I said that.

J: As you were talking through eye contact with Raechel, did she ever describe this place where she was when she was finished developing?

H: No.

J: Did she ever at any time talk about what it was like where she lived?

H: (long pause)... nothing except... that it didn't matter if... like here, it mattered if you looked different, or if you were different in any way. But there, they all look the same, so... so you didn't have that problem.

J: Did she ever talk about what it looked like where she lived?

H: Just the colors.

J: What colors were those?

H: Blue... green.

J: When she talked about those colors, how did she describe them?

H: She made me see them... she didn't make me... she let me see them... and they're beautiful. I don't know what they were... if they were... if they were sky or water... when I looked they didn't seem to be... they were just colors.

J: Did she ever mention to you family or who might have taken care of her when she was in this place before she came to Earth?

H: No... she didn't... there didn't seem to be any family. Not like a mother and father... because there wasn't a mother and father... I don't think there were any brothers and sisters, either. But I don't know that... there was no mother and father, but I don't know about the brothers and sisters.

J: Did she ever tell you how she happened to be in that ship that arrived in the desert?

H: She was supposed to be here... the other hybrid was already here... and she was supposed to come... everything was ready for her. And she didn't have any choice, she had to come... (whispering)... she had to come.

J: Did she know why she was coming?

H: Not really. But then she had no choice. She had to do what she was told.

J: How did she feel about that?

H: She didn't have any feelings. But... they just told her that it was time for her to go... and she couldn't question it... It didn't matter... she didn't have any feelings... not then.

J: What do you mean, not then?

H: Because after she came... she began... she was supposed to... the Project didn't work out with the older people... they couldn't... they couldn't fit in because... it wasn't feelings, it was... it was like love, hate, emotions. And the older people couldn't... they just couldn't seem to... they didn't work out. The Project thought that maybe... maybe if they tried with a younger one, that maybe it would, maybe they could be taught, maybe they could learn.

J: And when she first landed here in the crash landing, did she tell you what that was like for her?

H: Not much... not much... except that... that she was sort of trapped... and she thought maybe no one would find her, and she couldn't get out. So then, when someone did find her, he could talk to her... he did talk to her.

J: How did he talk to her?

H: With his eyes.

J: He knew how to speak the way she spoke?

H: That's right. Because he had spoken before... with other ones... and so... he took her out and gave her... took her... took her to a safe place. And then he told her that she could stay.

J: And did he tell her his name?

H: Not right then... not very long, though.

J: As they got to know each other better, did she ever tell you what she called him?

H: She called him by his first name... but I don't remember... she didn't call him father... anything like that... I don't remember what... I don't remember what, but it was his first name... oh... I should remember that.

J: Helen, I'm going to ask your deeper mind to answer me with your fingers for a moment. Just let yourself go totally into that place where your deeper mind will answer my questions. Was Helen ever told the colonel's first name by Raechel?

H: She didn't tell me. I don't know why she didn't... um... but she didn't call him father... but he wasn't her father.

J: I'd like the deeper mind to answer again and Helen can just allow her fingers to answer the questions. Did Helen ever hear the colonel's first name from anyone?

H: Don't know if yes or no. (fingers)

J: Did Helen ever hear the colonel addressed by some other name other than "the colonel" and his last name?

H: Don't know if yes or no. (fingers)

J: Is there any other information about the colonel that Raechel told you or Marisa that you are not allowed to speak at this time?

H: Yes. (fingers)

J: Yes. Is this information that you will allow yourself to remember and speak in the following weeks or months?

H: Not sure if yes or no. (fingers)

J: Was there some kind of condition or threat or some other way that you were told not to reveal this information?

H: Yes. (fingers)

J: Allow yourself to relax and go twice as deep as you are now. And if we come to a place where you're not allowed to let that information come out, then I want you to lift your middle finger so that I'll know that you're not allowed to answer that question at this time. Did the colonel ever mention any previous duty stations where he served?

H: No. (fingers)

J: Was there any other part of his life that he did talk about?

H: No. (fingers)

J: And now I'd like the deeper mind to allow Helen to speak.

H: The colonel didn't talk to me about those things.

J: Did he talk to someone else about those things.

H: Yes.

J: Who did he speak to?

H: Marisa.

J: Can you tell me what it was he told Marisa?

H: (long pause)... he told her about where he'd been before Nevada.

J: Where was that?

H: Nebraska.

J: Did he tell her where he grew up?

H: Yes.

J: Where was that?

H: Idaho.

J: Did he say where in Idaho?

H: Nampa.

J: Did he ever tell her the school that he attended?

H: Not the name... just... he went to school there... to high school and graduated.

J: And when did he leave there?

H: Right after high school.

J: And where did he go directly after high school?

H: Texas.

J: What happened in Texas?

H: He went... he went through training... like everybody else.

J: And when he finished that training?

H: Got a different place to go... but nobody would tell him where it was... and no matter who he asked, no one would tell him. They just said it was a mistake. But he knew it was not a mistake. But before he could go there, he... he had to go to Nebraska.

J: Do you know where in Nebraska?

H: He had to go to special school, and... it was at a big base... a big Air Force base.

J: Do you know the name of that base?

H: Crawford was the name.

J: And what kind of training did he have there?

H: It was a different school... different school than he'd ever seen, ever been in... all they learned about... was... other places. Spaceships... but all the other people in the class... they were all going to different places... different bases and they were all... nobody knew why they were there. They were just all sent... just all sent.

J: Was there anything that all of these people had in common?

H: Well, they had... they were all like outcasts from their families... didn't have any families... no wives, no girlfriends... maybe orphans... they were all different, but different reasons, but they were all the same, too... and... the colonel had a father and mother but they didn't want him... and he really didn't have any friends, either, any more.

J: Why is that?

H: Because he was different... everybody else just stayed home. He went away, and when he came back... they didn't bother about him...

J: While he was at these bases, what kind of security clearance was he given?

H: He had Top Secret and Crypto first... which he shouldn't have had.

J: Why is that?

H: Didn't need it then, while he was in basic.

J: So he was given that right away...

H: After two or three weeks. He shouldn't have gotten any clearance in two or three weeks, because it takes longer.

J: Was he given higher clearances or other clearances?

H: Before he went to Nebraska... just before he went to Nebraska, it was changed... and then... and then it was MAJIC... and nobody told him what that was because everybody said they didn't know, they never heard. But he knew that wasn't... that wasn't true.

J: What wasn't true?

H: That they didn't know. They didn't talk about it.

J: How did he feel about getting all this clearance and all of the information he was beginning to learn?

H: He didn't really know how to handle it... it seemed too much, it happened too fast. But he wanted to know more... and then... he found out he was going to a different place than the others. He was the only one... the only one that would go there.

J: And where was that?

H: It didn't even have a real name... it was called Four Corners... and they wouldn't tell him where that was, either. But by then, he was used to nobody telling him anything, so he just... just went along with it.

J: And when he got there, what did he find?

H: Four Corners?

J: Yes.

H: Not much. He thought he was in the wrong place, but he wasn't. He was... he thought there would be like a regular base, but... but all there was was old... funny old buildings... just, just old barns and things... on top of the ground.

J: Was there something else there?

H: Oh, yes. Oh, yes. Underground was the whole thing. Everything. That was just a cover-up... it was just to fool people.

J: Tell me more about what was underneath the ground.

H: Places to live... laboratories... big ones.

J: What did they do in the laboratories?

H: (long pause)... worked on different kinds of... things that made... like... things that made the ships run... things they got from the ones that they brought in that crashed... they take them apart... what was left... try to figure out... figure out how to... how the things worked... But he didn't go there very much because he didn't understand that.

J: What was his job?

H: His job was to go out and pick up the stuff... the people, but they're not people... the pilots... not pilots, either... the things that drove the ships.

J: What do you mean, things?

H: Well, he didn't know what else to call them... some weren't... weren't very easy to describe... and then some... some were like Raechel. But not very many of those lived... At first he didn't know why... why those ships could go so far and they'd crash when they got here... then he found out they were being shot down... in other places.

J: Who was shooting them down?

H: We were... he couldn't question very much.

J: When you said some of the occupants of these ships were very different, what did they look like?

H: (long pause)... like bugs, some did...

J: Can you tell me what kind of bugs?

H: Like grasshoppers... some of them. That can't be, but... but it was... it made him really upset... but it was his job so he had to do it.

J: And was he able to communicate with each of these that lived?

H: Most of them... the ones that wanted to, but some didn't want to... and he tried, but... then he couldn't with those, but most of them he could... he didn't know how... he didn't know why he was so good at that.

(Tape change--small amount of session is missing)

H: ...members of the team who went with him, but they weren't even going to look inside. They were just going to let it go.

J: How did he know to look inside?

H: He felt... he felt somebody was in there... something... because he couldn't see, he just felt there was something there.

J: Helen, have you or any of the people you know seen any of those buglike creatures since the time Raechel came into your life?

H: (long pause)... I don't know.

J: I'm going to count from one to three, and as I do, let yourself and your deeper mind look fully over the time period between when Raechel came and now. One, two, three.

H: Oh... oh... not... they didn't look like bugs, but their faces weren't really human.

J: Tell me what they looked like.

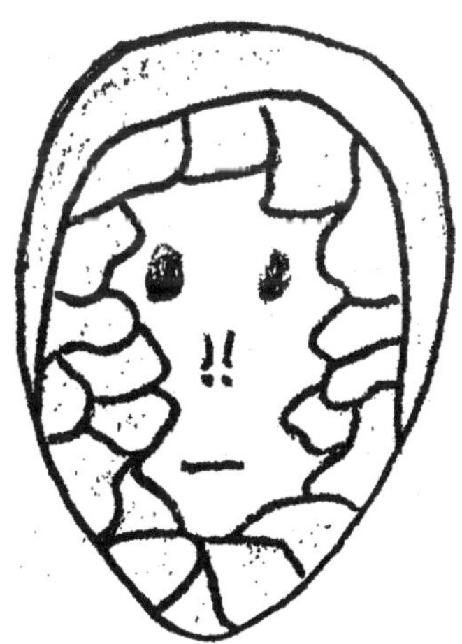

FIGURE 6. Helen's drawing of one of the unusual-looking people she saw at a restaurant in Eureka, northern California.

H: Um... they were... like they had layers of... like they had patches ... sewed on top of patches... but they weren't green... like bugs are... but... oh... I don't know.

J: Where did you see them?

H: In... when I was in a restaurant... they didn't look like bugs but their faces weren't real... they weren't the right color for people, either, but... they weren't... they weren't green.

J: What color were they?

H: Brown, not dark brown... kind of different shades of brown... but it was like patches... all over, and they both looked alike.

J: And did you communicate with them in any way, or they with you?

H: Oh, I think so... I think so.

J: What do you mean?

H: Well, they looked at me... through the window... really close.

J: What were you aware of as they looked at you?

H: That they'd been looking for me and that... they couldn't find me ... before... but why would they want me?

J: Allow yourself to look at them now, very closely, and to look at their eyes and ask them, why were you looking for me?

H: They wanted to make sure I was safe... what could they do?... what difference would it make?... what could they do?

J: Ask them why they were interested in seeing if you were safe. What connection do they have with you?

H: Oh... I don't want to be connected with them... they look bad.

J: But they wanted you to be safe.

H: Yes.

J: Ask them why they were interested in keeping you safe.

H: Because they know I was so upset... and they were afraid... and they don't know anything about cars, and they thought I would... they thought it was too big a trip for me to take... that's ridiculous... that's stupid.

J: Why were you upset?

H: Ah… ah… because I was so late getting started on the trip and it's a long… it's a long drive… and I wanted to start early and I couldn't because I couldn't… I tried to help the boys find each other… because they were coming up together… the one had come so far already from San Diego and he couldn't find the other one… no one would answer the phone in the house… no one would answer when I called. I couldn't wait any longer… and I knew I had to get there in time to go to the cemetery.

J: Why were you going to the cemetery?

H: (crying)… I had to go see Marisa. The cemetery was going to close… and I got lost, I took the wrong street, had to ask directions and nobody knew. Finally I saw a man coming along and he told me where it was, and then I had to leave. I couldn't stay very long because they were getting ready to close it up, close the gates… and I was upset over that. And I was so hungry, I hadn't eaten all day.

J: While you were there with Marisa, were you aware of anything at all between the two of you?

H: Just something she used to say… "whatever it takes, mom, you can do it"… it didn't… I don't know what she meant… she said, you'll do all right, you'll be okay… I said I don't want to have to hurry, I can't come back in the morning, I don't have time. I want to be here … and she said, it's all right, I'm not really here anyway… so I had to go… and I was upset. Because nothing… the whole day was awful. And when I went to the restaurant I was so thirsty and all I wanted was a nice, cold beer and the waitress brought me a warm one, and I was so mad. And I yelled at her… I said I won't pay for this, bring me a cold one… if you don't have cold beer, I want some cold water … this is ridiculous… so I got the cold beer and ordered my supper, and just as she brought it, I looked out the window… oh… I thought … I don't need this… I just… I can't handle this… I saw these two people, these two things, and I don't even want to look at them. But I thought, well, don't look… they'll be out of sight… don't look at them. But they weren't out of sight. They came right down… down the street, right by the window where I was, and they stopped and they looked… they just looked at me…

J: I want you to look at them very closely and I want you to tell me if you've ever had contact with these two people or creatures, whatever they are, before, in any form.

H: The eyes are all the same… all the eyes are the same.

J: What do you mean?

H: All these things have the same eyes… they all look different but… the rest of them… but their eyes are all the same… ah…

J: Like Raechel's eyes?

H: These are just big black eyes…

J: When you say they're all the same, who else has eyes like this?

H: The birds… (long pause)…

J: Is there anyone else?

H: (whispers)… the doctor… Oh… oh… (sobbing)… I don't know (can't understand)… can't get away… no matter where I go… but the other ones don't hurt me….

J: Is the doctor the only one that's ever hurt you?

H: Yes.

J: Did the doctor ever examine you or do anything at all with your body other than that time that you have described to us where she took you into her office?

H: No… I don't remember anything. So I don't know why she did it then. Well, I guess she did it because I went to her, but I don't know why I went. I should have gone someplace else.

J: When you speak, Helen, of all of the rest of them having the same eyes, do they all feel as though they are connected in some way?

H: I don't know... sometimes they look so strange that I'm really afraid. I'm startled because some of the birds don't look right... they're fierce... they've fierce eyes but they don't... they don't mean me any harm. But they look fierce... but that's how birds' eyes look. They can't help how their eyes look.

J: Helen, I'd like you to go back now to when Raechel first arrived on the ship when the colonel found her, and tell me the name of the project that she came to work with and that the colonel was working on.

H: It was the Humanization Project.

J: The Humanization Project?

H: Supposed to see how human... but I don't know... how much emotion they could develop... in... in the hybrids... they didn't... it didn't work... on anybody but the hybrids.

J: It didn't work with just the ETs?

H: That's right. They tried and it... I don't know... it just didn't work.

J: Is this what the colonel told Marisa?

H: Yes.

J: Where was the safe place they took Raechel to?

H: What safe place?

J: After Raechel was brought here and cared for and taught. How was she kept safe as they went out into the world?

H: On the base. They made a place for her to live, but somebody was always there.

J: Who was there?

H: There were two... two nurses.

J: What were their names?

H: I don't know... I don't know... but one was always with her.

J: Did Marisa ever tell you the names of the nurses?

H: No, I don't think she knew... maybe she did.

J: Did Raechel ever tell you about the nurses?

H: She didn't call them nurses.

J: What did she call them?

H: She just called them females... they had names but I don't know what they were.

J: And who began to teach Raechel?

H: A lady from the Project.

J: The Humanization Project?

H: Um-hm.

J: And what was it that she taught Raechel?

H: How to speak... how to put her thoughts into words... because she had to learn... she had to learn for the Project.

J: Was there anyone else who was a hybrid that could speak? Had this been done before?

H: Yes. There was another hybrid there. He was working on something else. He was... he was working on something else but he helped Raechel because they were... they were really alike... close... so... he made something for her to eat and to drink... and he knew how to do it because before... when they had the ETs... they couldn't keep them alive. There was nothing... it wasn't right what they gave them to eat and drink... so he made... he made his own things and it was the same for Raechel. It would work with Raechel. And he helped... he helped her learn to speak.

J: Do you know if Raechel ever saw him again after she left the base?

H: I don't know. I don't think she did but I don't know.

J: Helen, I want you to go back in time a short ways, and I want you to tell me about anything you know concerning the training in Texas and where in Texas it was that the colonel went.

H: Oh… it was where they all go to… Lakeland… Lakeland Air Force Base… think it's… I think it's near San Antonio… No… Wichita Falls, maybe… I don't know… it's one or the other… I've never been there.

J: And did you ever visit the area around Four Corners?

H: I think so.

J: When was that?

H: I don't know.

J: Was it before or after you met Raechel?

H: I never heard of it before… so… so it would… I don't remember. I don't know how I would go.

J: Were you ever at the base at the Four Corners?

H: (long pause)… I must have been… because I know what it looks like… but… but I don't know how I would go there… why I would go there… I don't know… I don't think… but if I didn't go, then I wouldn't know what it looked like…

J: Let your deeper mind take over for a moment. Let your deeper mind recall how you found out about what the base looked like. Let your deeper mind clearly look at all the information surrounding your knowledge of the base, and then let your deeper mind answer with your fingers as to what happened to allow you to know more about the base. Did Helen ever visit the base at Four Corners?

H: Yes.

J: And when Helen visited the base at Four Corners, was it after Raechel and the colonel left the base?

H: Yes. (fingers)

J: And did Helen go with the colonel and Raechel to the base?

H: Yes. (fingers)

J: And was it during the time that Raechel and Marisa lived together?

H: Yes. (fingers)

J: And did Helen go only once to the base?

H: Yes. (fingers)

J: And while Helen was there, was she taken to the base underneath the ground as well as above?

H: Yes. (fingers)

J: Was Helen at that time told anything about whether she could speak about this again or not?

H: Yes. (fingers)

J: Is it all right for Helen to tell us at this time what she was told about not speaking?

H: No. (fingers)

J: Was there a threat made of any kind?

H: Yes. (fingers)

J: Was there a threat of harm made to Helen's life?

H: Yes. (fingers)

J: Was there a threat made to anyone else's life?

H: Yes. (fingers)

J: Was there a threat made to Marisa's life?

H: Yes. (fingers)

J: To the colonel's life?

H: Yes. (fingers)

J: To Raechel's life?

H: Yes. (fingers)

J: To anyone else's life?

H: Yes. (fingers)

J: Do we know the other person or persons who were threatened with their lives?

H: Yes. (fingers)

J: Can Helen tell us who they are?

H: Yes.

J: Helen, who were the other people who were threatened with their lives if you spoke about your visit to the base?

H: My boys... so I can't tell (whispering).

J: When or if it is ever safe for you to give forward that information, it will be easily accessible to you. Until that time it is important that you do whatever you need to do to protect your family and yourself... Can you tell us any more about the surrounding areas of the base now so that we have a better understanding where it's located?... Where would that be?... What is it that you're aware of?

H: It's... it's just... it's hard to describe it because I know what it looks like, but... if I was there I would know where... where to turn... but it's really hard to tell somebody else because it's all desert there.

J: If you saw a map with roads on it would you be able to say where it is?

H: I already have.

J: You already have a map or you already have seen a map?

H: I've already seen a map and I've already done that.

J: And who have you told or shown?

H: Jean, some of the others.

J: So that they know enough how to get to the base?

H: That's right... they could find it okay.

J: Did the colonel ever mention to you or did Raechel ever tell Marisa or you any other organizations that he was affiliated with outside of the Humanization Project and MAJIC?

H: NRO.

J: What is NRO?

H: National Reconnaissance Organization.

J: And do you know what he did with that organization?

H: They were… they were like his boss or something… but… but about the same as ATIC. They all worked together… but nobody knew about anything… nobody outside knew… there wasn't any such thing… that's what they told everybody, but that's not true… just not true.

J: Do you know anything else about those connections that would be helpful for us in our looking for the colonel?

H: Um… no… I tried but I can't think… don't know.

J: Helen, I want to go again to your deeper mind and I want your deeper mind to answer some questions. Let your deeper mind move your fingers. Have you been contacted in any way by the colonel since the colonel and Raechel disappeared and moved from the apartment?

H: No. (fingers)

J: Have you received any information from any other source telling you about them?

H: No. (fingers)

J: In your visits from the birds and their invitation to look in their eyes and to go and visit that other place, have you ever been given specific information about that other place?

H: Yes. (fingers)

J: And deeper mind, Helen has mentioned to us a number of times the term "window." She has seen the man dressed in black in the car that delivered the food through the window. She again saw him looking like George Raft at the same time she saw the symbol that was on the food cartons and on the license plate, upside down, through a window. She saw the two strange beings with the patches on their faces through the window. Is there is a special significance in the term "window" for Helen when she speaks about that?

H: Yes. (fingers)

J: Is Helen free to know at this time the meaning of "window"?

H: No. (fingers)

J: Does Helen know about the meaning of "window" but it's not all right to tell it at this time?

H: Yes. (fingers)

J: Will Helen be allowed to talk about or be aware of what the window means in the next few months?

H: Yes. (fingers)

J: And will she be able to allow this information to come up naturally into her own consciousness?

H: (fingers. The answer is not to be told at this time - June)

J: Would someone else be able to assist Helen in finding out the meaning of the window?

H: Yes. (fingers)

J: Helen is raising her middle finger. Deeper mind, are you trying to tell us that there is some issue with her being helped to find out the meaning of "window"?

H: Yes. (fingers)

J: I want to assure the deeper mind and Helen that that information will not be taken or forced until Helen is ready to release that information, until it's safe, until she feels safe internally. It is important that Helen and the deeper mind know that that will not be forced before it's the correct time... I would like to ask one last question about the windows, if it's all right... Are the windows a way of alerting Helen in some way to the fact that the experiencing is continuing?

H: Yes. (fingers)

J: I'd like to ask the deeper mind if Helen was contacted or involved in any way with ET experiences before the age of five?

H: No. (fingers)

J: Before the age of ten?

H: No. (fingers)
J: Before the age of thirteen?
H: Yes. (fingers)
J: Before the age of twelve?
H: No. (fingers)
J: Was Helen contacted between the ages of twelve and thirteen for the first time?
H: Yes. (fingers)
J: And was that contact made in that secret place she used to go?
H: Yes. (fingers)
J: Would it be all right for Helen to tell us more about that first contact now?
H: Yes. (fingers)
J: Helen, I ask you to go to that moment just b efore that event and on the count of three I want you to be there, aware of everything that's happening. One, two, three.
H: ...um...(long pause)...I see a...I see a light, but...it's...the sun is out, so...I don't know where the light, the other is coming from...
J: Where are you standing?
H: I'm standing by the little creek...it's just a little creek and there's grass on both sides...and the bank goes up a little way but on top of the bank...in front of the trees...is a light...just a little light like...two or three feet around.

At this point, June felt Helen was tiring and she suggested they take a break. She picks up on this theme in the next regression.

Chapter 29

03/29/98: Third Regression with Dr. June Steiner and Helen

June (J):[1] How was it moving?

Helen (H): It was just kind of... skips along... skips along but it's not on the ground, either... and... it stops a little way away from me.

J: And how are you feeling while this is happening?

H: I can't take my eyes off it.

J: What color is the light?

H: Blue... really beautiful blue... like the sky.

J: And then what happens?

H: I want to touch it... but something tells me not to.

J: Are you close enough to touch it?

H: I'm close enough and I reach out, but just before I do... before my hand is on it... I get a feeling I shouldn't.

J: Why shouldn't you?

H: Because I might go inside it.

J: How would you do that?

H: I don't know... and I don't... I'd like to touch it, but I don't want to go inside it... because I don't know what's in there.

J: And then what happens next?

H: It's like I'm told... that's okay... we just wanted to... we just wanted to come and see you today... but we'll be back

1. The induction has been omitted.

another... we'll be back again... we don't want you to touch us today... and I'm thinking, this is... this is silly... a light, is talking to me... but it seems to be okay... so it doesn't do anything more... it sits there for a minute... and it skips along... back... backwards a little bit... and I think, well, I should have... I should be saying something to it, something more... and then I... and then it just goes away... it just goes away... but I can't tell anybody... can't tell anybody about it.

J: Why is that?

H: Because I was told not to.

J: Who told you that?

H: Just how I felt from the light... because there wasn't anybody... wasn't anybody in the light... but I hope it will come back.

J: Helen, I want you to go forward in time to the next time the light returns. Tell me where you are and what you're aware of.

H: I'm in the same place because I like to go there because I'm alone... I look up on the bank in front of the trees, and the light is there again... (long pause)... and this is when they... this is when they ask me, would you like to have a baby? (Laughs)... and I said, I don't want a baby, I'm just a little girl. Don't want a baby... I have to go to school.

J: And did you go into the ship this time? Did you reach out and touch the ship and go inside?

H: I didn't go inside.

J: What did you do?

H: I touched it.

J: And what happened when you touched it?

H: It felt like... I felt like an electric shock... and I couldn't take my finger right away... I couldn't take it away as quick as I wanted to... it's like it was stuck there for a minute.

J: What happened during that minute, Helen? Let yourself know everything that happened during that minute.

H: But I still didn't want to have a baby. I was too young. And they said, that's all right, we'll wait, we'll wait... and I don't remember... my finger came off it... and I was just standing there with my finger out, and the light was gone... I thought maybe I imagined it, but I don't think I did.

J: Helen, I'd like to talk to your deeper mind for a moment and let it answer with finger signals. I'd like you to go with your deeper mind to that moment that you touched the ship, the light, whatever it was, and in that instant I want you to tell me if something happened that you do not consciously recall.

H: Yes. (fingers)

J: Would you be willing to let that come to your consciousness at this time?

H: No. (fingers)

J: Is that something that you would be willing to allow to come to your consciousness within the next few months?

H: I don't know or I'm not sure whether it's all right. (fingers)

J: Is it all right if we check back with you in the near future?

H: Yes. (fingers)

J: Can you tell me, Helen, if whatever it is that happened during that minute that you touched the light, was it longer than one minute of our time?

H: Yes. (fingers)

J: And did you have an experience different from any other experience you'd had before then?

H: Yes. (fingers)

J: Thank the deeper mind for answering those questions. I'd like to go back for a moment to your birth with Marisa, and tell me if there was... actually tell me what happened when

Marisa was born. Tell me about the birth and about the conditions.

H: She was so little... she was so small... I felt so bad because I couldn't take her home with me.

J: How much did she weigh?

H: Four pounds and ten ounces.

J: Was she a healthy baby?

H: Yes, but she wouldn't eat very much. But she was healthy.

J: Was she full-term?

H: No.

J: How old was she?

H: I think eight months... I wasn't very healthy when I... before I had her... couldn't eat a lot of things.

J: Did that happen just during the pregnancy?

H: Yes... and it's happening now, too, sometimes.

J: Tell me more about that. What is it that happens? And what are those things that you can't eat?

H: I can't eat very much meat... sometimes I can't eat anything.

J: What happens if you do?

H: I feel really sick, nauseated... just like I did then... then sometimes I'm okay, but... it's new, now... it's just the last few months. I don't know why... I like to eat, but... food just looks awful sometimes.

J: When you first held Marisa, how did that feel?

H: (long pause)... not like I know it should have.

J: What do you mean?

H: I didn't feel like a mother... like a mother should.

J: Was Marisa your first child?

H: Yes... I didn't know how to feel... I guess she was so little I was afraid I'd break her.

J: And how long did it take you to bond with her?

H: A long time... it shouldn't take that long.

J: How long was that?

H: Years.

J: What finally created the bond?

H: I don't know... I think it was when she lost... no... she had gotten diabetes. She was so sick I thought she would die... it's awful.

J: What was awful?

H: It took so long.

J: But somehow there was a stronger connection when she got diabetes.

H: Yes... and why would that be?....

J: During that time before the birth of Marisa, and those years when she came down with diabetes, do you ever remember being visited by the blue light?

H: No... no, I don't.

J: And during the time when Marisa came down with diabetes, and you first met Raechel, do you remember being visited by the blue light?

H: No... no, I don't.

J: I'm going to ask your deeper mind for a moment to answer some questions with your fingers. Deeper mind, I'd like you to review Helen's life fully in the time just before Marisa was conceived to the time that you and Marisa met Raechel. Was there any contact of any kind between entities from another place and Helen—in any form?

H: Yes. (fingers)

J: Did that take place before the conception of Marisa or at the conception of Marisa?

H: Yes. (fingers)

J: Was it repeated again after Marisa was conceived?

H: Yes. (fingers)

J: Were they in contact after Marisa came down with diabetes until you met Raechel?

H: No. (fingers)

J: Were you contacted more than five times between the conception of Marisa and the time she came down with diabetes?

H: No. (fingers)

J: Were you contacted more than three times?

H: No. (fingers)

J: Were you contacted two times or less?

H: Yes. (fingers)

J: Were you contacted two times?

H: Not sure of response. (fingers)

J: Were you contacted any other time besides around conception? Between conception and when Marisa came down with diabetes?

H: Not sure of response. (fingers)

J: Was there any connection between that contact and Marisa's illness?

H: Not able to tell me at this time. (fingers)

J: Was Marisa in any way altered—was the egg or sperm that came to form Marisa in any way altered from its original form?

H: Yes. (fingers)

J: Are you able to go to that time when you were told or shown about that alteration?

H: Yes. (fingers)

J: I'm going to count from one to three…

H: One night… and I'm there by myself… and she says, it's so nice out, let's go take a walk. And I say, I don't even know who you are. And she said, that's all right, we'll get acquainted… I said, I don't want to go… and she says, well, come on anyway… and so I went… I shouldn't have but I did. I know now I shouldn't have gone... but it was such a little... such a little town and it was still light out, and I thought I... I went with her.

J: And you had seen this woman before, or you'd never seen her before?

H: I had seen her before... met her on the street.

J: What did she look like?

H: Nothing outstanding... uh... dark hair... I felt as if I knew her somehow, but I knew I couldn't... I don't think I did... because I had just moved to that town, so... and I had never been there before, so I couldn't... couldn't have known her there... So anyway we went for the walk...

J: What happened while you were on the walk? Did you talk?

H: Oh, yes... but I don't remember what we talked about...

J: Where did you go?

H: We had to stop to see somebody she knew... (long pause)...

J: Tell me about that.

H: Well, we went in, but it was somebody that wanted to see me....

J: What did this person look like?

H: Like a doctor.

J: Was it a woman or a man?

H: It was a woman and I don't like woman doctors.

J: Why don't you like woman doctors?

H: Because they always hurt.

J: Why did this doctor want to see you?

H: I don't know... but she said she needed to see me. She needed to make sure... make sure I was all right... I told her, I am all right... I don't need you to tell me that. But she said, well, you're here, so I will look anyway... I will make sure you're all right... so I lay... I sat up on the table... I didn't want to lie down.

J: What kind of a table was it?

H: It was like an exam table, examination table.

J: What was it made out of?

H: It was like it was covered with a brown plastic or something. It was an old-fashioned thing... it was an old-fashioned room... it was... but I didn't know there was a doctor's office there... ah... I shouldn't have gone with this lady. I should have stayed in the house, but... but I am... I'm here.

J: And what happened during the examination?

H: They made me lie down... and then they turned the light on and I couldn't see. I had to close my eyes, but then... then I don't remember... I don't remember... it's like... it's like... they gave me some anesthesia or something, but I don't remember the smell because... because ether smells funny and so does that thing on your face... I didn't smell that.

J: How did they give you what they gave you? What form?

H: It was in the light, I think... because as soon as I lay down, the light was so bright I had to close my eyes, and I don't remember anything, but the light doesn't do that... but there wasn't anything else either... but I don't remember what happened.

J: Was the woman who brought you to this place in the room?

H: Yes.

J: Was there anyone else in the room?

H: The doctor, the lady doctor.

J: Anyone else?

H: I didn't see anyone else.

J: And what instruments or furniture or anything else might have been in the room?

H: There wasn't much in there. There was this table that I was on, and a light up above... from the ceiling... and an old cabinet with two doors... two glass doors... really old... I didn't see... I don't remember anything else. It didn't have enough things in it. It should have had more.

J: Helen, I want you to go to the moment they turned the light on. I want you to be looking up into the light. I want you to be aware of what it felt like and what you saw. Be fully in the experience and tell me what you're aware of.

H: I could see the color of the light even... even though my eyes were closed... and it was so warm... it just really felt good all over, all around me, even though I didn't want to be there... and all I could see was just blue... it was blue... and really warm... but my eyes were closed, so I guess I didn't see blue... I didn't see anything, but I had the impression that I did...

J: And how long were you on the table?

H: I don't know. I didn't have a watch... I didn't... I don't know if there was a clock... I didn't look... maybe... I don't really know... maybe ten minutes... fifteen.

J: What time was it when you started your walk?

H: About 5:30 or 6, at night... it was still daylight.

J: And when you came out from seeing the doctor, was it still light?

H: No... it wasn't very dark, it wasn't really dark... but the sun was not out.

J: What time of the year was it?

H: Spring... early. Maybe it was... 8 o'clock. I don't really know, but by the time I got home it was dark... I didn't live very far away.

J: Did you go home with the woman?

H: She walked me home. And we went straight home.

J: And how did your body feel as you went home?

H: It hurt.

J: Where did it hurt?

H: Really deep inside it hurt... it felt... I don't know how to say it... it felt like... there was something there... just really deep and it just hurt... like an ache... and I kept saying, I can't walk so fast, we need to stop... but she said, no, we need to get you home.

J: Helen, point to the part of your body where it hurt.

H: (points to lower abdomen-pelvic area)

J: So after you got back home, then what did you do?

H: I just locked the door and went to bed... my husband was out on the road, he won't be home for two or three days. So I just went to bed and slept. It still hurt the next day, but it was better. But I didn't feel very good... I felt kind of... like I couldn't eat... didn't want to eat... was kind of nauseated...

J: And how soon after that did you find out you were pregnant?

H: I didn't have another period after that... so it was maybe... five or six weeks. I thought I was just late because I didn't... I didn't feel very good. But that wasn't it.

J: Is there anything else that you can remember to tell us about the time in which you carried Marisa? Anything about that time at all?

H: Nothing except that I never felt good the whole time... I was just really sick, sick to my stomach all the time... I was not really sick, I was... just felt... food just nauseated me... all the time... and I didn't get along very good with my husband... but that was not unusual... I should have felt better than I did.

J: Was your pregnancy and the birth different with Marisa than it was with your boys?

H: Yes, in some ways.

J: How is that?

H: Well, I had no idea what it would be like. No one told me... and it was... it was a long labor, really difficult... for such a small baby... but then the boys, the next child, that was difficult but he was so big... so I don't really think it was unusual.

J: And when your boys were born, did you bond with them any faster than you bonded with Marisa?

H: Yes... that shouldn't have been... I should have bonded with her right away.

J: Just let yourself begin to go deeper and deeper, more and more relaxed, realizing that you've looked at many things this last session, discovered, re-experienced.... Just let all of that material become clearer and clearer, more and more in the next few hours, days, and weeks, and come forward for you to write down, remember. Your body is going to feel wonderful, relaxed, as though you've healed and accomplished a great deal. And the next time that I ask you to look high up into the back of your head and close your eyes, take a deep breath, you will immediately go five times deeper than you are now, easily and quickly into hypnosis, more and more comfortable. And you can begin to let your mind, your body, your spirit, your emotions all come back to a very comfortable, relaxed, balanced place. And as I count from one to five, bring yourself back very slowly....

Chapter 30

03/29/98: Fourth Regression with Dr. June Steiner and Helen

June (J):[1] Is the colonel's first name George?

Helen (H): I don't know. (fingers)

J: Is the colonel's first name Rich or Richard?

H: I don't know or it's not all right to say. (fingers)

J: Is there a good reason at this time why Helen is not able to recall the colonel's first name?

H: I don't know or it's not all right to know. (fingers)

J: Is the answer I don't know?

H: (not sure of response)

J: Just let the deeper mind do all the work. Let the deeper mind answer each question. I want the deeper mind to go back to when the colonel took Helen to visit the base. I want the deeper mind to look fully at the whole trip, at who went, at how they got there, the vehicle they took, and who else might have joined them. And just let the deeper mind remember clearly everything about that trip. And when I ask Helen in a few minutes to tell me what she knows about that trip, everything will come forward easily and clearly. When was the last time Helen had contact with the blue light? Was it within the last six months?

H: Yes. (fingers)

1. A subsequent regression--beginning of tape is missing.

J: Good. Was it within the last three months?

H: Yes. (fingers)

J: Was it within the last one month?

H: Yes. (fingers)

J: Was it within the last two weeks?

H: No. (fingers)

J: Was it within the last three weeks?

H: No. (fingers)

J: Was it a month ago?

H: Yes. (fingers)

J: Did it occur when Helen was at home?

H: Yes. (fingers)

J: And when the blue light was seen, did anything else occur as well?

H: I don't know or I can't say. (fingers)

J: Helen has mentioned several times green bugs. Is there any connection between green bugs and Helen's experiences with the ETs or the hybrids?

H: I don't know or I can't say at this time. (fingers)

J: Is it that Helen does not know?

H: (unsure of response)

J: Thank you for answering my questions, and now I would like to ask Helen to tell me what she knows about how she got to the base with the colonel. Helen, I want you to go to the time when you traveled to the base where the colonel worked at Four Corners, where he met the hybrids, where he picked up the pieces of the ship, and where he met Raechel. Go to just before that trip took place and tell me what you're aware of.

H: (long pause)... I can't remember... I can't remember... making the trip... just... until just before... until just before going in the road... off the main road on the old road... on the old dirt road.

J: Was there a marking of any kind as you went off the main road?

H: Yes, there was an old cattle chute, a cattle loading... place, an old corral.

J: Was there anything written?

H: I don't think so.

J: Take a good look as you turn off at everything around you. Tell me everything that you see.

H: There's just an old corral, but it looks really small... and a lot of the fence... a lot of the posts are falling down, but you can see... you can see that they probably have used it not too long ago, but yet there's no tracks around the corral... but just past it is this old road that turns off to the right because that's where the corral and the cattle place... it's on the right-hand side of the road... just this old road that looks... is supposed to look it hasn't been used for a long time, but it has.

J: What is the road that you're turning off of? What's the highway?

H: It's the only highway south from... it's the only main highway south... from Ely.

J: And about how far from Ely have you come?

H: Um... maybe ninety miles, eighty or ninety miles. I didn't look.

J: Have there been any other important road signs along the way?

H: I don't think so... there was one before we turn off... there was one that says how far to Las Vegas, but I don't remember how far that was.

J: Then just take the small road. Let yourself, you're being taken down that small road, and tell me who you're with.

H: (long pause)... I don't know who I'm with... I haven't seen this person before.

J: What do they look like?

H: It looks like the colonel... but he doesn't have a uniform... and he has his fatigues on... not the shirt, just a T-shirt... just the T-shirt and the pants because it's so hot... it doesn't look like the colonel...

J: What do you mean, he looks like the colonel, but he doesn't look like the colonel?

H: Well, he says he is... but he doesn't look like the man I saw in the apartment with Raechel... but he's the same size... his face doesn't look the same.

J: Does his voice sound the same?

H: Yes.

J: How do you feel with him?

H: Well, he's been all right... we talked about the scenery and the ... he talked about it. I didn't say anything because I had a hard time keeping awake.

J: Why is that?

H: I'm so sleepy... but I'm... I'm awake now and I can see... it's like it is the colonel, but his face is different. The rest of him looks the same... and he sounds the same... I don't know how his face could change.

J: And did you sleep during part of the trip?

H: I guess so.

J: Were you tired when you started?

H: Not really... but as soon as I got in the car... I guess I must have fallen asleep.

J: Did you have anything to eat or drink in the car?

H: I wasn't hungry... He had some sodas... and I remember we got out of town... and he asked me if I was thirsty, and so I said, yes... and... and so he had a little cooler with some sodas in it, so he pulled off the road, got two cans out of the cooler, and he had one and I had one... and I guess I fell asleep after that... but that's a long time to fall asleep.

J: What do you mean?

H: Well, from Sacramento... clear to south of Ely... that's a long way.

J: About how long is that?

H: Five or six hours at least... I think... it's not much less than that.

J: And when you woke up did he say anything to you about having been asleep?

H: No, he didn't say that. He said, how do you feel? And I said, well, I guess I feel okay. I guess I must have fallen asleep. And he said, yeah, you were really tired. So I thought maybe I was. I must have been if I slept all that time. So then... we had turned off and we were... looked like we were going to nowhere in the middle of the desert on this old road... and so I said, where are we? And he said, we're almost there. It's just not very far, now. Well, I don't see anything (Helen said). Well, just wait... it's over... he says, it's just down... down behind this... this little... it was like a little hill, not very high, but then the road went down on the other side of it... and then, I could see... could see we were... we were there because it had a big, high fence around it. Really high.

J: About how high?

H: Maybe twelve feet, ten or twelve feet.

J: What was it made out of?

H: Heavy wire... like squares, heavy, real heavy-duty... and then it had like rolls, rolls of wire on top of that, up another, another foot or ten inches, or a foot, and that, I think, was electric. I don't know but I think it was. And there was a big gate, big iron gate.

J: Was it open or closed?

H: It was closed.

J: What else did you notice?

H: There was a guard there... and a big dog... and there wasn't any guard shack. That was... bases always have a guard shack... this one didn't. It had the gate and the man and the dog. So there was no chance the guard would miss anybody that came over that hill.

J: So then what happened?

H: We drove up. The guard walked out, the dog right beside him... and I rolled the window up because I'm afraid of that dog... and... the man who was driving took something out of his pocket and showed the guard. He just saluted and he didn't touch anything, but the gate opened. I didn't see him touch anything, but it must have been on his belt or in his pocket. The gate opened and we just drove through. I put the window down because it was really... it was hot.

J: How many were in the car?

H: Just me and him.

J: And then what happened?

H: We went on a little ways further... and it was just nothing but old... old barns and sheds... and another old corral out there behind... and so he just... just pulled in and there was a truck... two trucks behind... behind the barn. You couldn't see it from where... from the road, but if you drove around behind you could see two. And... we pulled in and parked, and he said, well, come on, get out. So I did. I could hardly move, I was so... I was really stiff.

J: And as you got out and closed the door of the vehicle, what kind of a vehicle were you riding in?

H: It was an old station wagon... I don't know what kind... a big one.

J: What color was it?

H: It was kind of brown... kind of brown and tan.

J: And what was the license plate?

H: I didn't see the license plate... because I didn't go behind it. I got out and I walked in front... and I didn't look back at it.

J: And when you were there, did you meet the two women who helped take care of Raechel?

H: I only met one.

J: What was her name?

H: I wasn't introduced. I mean... I saw her but I wasn't introduced.

J: So you didn't actually meet her.

H: Not really, no. I didn't. I was not introduced to her but I did see her.

J: How did you know it was one of the people who taught Raechel or took care of Raechel?

H: The man I was with said so.

J: And did you meet the other hybrid?

H: Yes.

J: And were you introduced to him?

H: Not by his name. Just... that he was responsible for... for helping raise Raechel... partly responsible. No name. It was as if nobody wanted me to know who they were. Just faces.

J: And as you looked at him, tell me what he looked like.

H: He was little, really slight built, not very tall... he looked sort of like Raechel. His skin was... his skin was sort of like hers... really smooth, really smooth-looking... and kind of... kind of greenish... greenish-yellow, but a little bit lighter than hers. And he had big eyes like her, but his were blue, really pretty blue.

J: Did you ever look into his eyes?

H: Yes, I did.

J: And what happened or what did you see when you looked into his eyes?

H: It was... his eyes looked friendly... and I felt that... I felt that he was thanking me... for being a friend. But he could talk, but he sounded squeaky, really squeaky little voice... and he didn't say so... not with his words, but he told me with his eyes... he didn't like to talk because the words weren't right, the words didn't sound right.

J: So you, too, knew how to talk without words.

H: Yes.

J: And where did you learn how to do that?

H: I could do it for a long time.

J: When was the first time you knew you could do that?

H: (long pause)... when I first... when I was a little girl... and they wanted me... they asked me if I would like to have a baby... and at first I talked... I spoke... but then I found out I didn't have to... just think and it was easier.

J: Did you continue communicating that way with them then over the years?

H: Sometimes... sometimes it was just easier that way... it was quicker. You just think, and they pick it up. It's easy.

J: Was there anyone besides the colonel and the ones that contacted you over the years that you could talk to that way or understand that way?

H: Oh... I think I could communicate with the ones that come now. I've been afraid to, but I think I can do it now. I didn't try before. I think I can do it with the birds now... I could do it with Raechel.

J: Did you ever do it with the doctor?

H: No, but she... she did it with me. She did both ways. She talked, she spoke, but at the same time she did it with her eyes.

J: And did you understand her?

H: I don't think I understood... saying... it was too loud... but I could turn my mind off... I didn't have to take what she said with her eyes.

J: Did you ever communicate with Marisa that way?

H: Not directly.

J: What do you mean?

H: We could do it long-distance. Wherever she was, she could think of something and I would pick it up, and I could do that to her, too, almost always... we didn't try... we just did it... she was really surprised at first, but she got used to it... and then after a while we hardly had to even call. We did... but we already had said what we said on the phone, then later... we said it first... with our minds... she wasn't sure sometimes, so she'd call me on the phone... and I'd say, I know that, you just told me that... then after a while, she just... she just got used to it.

J: Did Marisa ever question the fact that she could do that, what that might mean?

H: Oh, yes... it really scared her at first... and I told her there was nothing she could do about it... that it was just something that she... it was an ability that she had... and... she couldn't do anything about it... she couldn't stop it. And... that she had to get used to it because it would always be there... and she said, well, how do you handle it?... and I said, sometimes it makes me nervous, too, but... and I get really upset and I get frightened, but I can't stop it. And I said, it's really nice to be able to do this... it's a gift... think of it as a gift... but then she saw some really bad things happen... she could see... that was different, though. She could see things in the future that would happen... and that wasn't a gift.

J: What do you mean, it wasn't a gift?

H: Well, maybe it was... maybe it was a gift, but it frightened her really bad because most of what she saw were car accidents, people being killed, being murdered, things like that. She couldn't do anything to stop the things from happening, and... and that made her very upset... and it bothered me, too, but I didn't know what I could do about it.

J: Were any of your other children able to do that?

H: One is just starting now.

J: Who is that?

H: It's Carl... and it's very upsetting to him. He has too many other problems to deal with this now... but... he can't stop it... I mean, he can't do anything about it. He has to accept it. He sees things that happen in the future... I don't like to see that happening to him, but... but I don't know what I can do about it. I can't stop it for him. And I tell him he has to... he has to learn to live with it... because it's the way we are.

J: Helen, just let all that be. And I want you to go back again to the base with the man who helped Raechel speak. And tell me if there's anything else that happened with that man or on the base that you haven't yet told us.

H: I don't think there's anything else.

J: And I want you to get back into the car, the station wagon-type car that you came in. Notice if you see the license plate as you get in, or as you approach the car.

H: Oh, I still don't look at that... but I saw the one next to it on the... I look at the truck that's parked beside it, and it's a different truck than... than when we came... and it's parked out closer to the building. And I see the front license plate... and it's on... it's on the right... as I look at the truck, it's on... the left-hand side and that's not right. It should be in the middle, but it isn't. It's on the left-hand side... and it's the black license plate that I saw before.

J: What's on the black license plate besides black?

H: The triangle... and it's got the lines through it... it's the same one.

J: And when you see it, what do you feel?

H: I think, oh God, what is happening to me?... but it all begins... it starts to all get connected now somewhat.

J: Do you say anything to the colonel?

H: No. I don't let him know that I know. I just look away. I don't have to keep looking at it. I've seen it before. I don't want anything to happen to me. I want to get home.

J: Then after you get into the car, do you drive straight home?

H: I think so. I don't remember anything after going through that gate again. Not a thing.

J: What's the next thing you remember?

H: Getting into my car... at the parking lot at the apartment house where Marisa lived. By myself. I don't know... I don't even have... I don't even have any... clothes... any suitcase with me... I don't remember taking any... but if I did, I must have left it someplace because I don't have one now. But my clothes are clean.

J: Are they the same clothes you wore to the base?

H: No... someone must have taken my clothes with me, but... I didn't. I guess I changed them, I don't know. Maybe the girl did, but... they're not the same clothes... .well, anyway, I don't have the other ones with me... all I have is my purse... I don't know how long I've been gone. Well, I had to be gone... had to be gone two or three days. I don't know... I don't remember, but this man is not there... and there isn't any station wagon... and I didn't even go up to the apartment. I just get in my car and I drive home.

J: And when you get home, is there a calendar anywhere that you can look at?

H: There's one in the kitchen... but I don't know... I don't know what day I left... I must have missed work... whenever I went. If it was... three days, it would have to be three days... it takes a long time to drive over... and time to drive back and whatever time we were there... so no matter when I went, I had to miss work. But I didn't call in.

J: Did you ever talk to anyone about this trip?

H: No... no. Because I wasn't supposed to.

J: Who told you that?

H: The man I was with.

J: Did he say anything else besides for you not to tell?

H: No... he said I should never tell... I don't know... (long pause)... it just seemed like it was the colonel, but... but his face wasn't really quite right... when he said, you can't tell anyone, you can never tell anyone... his voice didn't sound at all like the colonel. I knew he meant what he said. I knew what he meant, too.

J: Did he ever say what he meant?

H: He said there will... no one will ever find a trace of you or your family if you ever say a word... and I said, okay, I will never tell... but I don't care now....

J: Why do you feel differently now?

H: What they're doing is wrong... what they did to me was wrong... they never asked me, they just did it... they messed up my life... messed up my daughter's... and I can't forgive them for that.

J: Just leave the trip behind for now, Helen. More will come forward if there is any more in days to come, weeks, months. And I'd like you to tell me if you have any reason to feel uncomfortable around bugs, especially green ones.

H: No... because they've never harmed me.

J: What do you mean, they've never harmed you?

H: (long pause)... well, sometimes they look scary, but... they've never done anything....

J: What kind of bugs are you talking about?

H: Ones with scales on.

J: And where have you seen them?

H: Well, I don't think they were real bugs... they're supposed to be like people... but they weren't... but they weren't green, either.

J: Have you ever seen green bugs that frightened you?

H: No.

J: Have you ever seen anything that looked like a green bug that frightened you?

H: Not green.

J: What kind of bugs have you seen that have frightened you?

H: Kind of big, long, brownish bugs with scales, but it was supposed to be faces... but I don't think there was a face... not a real face... like... like... like scales or... or the markings like turtles have on their shells. They overlap and they're kind of... kind of rounded things like they're all sewed on top of each other... they look... they don't look like bugs... but I don't know what else they look like... they're supposed to be people, but they're not people...

(blank spot in tape)

H: ...anyway... they didn't look... nobody noticed that they looked so strange....

J: Just let those two strange, different-looking people go out of your awareness, and tell me if you have ever been in contact with any other forms of life other than humanoids or the hybrids like Raechel and the man who helped her talk.

H: No... that was enough... that was enough.

J: And just let yourself relax and go deeper and deeper into a very, very wonderful place. A place where you can relax and let go, and let every breath you take bring more and more relaxation and healing into your body, your mind, your spirit, and your heart. And just feel with each breath more and more healed, and more and more relaxed. And know that everything that you have uncovered and recovered in these last few days will become clearer and clearer and you'll understand it better. You'll integrate it and be able to take it in, and it will help to improve your life. You'll be able to look at it without fear. Just let yourself float deeper and deeper and more and more relaxed. Let your body come back into a wonderful sense of well-being. Let your heart be light, your emotions be happy, your spirit be strong. As I count from one to five, you'll be coming back into the room this Sunday afternoon, on March 29, 1998, bringing back with you everything that you've learned, bringing back a new sense of strength to face whatever it is that you're learning. You'll remember everything that you need to remember to complete the journey. You'll come back knowing that you can go just as deeply back into hypnosis whenever I ask you to raise your eyes and then close them and take a deep breath and relax. So now, one, taking another deep breath; two, beginning to move the energy about your body; three, moving your hands and your feet, becoming more and more awake; four, feeling very, very much energized; and five, opening your eyes, feeling awake, refreshed, and very, very good.

"Doing extensive research, and finding nothing, is an answer too,"
—former intelligence officer.

Chapter 31

Raechel Is Described by the People Who Met Her

The fact that Raechel was real and was at one time Marisa's roommate was verbally confirmed early in the investigation. There is a tendency for remembrances of others to mellow as the years go by but memories of Raechel seem to remain quite strong to this day.

12/10/98 Synopsis of a telephone conversation with a former boyfriend of Marisa's.

A former boyfriend remembers Raechel as, "unusual, with an otherworldly quality," "someplace else" in her thinking, didn't quite fit in. He said that she "sort of made sense," but seemed to have no fund of knowledge, and was "on a different wave-length." There was something unique about her voice, it was sort of mechanical-sounding.

12-15-98 A telephone interview with a former boyfriend of Marisa's.

"I do remember one of her roommates was a little bit... like unusual, I believe I met her there once. I kind of remember Marisa thinking that, she might have been a little unusual, a little different.... that she was... you know, like tuned in to other.... She might have been tuned in to something that might have been, you know... extraterrestrial or supernatural, or something along those lines.

"Marisa was wondering... she thought it odd or strange because of the way this woman talked about her experiences... She was maybe just a little bit disengaged, I guess, was kind of my impression. Maybe a little flat or... hollow or disengaged.... The one kind of fleeting recollection that I have of the one time that I met her, was that she was generally unremarkable, at least to me."

04-20-98 A letter from a former roommate and friend of Marisa's.

"I am fairly sure Marisa met this girl through the placement office at Lost River and was probably set up with Raechel through the counseling department. I know that because of Marisa's sight disability she was in steady contact with her counselor.

"When I visited Marisa that day at her new apartment I remember sitting outside together and she started telling me of this girl Raechel who had been her roommate. I remember my response to what she told me as being a bit "freaked out" as we put it in those days and remember we were laughing and I was telling Marisa to stop from time to time in disbelief (not of Marisa's story, because I do believe what she told me was true, but because what she was telling me was too weird).

"I remember her saying that this girl couldn't go out in the sun. That Raechel was reclusive and Marisa didn't socialize with her much (let's face it, Raechel sounded a bit strange). Marisa was a very social person and I think she puzzled over this girl's reclusive manner. She said that Raechel wore sunglasses and that her skin had an odd texture. She said, I think, it had a greenish cast to it. I remember her mentioning the girl only drinking water that came in containers. That Raechel didn't eat regular food and only special food that came in boxes. (Marisa and I were great food fans so this was important to us both, although Marisa had to watch her diet. We were both pretty health-oriented and lots of green vegetables and healthy stuff was important to us - so I know this was strange to us that someone couldn't eat fresh food we considered healthy). Like I said, I never went into the apartment Marisa and Raechel shared, so I never saw the containers.

"Marisa said that Raechel kept her body covered and protected from the sun. That was understandable in that we both knew people could have allergies. But the color and texture of Raechel's skin was what sounded creepy. And I think because Raechel didn't really ever talk that much about what she could or couldn't do made it feel creepy. If someone has differences it's a lot easier to accept if you know the reason, but when Marisa was telling me this, my feeling is that she was puzzled and not at ease about the whole matter. That's what brought on our conversation, not meanness or girlish cattishness, but discomfort with things strange and made creepy feeling because it was not explained.

"Marisa never mentioned anything about the girl's family to me. But I vaguely remember her saying something about odd visitors at the apartment. Odd in that the people who came to see Raechel were not other students like whom Marisa and I had friendships with.

"Then Marisa told me that the girl disappeared. That she didn't know where she went. That this roommate just was gone and Marisa had no idea where or why. Marisa was still shaken up over the episode, and I'm sure her husband (whom she married later on) heard a lot more of the story. I do remember him interjecting on the story to tell me it was true or something...."

10-26-97 Interview with Helen.

"Marisa was about 5'4" or 5'5", maybe, and it seems as though Raechel was just a little taller, not more than an inch. No more than 5'6". She probably weighed about 115 to 120. She wasn't heavy, she wasn't thin but... She had long legs, and long arms. The torso was relatively short. She was actually of an average build, it was just... just the facial features that were so striking. Her high cheekbones, too, and the color... skin coloring... was certainly unique. It was yellowish-green."

"Could that be like jaundice?"

"I thought of that, too, and medically speaking, it could be and it could also be from eating the green stuff, but in her case it was not an unhealthy color. It was a beautiful skin color, but it was so unusual. And the eyes, avocado-green, and their placement on her face. She was really a beautiful thing. I don't know, other people might not have thought she was beautiful, but I thought she was."

05-25-98 Interview with Marisa's husband.

"Once in a while I'd see her... Marisa and the strange one stayed together. I met her and saw her, she had hair, and then one time she says, yes, well, she's got no hair now. All of her hair fell out. I'd seen her with a full head of hair. Just seemed like it was short and not real long. The style back then was, it wasn't... it looked... I didn't pay that much attention to it... but Marisa says, yes, she's bald, completely bald.

"There was another incident where Marisa said it looked like Raechel had slit her wrists. Marisa said she had big scars across her wrists.

"Raechel wasn't attractive to me, so I didn't really pay any attention to her. I don't remember her being busty, or anything attractive.

"She didn't wear glasses. The first thing I usually look at on a woman, I like to look at their eyes and then work my way down. As far as her eyes, I don't even remember what they looked like. It's kind of like there wasn't anything to look at, so why even look the rest of the way down.

"I would say the image of her face would be just a face, nothing, nothing there, nothing. She looked to be Caucasian. The color of her skin was kind of on the light side. She was 5'5", 5'6"... somewhere in that range.

"Marisa said she had some really weird feelings about her, and when the men in black were there... she just said from then on, I'm not going to stay here with this, with her in the house, this is not safe, not so much Raechel, but as what was going on around her. Raechel was strange... but there were more things going on around Raechel, that dealt with Raechel, but that basically she had no control over."

06-06-97 Interview of Marisa's brother Carl remembering Raechel.

"I met Raechel, met her at my sister's apartment, upstairs apartment, many years ago. Quite an unusual gal. I remember dancing with her, hugging her, something... just cool skin, just kind of clammy feeling, just didn't feel right, didn't seem to feel right to me, and I don't remember what happened... I can't remember a whole lot of it. I think back, the more I think about it, the harder I think, the less I remember.

"I don't think she had sunglasses on. I know she didn't have sunglasses on. I don't remember her eyes other than they were set apart a little farther... and big old, big eyes. The more I think and try to go back in time and think about it, the more confused I get. I remember less of her than probably anything I've ever tried to remember.

"I want to say her eyes were black or dark brown, honestly, right now I'd like to remember, but it's just one of those things that I think I've got blocked, a mental block. I just can't draw anything out."

01-09-98 Carl remembers a little more.

"I remember going out with Raechel. We all went out one night, Marisa, her boyfriend, Raechel and I. I remember dancing with her. I don't remember where we went or how the evening progressed, but it was like a group going out.

"She was awfully shy, awfully quiet. She was kind of a distant person, real distant, and when you dance with a woman you try to get a little close. She just didn't have the warmth.

"I wasn't really attracted to her, but yet, I don't know, she was just kind of cold to touch or feelings. She was more cold than warm.

"She was a very strange girl, very quiet, kind out of touch with everybody. I believe I only met her one time....

"She was smaller than me, thin-framed.... I want to say she had dark hair.... I want to say her skin was more like leather than skin, really cold... a weird-feeling kind of skin... when you're a young man in the service... but the skin was... was just kind of, it wasn't, didn't... she was cold to touch... she was almost like she was dead, kind of.

"I think it was more of being forced into dancing with her and being with her by my sister than anything. It was more of a setup so she'd have some company. I think that it was one of them "sister love" deals... all I remember is she was like a zero compared to girls I've been around as far as conversation and, you know, happy and bouncy, she wasn't any of those."

07-09-98 Helen is interviewed about Raechel.

"When Marisa first started talking about the food and stuff that she could drink, I suggested maybe she had some sort of a physical problem. That maybe she had to be on a particular diet because there are a lot of disabilities where you can only eat and drink certain things. Marisa thought it was sort of strange, and I did too, that when she wanted to try some of Raechel's food, Raechel said no, she couldn't, that it would make her really sick.

"Marisa started talking about the men that came to visit Raechel. She was in one of those periods when she could see a little bit better, and she looked on the boxes and discovered the logo. Then she found it on the jugs, and saw it on the license plate.

"After the colonel talked to Marisa of Raechel's origin, Raechel cut both of her wrists in an apparent suicide attempt. She received no medical attention for this, did not seek any--apparently she stopped the bleeding by the same technique she used when the colonel discovered her in the crashed vehicle."

The suicide attempt was also remembered by the man who was later to become Marisa's husband.

11-07-97 During a regression Helen remembers Raechel's eyes.

H: Well, her eyes were large but not like the usual picture, you know, like the picture on the cover of that book. They were not so high, but they came out onto the sides, because the glasses she had were the wraparound, you know, the old-fashioned ones. What really struck me was their color, avocado-green... that's the closest thing I can think of.

10-03-98 Regression with Helen and June, exploring Raechel's looks and actions.

H: She didn't fall like a regular person... she didn't bend, I mean she bent at kind of a funny angle. Another person would have tried to catch themselves, but she didn't know what was going to happen. She didn't know. Everybody falls sometime in their life. It's like she never did before... and so I knew I had to reach out and get hold of her. But this is so weird, that she just... well, anyway, I took hold of her. I got hold of her arm, but she didn't try to catch herself like a person would. She just kind of fell over, like she would bend at the waist or something, it was really strange. Marisa couldn't see what was happening, she could hear it, but she didn't see. During this, while I was trying to get hold of Raechel and keep both of us from going on the floor, a lot of things started to happen all at once. From what I could see... because her glasses went down, I could see the eyes, and I could feel her arm. Oh, God... this is not like anything I've ever been in before.... Oh, but I can't drop her... I want to... I'm kind of afraid... I don't know what I've got hold of here, but... but I don't... I hang on... I looked in those eyes.... Oh, God....

J: What do you see as you looked into her eyes? Let yourself look deeply into her eyes. What is it you see?

H: Just that green... the whole thing... oh, it's like I go inside the eyes, but I'm not because I'm there.

J: Perhaps it's like when someone says the eyes are the window to the soul... and it's as though they're looking into the person. Is that what it's like?

H: Kind of... but there was no limit to what I could see.

07-16-99 In a subsequent regression, Helen remembers a few more details.

J: I want you to be there at that moment, Helen. You're reaching out, you're touching Raechel. I want you to feel it, and see it.

H: I don't like to...

J: Why is that?

H: Oh... because she didn't feel real... oh... she... oh...

J: Feel her arm and tell me...

H: Oh (crying out)... Oh, it felt spongy and it was cool, and it was a hot day. She shouldn't have felt cool, not that kind of cool, and it was spongy, and it... and I couldn't let go... because if I did, then she'd fall. Marisa couldn't see, she couldn't catch her, so I had to hang on... and she didn't go down. But her scarf slid, kind of back a little. Her glasses came down.

J: And what do you see? Look at her face.

H: Oh....

J: What's the first thing you see?

H: The eyes... big... big eyes... black slits....

Chapter 32

Trigger Events—Eyes and Windows

During Helen's regression sessions she would be answering questions, then suddenly skip over an event or say something that didn't make logical sense within the context of what was being said. When questioned about this leap in logic, she avoided the question, or had an unusual emotional reaction to what was being discussed. When pressed for details, she said she didn't know, or was afraid to say.

This may signal what is called a trigger event. Something else has happened at this point and the person under hypnosis doesn't want to deal with it. Saying anything that comes into their minds, they are often concerned about sounding foolish. They censor themselves, remaining silent about meaningful events. Taking the person back to the events just prior to the trigger event is a helpful technique. Key questions usually help to uncover skipped material or deeply buried material that the person has trouble remembering. Asking questions about material already verbalized can help get the person through the situation. When the person says "I don't know," restating the situation helps.

Using these techniques during subsequent regressions, a much more detailed experience concerning Helen's interaction with Raechel was revealed.

In an earlier regression Helen refused when asked to go to the place with the windows that she went to with Raechel. Dr.

Steiner did not pursue that line of questioning and proceeded on to another subject. In following regressions she takes Helen back to the windows and the same situation to explore this trigger event. During these regressions, still another trigger event is hinted at, then immediately glossed over.

10-03-98 Helen is explaining further about what happened when she went to visit Marisa, and Raechel was the only one home. While standing in the kitchen Helen looks into Raechel's eyes, then finds herself in the window room.

J: How did you get on the other side?

H: I don't know, it was like one minute I was on the outside and the next, I was on the inside. I went through it, but there wasn't a door.

J: I want you to freeze-frame that moment when you went through the window. And I want you to go deeper and deeper to that place where your cells and your being are in touch with what happened that allowed you to go through that window. Tell me what you were going through and how you managed to do that. Because your mind and your body knows what that is, whether you understand that or not. Just tell me the process by which you got through that window.

H: Um... I put my finger on the window, and she put hers on the other side, just on the other side of the glass from mine. She kept looking at me, in my eyes... and I felt all warm and... not hot... but all warm and... I don't know... a feeling... I've never felt like that before... but while I was still all warm... I was on the other side. But I couldn't do it until she touched her finger to mine on the other side of the glass.... It didn't hurt.... It should have.... It should hurt when you go through glass.

J: Did you feel anything at all going through?

H: Like I was really tall and long and thin.

J: Here you are, now, on the other side of the window, and where are you?

H: I'm in a big room, a big, round building. It looked like there are a lot of... all these rows of circles of... big circles... of windows... it looked like they went all the way around and then the ones towards the inside the circles, they were smaller circles. I didn't see any people in there. I don't know what she was trying to show me. She said I want to show you where I live... and it seemed a funny place to live. It looked like lab counters, or kitchen counters or something on... not the first two windows, like from the third one on in toward the center... but I didn't see any... any people or any things.

J: Was there furniture of any kind?

H: I stood there inside, between the first and the second row of windows... then from the third window it looked like counters but they went around to...I don't know where they ended because it was... a curve and I couldn't see beyond where it went around to...the curve, but it looked like there was... and that was on the side toward me, where the counters were. Then, I don't know if there were counters to... inside the windows to the right... but across... it's so hard to explain... but I could see... it was something lower and it looked like... like something to sit on, like benches against the wall... well, that's... that doesn't make any sense, but there was nobody sitting there. They were lower... they looked like benches. The counters were high, were... not real high, though, but where you could do something on, you could write, you could do something. But the benches... were on the opposite wall from where the counters were, oh, this is confusing.

J: Don't try to make sense out of it.

H: There were benches facing where the counters would have been if there were any, but there was nobody there.

J: How long did you stay in this place?

H: I don't think I stayed very long because I didn't feel comfortable there. It really wasn't very interesting, it looked really cold and bare. It didn't feel cold, but there was just the benches and the counter and the windows. I said to her again, well, this is really a funny place to live. She said this wasn't all of it, but she said, maybe we need, maybe you need to go back. Maybe Marisa has come by now, and I said, well, now I have to go back. Do I have to go back through the window again because I still don't see a door... and she said this time we're both on the same side, I'll just touch your hand.... I'll hold your hand.... You put your finger on the window just like you did before... and I'll just put my finger on yours, and then we'll both be back in the kitchen. She said don't be afraid, we'll go together... and then we did... and then, the next thing I know, she was standing across from me where she was to begin with... and I'm still there with my hand on the kitchen table, feeling... feeling how cool it was.

07-16-99 During this regression Helen remembers more about Raechel's eyes, and another trigger event is explored.

J: What do you mean black slits?

H: Vertical slits like a cat's eye... her eyes... oh... they're all green... the whole thing... I mean... other than the slits.

J: Have you ever seen eyes like this before?

H: I don't think so. I was... I wasn't really so much afraid as... I just didn't believe what I was looking at. I was fascinated, I couldn't take my eyes off those eyes... for a few seconds.

J: And what happened during those few seconds as you were looking at Raechel's eyes, Helen?

H: I could feel how frightened she was. She was the one that was frightened, not me.

J: Why do you say that?

H: Because she knew I'd seen what she looked like and she didn't want that... not yet....

J: How do you know that? Did she tell you that?

H: She didn't say it.

J: What do you mean?

H: She didn't say it in words... it was just in the eyes. She looked right back at me and she was so frightened that I was going to say something about it. She was afraid I would say something to Marisa... or if... I'm not sure why she was so frightened, but she was. Then I stopped being afraid of her... felt sorry for her. It wasn't because she looked strange. I wasn't sorry about that.

J: I want you to go to that place inside of yourself where you know clearly why you felt sorry for her. Tell me what you're aware of.

H: She was afraid I wouldn't accept her...

J: Accept her for what?

H: ...as my daughter... and I thought that was ridiculous.

J: How did you know that, Helen? How were you communicating with Raechel at that time?

H: The eyes.

J: In what way were you communicating with the eyes?

H: She just stared, just looked really deep, but not as deep as I had to look in hers. She wouldn't let me go.

J: What do you mean, she wouldn't let you go?

H: Her eyes just held mine and then I thought well, how can this be? How can this be? This is not even a person because she didn't feel right and she didn't look right... her skin was not right, it was that funny color. What kind of a sick joke is this, she wants to be my daughter.

J: Did you say anything to Marisa about Raechel at that time?

H: I knew I had to talk to her about it, but at that time I didn't know how to explain it to anybody else. I couldn't really explain it to myself. I thought I would get it straight in my mind and then I would talk to her in a day or two.

J: I'm going to count backwards in time now, Helen, to the moment when Raechel's glasses slipped down and you're looking directly into her eyes. Be there looking into her eyes, experiencing it directly. I want you to tell me about the word "window" of Raechel's eyes. What does that mean? Looking into her eyes... as you said, being pulled into her eyes... communicating through her eyes. You called them windows last time we talked about this in October. What did you mean?

H: It was like looking in through a window, to see what was on the other side. Like I went inside her eyes, but I didn't... I mean... not that time.

J: What time did you go into her eyes?

H: The next time I went back to the apartment.

J: Tell me about that.

H: I went to see Marisa that time. I think to take her something, doesn't matter... but she wasn't there, but Raechel was... and she said she didn't know when Marisa would be back. "I... do... not... know," was what she said.

H: I said, well, I have a little time. I can wait a few minutes. And this was in the kitchen and we both stood there. I should have gone in the living room and sat down, but I didn't. I stood there in the kitchen with my back up to that old... oblong table... that porcelain top or whatever, enamel top... and I stood there with my hand kind of behind me on the table... and Raechel was kind of by the refrigerator, between the refrigerator and the stove. And she told me that she didn't know when Marisa would be back. So, that was all she said for a minute, and then that was when she said, "I... wish... you... could... be... my... mother." And I said, "I can't, I can't be your mother." She said that it would be nice to have a mother like Marisa's. And I said "Well, maybe so, but it doesn't make any difference, I can't be your mother."

J: How were you feeling when you said that, Helen?

H: Awfully upset, my insides were just churning, and they shouldn't have been because I should have been able to say, well, this is really flattering, but I can't be your mother. I could be a friend. This is what I should have said to her, and I should not have worried about it, but I did. I was really, really upset because I had a feeling that... how could I?... but I did... I thought for a minute maybe I was her mother. I didn't think I was, I didn't remember having a child like that and I didn't have a child like that. She just kept looking and I just kept looking back. I shouldn't have done that, either, but I couldn't help it. That's when I went in through the window... the first window.

J: Tell me what happened.

H: That's when she started to talk about... she was going to take me to see where she lived... and then I was...I could see a lot of windows inside of each other. It was like circles, a big, round room, and it was like a maze is what I think, but the hallways didn't go different directions. They all went around in a circle and the outside circle had a little opening into the next circle, and then that one had an opening into the next one towards the center. I could see that from where I was on the outside. And then Raechel was on the inside. She said, "Well, come... on... in. I... want... to... show... you... where... I... live." I said "Well, this looks like a funny place to me. I can't. There's no way to go through." She said, "Put... your... finger... on... the... window." I said, "What good is that going to do?' And she said, "Just... do... it." Then she put her hand in the same place on the inside, and here I am on the other side, the same side as her, on the inside. It felt good in there, really comfortable, and yet, I didn't know why I was... what I was doing.

J: What was it like in there?

H: It was all white, really light-colored. Everything seemed to be all white, but there were… oh, let's see… I don't know how to explain it. Each circle, on the outside part of it… it was really weird. It had like a counter like they do in banks to write on. Little counters that ran along the inside of the outer wall. There was a little, narrow walkway, a corridor, and on the other wall of that same outer circle was a little bench. The counters and the benches weren't continuous, they were about four feet long and then there was a little gap before the next one. They were in little pairs… like a chair and a table, but if you sat on the bench, you'd be down too low, you couldn't write on the counter. I don't know what they were for.

J: Did you ever sit on one of the benches, Helen?

H: I don't remember. I leaned on the counter, though.

J: What happened when you leaned on the counter?

H: I felt like I was part of it, but I was separate. As soon as I felt like that, I raised my arm and it came right off, so I stepped back in the middle… no, I didn't step in the middle, I stepped in the space between that and the next counter. I didn't touch anything… just put my arms down at my sides and I didn't touch anything.

J: How many windows did you go through, Helen?

H: Just one. But I could see through, there were a lot of them. I don't know how that could be because the room didn't look that big around. There were so many circles of passageways to the middle. I couldn't see the middle. It should have been just a huge, huge place, but it didn't seem that big. It seemed to be round, maybe it was oval.

J: Just let your deeper mind look very carefully at everything that's there. Don't try to figure it out, just let your deeper mind take you deeper and deeper into the experience. I want you to look all around you. I want you to look at the windows, I want you to look at the shape and the size of the room. I want you to see whatever is in the room, just see... I want you to become very aware of how you feel as you're looking at the room and at the windows. Tell me everything that you're aware of.

H: I don't know where she is. I can't see her. I can't see anybody. Just all those circles or rows. I felt like I was not really in control. I felt like... like I was going to faint. I was light-headed. I didn't know if she was going to come back. I was afraid that I couldn't get out of there. But I didn't say anything. I kept thinking, I wish she'd come back and take me back... she didn't come for a while. Then when she did, I felt all right again. I didn't have that... didn't have that queasy feeling in my stomach and I didn't feel dizzy any more. But I was still there, where I had been in the first place... not... not touching the counter. I was still there with my hand, my arms right at my sides... because I didn't know what would happen if I touched anything more.

J: Helen, I want you to stop for a minute and look around and see the counters and the windows, see the shape of the room, and I want you to go back, as far back as you can and tell me if you have ever been in this room or one like it before now.

H: No. I've never been in one like that. I don't ever want to go back there. I was so afraid that I couldn't get back to where I should be.

J: Have you ever looked into the windows of eyes similar to those that pulled you in?

H: Not really... the eyes were not the same, but the colonel... he didn't really pull me into his eyes. He told me a lot of things with his eyes, but the men that came in the van, the first time... the one man... I didn't feel the driver, he tried to pull me in, but the passenger... he was staring but I don't think that he was... I didn't feel he was trying to pull me in but the driver was.

Helen had an emotional response to the counters, saying her hand came off the counters, then in other sessions saying "I kept my hands from touching the counters, I didn't touch anything. I didn't know what would happen if I touched anything more...." Why did she indicate that she was afraid that her hand wouldn't come off the counters? Hands normally come off a counter when placed on one. Did something happen when she touched the counter that made her want to avoid touching them? Frightened and resistant, Helen wasn't ready to elaborate at this time. However in the following session she relates, with some reassurance from Dr. Steiner, a bizarre and frightening experience concerning the counters, and her time in the oval room.

07-17-99 Exploring the very frightening "counter" trigger event.

J: In our last session we talked at length about Raechel, about the windows that you saw as you looked into Raechel's eyes and how you were pulled in and allowed yourself to go to that place; how in that place you knew what was being said, and you could communicate with Raechel clearly; and in that place you described the windows in a new way, more clearly and more defined than you had before. And as you defined those windows you talked about a counter and a bench in each window. I want you to be inside that place, an oval-type room. I want you to look around you, to be fully present there. I want you to notice the counter. I want you to walk towards the counter now of one of the windows, and I want you to reach out and touch the counter, and just let yourself feel and respond fully to the experience. And tell me what you're aware of.

H: Hm... it wants me to touch it... but how can a counter....

J: Just touch the counter, Helen.

H: I do. I am touching it... oh... I... it looks hard.... It looks like a piece of board... like a... like it's made of wood or plastic, but... it feels soft... not real soft, but... oh... it feels kind of like Raechel's skin... but it's warm, not... real warm, but where her skin was cool...

J: And as you touch the warm counter, what else happens?

H: It doesn't want to let go of my hand.... There's nothing.... It's not sticky.... It doesn't want to let go... oh....

J: Just let your hand be there.

H: I don't want it to be there.

J: It's all right, Helen, just let your hand be there. You've gone through this experience in the past and been all right, so let your hand be on the counter and tell me what happens.

H: Oh... oh... I don't know....

J: It's all right. Just go with it.

H: It wants me to move my hand farther, and... I'm afraid... oh... I'm afraid of the counter. It won't let go....

J: It's all right, Helen. Let yourself be with the counter completely.

H: I pull and I pull... it's like it's... it's like it's glued on... and I pull and I get one finger loose and the rest are stuck tighter... but I keep that one up that I pulled off, and then I pull another one, and then my hand is stuck tighter, the palm of my hand. I'm so... I'm really afraid... and I can't, Raechel's not there... I don't call.

J: And what's happening with your hand? Is it stuck?

H: It just feels really, really warm and it tingles all over... oh... oh... I don't know... I'm afraid... I'm afraid to let the hand stay on there.

J: But the hand is on there, Helen.

H: I know.

J: What's happening? Just let go into what's happening, one moment at a time. Just let go.

H: Oh... oh...

J: You're going to be all right. Go into the experience.

H: Oh... oh... all of a sudden... it just stops pulling, but I'm still stuck, stuck really tight to it... and I don't dare put my other hand on because I'm afraid that will get stuck, too... then I'll never get away... I don't know what it wants.

J: Ask it what it wants.

H: It wants me to stay... not there on the table, the counter... but it wants me to stay... it says it wants me to stay in that room... but there isn't really a room. It's just a whole lot of corridors that go around and around.

J: I'm going to ask you to stop right here, Helen. I'm going to count from one to three, and if during that time that your hand was stuck to the counter you were shown where here was in any clear way, or you were taken anywhere, you'll be able to go there at the count of three. One, two, three.

H: Hm...

J: What are you aware of, Helen? Where are you?

H: I'm not there anymore.

J: Where are you?

H: I don't know.

J: Just look around you.

H: I'm in a different room. This is not white... where the counters and the benches were was white... this is like... oh... it's a funny color... it's like blue-gray... really dismal-looking... kind of cloudy.

J: Is there anyone else there?

H: Oh, yes... well, that's where Raechel went.... She's there... oh... she's... she says, come over here.... What's on this wall?.... It's a... it's a big room... it's like tanks...

J: Tell me more about the tanks.

H: They look like fish tanks... that's not fish in there...

J: What's in there?

H: Little babies... and they're so little... but they can see... just... just floating around...

J: Who is showing you the room, Helen?

H: Raechel.

J: And what is she telling you about this room?

H: She says, "This... is... where... I... came... from." I said, "I don't want to look at it. I don't want to believe this... this is... this is sick and it's bizarre." She said, "I... do... not... care... if... you... do... not... want... to... look... at... it... you... have... to. It... is... time... you... knew. You... do... not... have... to... remember... it... but... you... have... to... see...

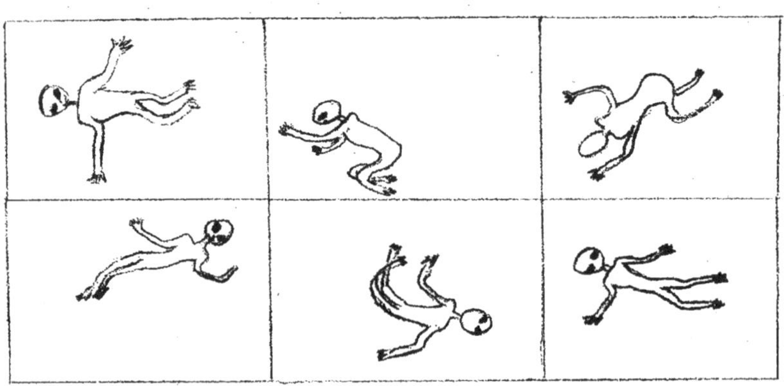

FIGURE 7. Helen's sketch of the double high row of tanks containing fetuses.

it… now." The babies weren't… weren't pink or white, they all had that awful greenish color.

J: Did anything else happen in that room, Helen, while you were there?

H: No. I just felt really sick to my stomach. I ask her if she can take me out, take me back. I can't handle this… I said I need to think about this.

J: Why did they want you to stay here, Helen?

H: I don't know, but I don't want to be there…. It's just… oh… I don't want to look at these things. They don't even look real, but they are. They're alive.

J: Is anyone attending to them, Helen?

H: No, they want me to do that and I can't do it.

J: What do they want you to do?

H: I don't know, they don't tell me that. She doesn't tell me. I said "I can't stay here, I can't look at these things. I'm sorry that this is where you came from, but there's nothing I can do about it. I can't do this. I have to go back. Marisa needs me. I need to take care of her. I don't need to take care of these things." She didn't like it when I called them things. She said, "They… are… not… things…. They… are… from… people… like… you." I said, "I don't care, Raechel. I can't look at these things, I can't stay here…."

J: And then what happened, Helen?

H: She just kept her eyes locked on mine. I say, "Raechel, I want you to take me back right now. I'm not going to stay here, this is not right, to bring me in here and show me these… whatever they are."

J: What are they, Helen?

H: They're like little babies, but they just swim around, and even the stuff they're in, it's greenish-colored, too. But I could still see that the skin was greenish, and the hands had four fingers like she had… they're all the same length, the fingers. I look at that. I don't want to be here. She says, "Well… it… really… does… not… matter… what… you… want… But… I… will… take… you… back… Maybe… we… can… find… something… else… for… you… to… do." I say, "But Raechel, I'm not looking for a job." She says, "It… does… not… matter… what… you… want." I say, "I don't want to argue and I'm not going to, but I want to go back right now." I just kept staring at her, and we didn't go back to the counters and the benches… We… I'm back in the kitchen.

J: Stay in the experience, Helen, totally and completely in the experience, and tell me what you did. Tell me what is going on in the moment.

H: I'm in the kitchen where I was to begin with… my hand is still on the table behind me… and… she's still staring at me, but she's not… she was… between the stove and the refrigerator. Now she's closer to me and she's beside the jugs of water. She's not touching me, she's just staring at me. I'm sick… I feel sick… I never… I've never seen anything like this. The babies, there were a lot of them, some were bigger, some were small, some were really, really tiny… just swimming around.

J: Does anything else happen in the kitchen that day that's important for us to know?

H: I don't think so…. It isn't as if… I'd really gotten my way… though I did to a point. I got back out of that God-awful place, but she says maybe I'm not what they're looking for, and I say I'm really glad about that. I don't want… I don't want to do… I don't want to be there again, ever.

Chapter 33

The Humanization Project

When Helen refused to take care of the babies in the tanks, Raechel told her they would find something else for her to do. Further exploration of the Humanization Project revealed Helen's role in it.

07-17-99 Regression.

June (J): I want you to go back to that time when Raechel said they may have to find something else for you to do because you don't want to take care of whatever is in those green tanks. I'm going to count from one to three, and on the count of three I want to know, did they find something else for you to do? One, two, three.

Helen (H): I don't think so... except I can, I could communicate with the colonel through my eyes... I could do it with Marisa and I could do it with the boys. What difference does that make to them?... or to her?

J: I want you to take a moment, Helen, and let yourself be fully in touch with why you have those abilities. Let yourself see and feel and know what it is that you're doing with those abilities and why.

H: I don't know... just that I can do... I can do these things, but well, what's the point?

J: I want to take you to another place, Helen. I want you to imagine that you're stepping into an elevator or going down deep into the middle of the earth, and as we go down deep into the middle of the earth, you're entering a new stage of trance, and in that stage of trance you're going to one of the compartments within yourself that you know is totally and completely safe from harm. A place where you know the answer to this question because you have been in contact with this entire experience in this place where it's been safe, and perhaps not let the rest of you know what's going on to keep you safe. I want you to continue down and I'm going to count from one to ten and at ten you're going to be down at the center of the earth and the center of your own being, to a place within yourself that has been allowed to know the answers, and your deeper mind has said it was all right for us today to go to that place to allow new information to come forward. One, two, three.

H: They don't... they don't want me to give up, but it's not much of a job, not much of a part.

J: What is the part, Helen?

H: I would have done it, anyway. Just to tell, to tell about Raechel... and about Marisa. That was my part... is my part, I don't know why it's such a big deal. I mean, it's like I was given an important position.

J: Why do they want you to tell about Raechel and Marisa?

H: They say that people will believe me. I don't know why that would be any more than anyone else.

J: Do they want this information to begin to come out?

H: Yes, maybe they know me better than I think they do, because they know once I start, I won't stop.

J: Who is they, Helen?

H: No one that I've seen or talked to, either, but I guess it was the people that were raising these things in the tanks.

J: How do they communicate with you, Helen?

H: Just with thoughts.

J: Are they of this planet, Helen, or do they come from somewhere else?

H: They're both places.... It's working here.

J: What's working here?

H: To do the raising of these things, but nobody knows. Nobody is allowed to know, except a few people. It's so awful that nobody really wants to know.

J: What is it that's so awful about it, Helen? Is it the actual way in which the babies are raised or is the end result? What is it that you say is awful?

H: I think it's the way they're raised. The end result is no worse than the children we raise ourselves. Sometimes it's better.

J: And what happens to these children after they're born?

H: They are adopted out. Some people know what they're getting, some people don't and that's when the trouble starts. They try to take them home and raise them but they don't fit in. Sometimes they just disappear.

J: What do you mean, disappear?

H: They're taken back. They go out to play or they go somewhere, maybe with a family, and all of a sudden the child is gone.... It never comes back.

J: Helen, what is the purpose of this whole project? The project the colonel worked with, bringing hybrids through, the raising of babies, the adopting them out, what is the purpose?

H: I don't know the whole purpose. All I know is just a little bit.

J: What do you know?

H: It's just a giant experiment to see if they could fit in... like to replace.

J: To replace what, Helen?

H: Real people.

J: Why would they want to replace real people?

H: I don't know. I'm not told that... that's what I don't know. What is the point of the whole thing?

J: The colonel never told you what the point was, Helen?

H: Not really.

J: What did he say?

H: He just said that she was part of the project... to see how far they could get. To see to what extent the emotions could be developed, but he didn't say why they wanted to do that, but he was part of it.

J: Is it possible, Helen, that... the different ways in which you're contacted through the men in the van, through birds, through music, through smells—are they in any way connected?

H: Yes, I think they are.

J: In what way?

H: To let me know I'll never be out of touch with them, I'll never be free, and just when I think I may be, it happens again, and so now I don't try to fight it. I'm not sure what the point is. It's not threatening to me any more, at least I'm not afraid of it. Actually I'm not even surprised.

J: Go into that space, that private, safe space where nothing is masked or hidden. Helen, what is the name of the Project?

H: The Humanization Project.

J: And the code name?

H: I don't know the code name. I was never told. But there is one.

07-18-99 Regression.

J: Is there anything else that we need to know about the hybrid children? Is there anything that would be important for us to know about it scientifically or philosophically that you're aware of?

H: Um... they have no soul, so many don't. They're creating so many problems.

J: You say so many don't. Do some have souls?

H: Somewhat, there's too much alteration, but I don't know what that has to do with the soul, but it seems to. The children don't have any souls. They want to kill people, they're not supposed to do that.

J: Who wants to kill people, Helen?

H: The children do. They don't seem able to think good thoughts.

J: Was this true of Raechel and Marisa?

H: No.

J: Why were they different?

H: I don't know. I guess they were the right combination and a lot of them are. But there's so many that go bad. But they usually program to kill themselves. They kill other people, but then they destroy themselves. I don't think this experiment is a good thing.

J: Do you know why it's being done, Helen?

H: Not really. It's just an experiment. That's all I know about it. But there is usually a reason for every experiment. You have a goal, and I'm not told of the goal.

Chapter 34

The Colonel, Helen, and the Underground Base

Helen was puzzled as to why she seemed to know so much about the Humanization Project and the underground base called Four Corners. When questioned she would answer, "I don't know, but I'm sure it's true."

One of the researchers was familiar with a government program called STARGATE. In this program participants were trained in remote viewing to be psychic spies, able to travel to places psychically, using their minds to reveal intelligence information that would not have been available otherwise. The results were often phenomenal.

Remote viewing research began at the Stanford Research Institute in California in 1972 and was funded by the CIA. In the December 7, 1995, issue of *Nature*, vol. 378, the project is described, "A $20-million 20-year US government programme to employ and evaluate paranormal spying techniques...various US government agencies secretly used up to six psychics at a time to help locate hostages, track down alleged terrorists and help drug enforcement officials.... The reviewers agreed that the results were statistically significant."

Helen agreed to try remote viewing even though she insisted she'd never been to the underground base. She was soon able to point to a specific location on the map, assuring us it was just a guess. During the first regression, only her deeper mind would answer questions concerning the underground base, although she did say she had been there. In subsequent regressions she seemed to recall a certain highway sign, and described some structures. Armed with the remotely viewed location marked on a map, and the new information, a volunteer investigator drove to the area. The sign and the structures were right where Helen had indicated. The investigator videotaped the area, and some other sites that had similar descriptions. When shown the tapes, Helen was able to pick the correct site. Due to the low clearance of the investigator's vehicle, driving down the road was impossible.

In the following pages, information on the Colonel, Helen, and their trip to the underground base comes out.

11-07-97 Interview with Helen.

"Well, it was surprising that the colonel would go into that much depth because I don't think that Marisa would have required that much of an explanation. She and Raechel got along well, as weird a relationship as it was. I don't think it really meant all that much to her to find out all this information. But I guess he felt that she should know.

"I feel you deserve to know the truth about Raechel. She is so much different from you and yet you two have become such close friends... and you've been wondering about her, too, because she doesn't act like your friends, doesn't act like you. She is not from here. I rescued her in a crash near Four Corners and for some reason I took a special interest in her because she wasn't like all the other ones who had arrived. She was like one who helped me, he knew how to sustain her life. For some reason I wanted to keep her with me. I knew about the Humanization Project which had never had a young person, I don't remember the exact word, but a young person.... I thought that maybe she would be a good candidate for that project. That's when I contacted ATIC about what had happened. They gave their permission, but they said I had to adopt her and raise her as a human. I didn't know how I would do this because I'm not married, and I'd never been around kids much. But I had help from everyone else there." These aren't the right words, but this is what he said to her.

"Marisa did tell her that she was still the same person she was the day before... earlier that day. But I think just because my daughter could accept it, Raechel was smart enough to know, and certainly Harry was, that not everybody else was going to, and those two girls were not going to be together the rest of their lives, either. Sooner or later Raechel would have to be out in some other situation. She would not be accepted, and she knew that."

07-09-98 Interview with Helen.

June (J): Did the colonel show any emotion when he was talking?
Helen (H): No.

H: It was on that trip, that bothered me. It was supposed to be the colonel and it didn't look like him. It was almost as though that was the true colonel, on the trip, but the features didn't look like the same one that I had talked to in the apartment....

J: How did you get in the car with him?

H: I don't know.

10-03-98 Regression.

H: His emotions weren't the way they should have been.

J: What were they like?

H: Cold... he seemed to be... warm, like a normal person... but when he looked at me, just before I got all this information, his eyes were really, really cold and hard, really piercing.

J: As you're looking at his eyes and noticing how hard and cold and piercing they are, what color are they?

H: Blue, I thought they were dark before, but I know now that wasn't right. That's what I was supposed to see. He said he had worked in the Project with others and he had learned to communicate with them. When he told me that, I did not realize that I was being told the information with the eyes. I thought it was with a computer or something. He didn't tell me it was with the eyes, but that was how he was doing it. How could I have not.... Why didn't I know? But I didn't, anyway. But I'm sure, now, that's how he learned, from the others in the program, the adults at the underground base.

J: And how did you know you were at the base?

H: Because the colonel said we were.

J: Was there anything at the base that would let you know it was different from any other place?

H: It was underground.

J: Was there a fence around the base?

H: Yes.

J: And how did you get through the fence?

H: They opened the gate.

J: Who opened the gate?

H: The guard did.

J: Why did he open the gate for you?

H: Because he knew the colonel.

J: And how did he address the colonel?

H: Sir.

J: And did the colonel have to give him any identification?

H: No. He didn't, but he should have. But he didn't.

J: Did he say anything?

H: No, neither one said anything. They just looked at each other. The guard said, go ahead, sir.

J: At any time during that visit on the base were you given information by the colonel through his eyes?

H: Yes.

J: When was that?

H: When I first got there.

J: Tell me what happened.

H: He explained that this was where it all happened, where it all started.

J: Where what all started?

H: Where he had gotten Raechel, where they had lived, and how they had lived. How she had been brought up. But then he took me to the places, too. But it was more through the eyes.

J: He took you through the base with his eyes rather than taking you through the base actually?

H: No, he took me actually. I didn't go to all those places actually, but I was there and he described it through his eyes, with his eyes.

J: And where were you when he did that?

H: I don't know. I was in the first place that we went into which was under the ground, but you had to go in through an old barn door. I don't know why he took me there because I didn't get to see much. He took me downstairs where there were a lot of rooms, where the people stayed, like a barracks, but they were all separate little rooms. And he took me in and he said this is where you'll stay. I was tired from the trip and I sat down on the bed... and that's where I got a lot of information about the lab. I didn't really go in there, in the lab. But I knew what it looked like because he made a picture in my mind, where I could see it.

J: Why did he want you to know about those places?

H: I don't know. If he took me there, why couldn't he have just shown me? Taken me in and let me look? I think he was not supposed to do that. I think it was all right, well, not really all right that I was there, but it was as far as I could go... as far as he could take me. There was nothing that would stop him from putting the picture in my mind because nobody would know.

J: Why would he want to do that?

H: I don't know.

J: Remember his eyes. Let yourself remember looking deeply and intently into his eyes. Remember you beginning to receive the information and remember anything at all that he said about giving you that information and why. What was the purpose?

H: Because I was Raechel's mother. But that's not what he said.

J: What did he say?

H: Originator.

J: What was the word?

H: Originator.

J: Originator.

H: And I never heard the word used like that before. And so I asked him back, what are you talking about? And he said, that's where she originated, with you. So you need to see what happened after I got her. I don't like being called an originator… but I guess that's what I was.

J: How old was she when the colonel got her?

H: Thirteen or fourteen. He was not exactly sure.

J: And why was he given the care of Raechel?

H: Because they'd taken something from him and added it to her. He didn't say what.

J: So the colonel was related in some way…

H: Yes.

J: Was the colonel Raechel's father?

H: In a sense… that was after they'd taken her from me. He didn't go into detail on it. I don't think I asked. I couldn't believe it. It was true, but he was not her only father.

J: What do you mean?

H: Because there were things they'd taken from the others that they added to her.

J: From what others?

H: Some of the others that were where she'd been after they took her from me and before she got there. I don't know where that happened. I don't where it happened when they took something from him.

J: Was that different than the way most hybrids were created, or is that typical?

H: I don't think that was typical. I think it was a new experiment.

J: What was the purpose of the experiment?

H: To see how well she could fit in. How an entity like that could fit in with normal humans, what their reactions would be, what they could feel, would they be accepted? But they messed up with her because she was pretty good on all the counts except the color of her skin and her eyes. Otherwise they did a pretty good job.

J: What was the purpose of creating a hybrid that could fit in with the human process?

H: He did not give me a reason for that except it was something the government wanted to do. He said it was a necessary thing and it would never stop.

J: What do you mean?

H: I don't know how many governments it was, but I think it had to be beyond our government. It had to be other civilizations, other planets, but I don't know what the purpose is… was.

J: I'm going to count from one to three, Helen, and I'm going to ask you during that time to go directly to the colonel's eyes and ask what was the purpose of this program… to have hybrids in with the humans. One, two, three.

H: He said they were not strong. They needed a breeding program. It's all it was, just a breeding program. Just like when you raise cattle, you take the best ones and mix them together until you get what you want. They wanted hybrids that were physically strong, with good immune systems that they could get from humans. They wanted some emotions, but not destructive ones. They wanted to hang onto the intelligence they had. And they had a hard time getting everything mixed up just right. Raechel was the closest that they had come.

J: Why was the United States government involved in this?

H: He did not say. He knew... but he did not tell me that.

J: How long did you stay at this base?

H: Not very long, I think maybe twenty-four hours or less. But I seemed to have lost track of time.

07-17-99 Regression.

H: Helen, I want you to go even deeper and take yourself back to when you were taken onto the base by the colonel. I want you to be there in the moment. Tell me what's happening to you and tell me anything at all that would help us to understand what was going on at the underground base and the reason for it. One, two, three. Where are you, Helen?

H: I'm in where they eat, in the mess hall, but there wasn't any food right then.

J: Be there in the moment, Helen. Take yourself as deep as you need to go.

H: Some people come in, not very many.... There's a guard... his dog... I'm afraid of the dog... and it comes up and licks my hand so I guess it's all right, but I'm still afraid... and there's a woman... and she's a nurse.

J: What's her name?

H: I'm not told her name and anybody's name. It isn't very polite to introduce you to people and they don't tell you their name, but that's how they did it.

J: Were you told anyone's name while you were there, Helen?

H: No, it was like, this is the guard, you met him at the gate… and this is the nurse. She's the one who took care of Raechel and helped me with her.

J: I want you to be with the nurse right now, Helen. Let yourself go as deep as you need to go to be in the presence of the nurse. Look at her, tell me what you're aware of. Where are you?

H: I'm still in the same place and she's looking in my eyes. But she can't talk with her eyes. She just looks, her eyes are sad as if she'd like to tell me something, but she can't. She says I hope everything goes well for you. This is a funny thing to say when you meet somebody… I hope everything goes well for you.…You should say, I hope you have a nice time here or glad to meet you, not that, it sounds strange.

J: Helen, why did the colonel bring you here today?

H: He wants me to know that although I'm already aware, well somewhat… of Raechel's origin, that it was just regular people that helped him with her. I wasn't worried about that. He didn't have to do that. He wants me to know that there really is a place like this. But then he tells me I can't go in the underground part because there are some things that even he can't do… is not allowed to do. And that's one of them… so, he just tells me about it with his eyes. He said, this is the best I can do… this is as close as I can take you.

10-03-98 Regression.

J: Did you ever see the colonel again?

H: I've seen the same eyes.

J: The same eyes as the colonel's eyes?

H: Yes.

J: Where did you see them?

H: The man in the van.

Chapter 35

Helen, Her Mother, and Her Aunt

If a person suspects an abduction, has repeated UFO sightings, and other unexplained experiences, there is a good chance his parents or children have had similar experiences. Members of Helen's family were interviewed to see if they had ever had any unusual experiences.

Many abductees tell of miscarriages and abnormal pregnancies. Did this apply to Helen as well?

06-21-98 A letter from Helen.

"On June 21, 1998, I talked to my aunt in Florida and asked her again what she had seen in the sky as a child (she's now in her 80s). She told me that her mother would get all the children up and dressed so they could go outside to see the 'lights and things.'

"Apparently the house and windows would usually rattle and shake when the lights appeared, though not always. My grandmother would tell the children that it was just like what she remembered happening to her home when she was a child in Switzerland. She told them it was probably an earthquake. They lived in upper New York State and I don't believe there were any earthquakes at that time, certainly nothing that could even have been detected, or rattle the whole house. When they went outside, my aunt recalls seeing many lights and objects, various colors (red, blue, and green) and shaped in round, oval, triangular, and some that changed form as she watched. Some came in very low and she wouldn't go into any more detail on that. They flew alone and in formation, and all the children were really fascinated. My grandfather never saw them—he refused to get up and go outside or even to look out the window—told them all they were crazy."

10-03-98 Regression.

June (J): I'd like to ask you about your own mother. Tell me what you're aware of.

Helen (H): She really didn't want me.

J: How do you know that?

H: She told me that.

J: What did she say?

H: That she'd never really wanted me. I was never her child.

J: What did she mean, you were never her child?

H: Nobody will tell me. She wouldn't tell me.

J: Did other people ever say that you weren't her child?

H: No, it's so bizarre.

J: What's bizarre?

H: I think the woman who is my aunt is really my mother. My mother told me about ten years ago that I was never her child, that she didn't want me, never wanted me, never wanted any more contact with me. She wouldn't talk to me after that and then she got to where she had somebody from my brother's family there all the time and I never could get through to her. I was not allowed to talk to her, so I talked to my Aunt Helen. I told her about it and I told her it was so strange. She was always so much closer to me than my mother, the woman I thought was my mother. I asked, are you my mother? And she said, it was just so long ago, I don't want to talk about it. She won't talk about it, either. So I don't know, I wish she was my mother. She's a lot nicer person.

J: Helen, I want you to go into your deeper mind, and I want to ask your deeper mind to answer some questions about your birth... about your conception. Go as deep as you need to go to be in touch with that information. When you were conceived, Helen, who was the person in which you found yourself? Now I'm going to ask a question of your fingers. Was the woman who was supposedly your mother, your real mother?

H: (no - fingers)

J: No. Was your aunt your real mother?

H: (no - fingers)

J: No. Was your real mother someone who gave you up for adoption?

H: (I don't know - fingers)

J: I want your deeper mind to become very aware of the first time you were aware of the mother you thought was your real mother. Was it under the age of one?

H: (no - fingers)

J: No. Was it under the age of two?

H: (yes - fingers)

J: Yes. Was your conception a normal conception?

H: (no - fingers)

J: No. I want you to be very, very clear looking at your conception so that you know what wasn't normal about it. Is it all right for Helen at this time to talk about her conception?

H: (yes - fingers)

J: Yes. Helen, tell me what you're aware of about your own conception.

H: It was... oh.... It's so mixed up... so mixed up.... Oh... they took... oh, God... they take an egg from my aunt.... They do something with it.... Then it's put in my mother.... She carries me.

J: What was done to the egg and who did it?

H: I can't see, but I'm all mixed up.... My aunt can't have children.... She can't have children. She has no uterus, she can't have children. That's why, because they want to use her... they did what they could... they took the egg.

J: Who's they?

H: I don't know... but they took what they could from her, they didn't know that she couldn't have children, that she couldn't carry a baby until after they made the plans. I guess I belong to both of them, sort of. No wonder my mother said that.

J: I'm going to count from one to three and on the count of three, Helen, I want you to tell me who "they" were who took the egg from the aunt and put it in your mother. One, two, three.

H: I think they're the people who used to come with the blue and green lights that I saw when I was a child, but my aunt saw them when she was a child, too.

J: Tell me about the blue lights and the green lights.

H: They were like the lights that I saw when I went with Raechel. They looked like that. My aunt described them like that, too, but she saw crafts, and everybody did in the family, all her brothers and sisters. I think it was the people that came in those crafts that were responsible for what they did to her and me, and to my mother.

J: How did you feel when you saw the blue lights?

H: Fascinated, they were so pretty, the most beautiful shade of blue.

J: And did anything else happen during those times when you saw the blue lights?

H: I don't think so. I was a child when I saw them. The lights were a long way away.... I thought they were. When I talked about them, everybody said they were northern lights, but they were not northern lights, they were totally different. They were something that appeared on a pretty regular schedule.

J: Was there anything unusual about the way they would act?

H: No, they were not coming through the sky. They were already on the ground, but they must have been enormous. You could see so much light and they had to be quite far away, so beautiful. They were not northern lights.

Chapter 36

Helen's Pregnancies

In an earlier session Helen said she went for an evening stroll with a woman she didn't know. When asked why she would do this, all she could answer was, "I don't know, it doesn't make sense." Helen said she hated women doctors because they always hurt you. Dr. Steiner asked why. Further explanations on both these questions came up unexpectedly during the following regressions.

10-03-98 Regression beginning with Helen stepping back away from Raechel and touching the kitchen table in the girls' apartment.

J: Tell me about that kitchen table, Helen. I want you to feel the coolness of it and your hand on it. I want you to tell me if it reminds you of anything else. Have you ever felt that same texture, substance, coolness?

H: Same coolness, like in an operating room or exam room.

J: I want you to imagine yourself in a operating room or an exam room with that kind of coolness and tell me what comes to mind.

H: Awful lot of pain....

J: Where do you feel the pain?

H: (demonstrating)

J: In your pelvic area?

H: Um...

J: What's happening?

H: I don't know for sure, but they're doing something.

J: Who's they?

H: Supposed to be a doctor… supposed to just give me an exam but… this is more than an exam….

J: Tell me what you mean.

H: I feel like they're putting something inside of me.

J: What does it feel like?

H: It hurts, it hurts really bad. I think they're putting… I don't know.

J: What are they saying to you as they do that?

H: They tell me to hold still, be quiet, it'll be over pretty soon.

J: Do they tell you why they're doing it?

H: They say I'll feel better, and I tell them I felt good when I came in here, that I feel terrible now. They say, it doesn't matter, you'll be all right, you have to do this. Nobody will ever know after it's all done.

J: What is it they won't know?

H: What they're doing. I don't know what it's called, but they put something up inside my cervix. Because it hurts when it's opened up. But they tell me this is all right, this is okay, it's not going to do any harm. No one will ever know the difference.

J: No one except…?

H: Me.

J: You. What is it that you will know about the difference?

H: That Marisa is not entirely human.

J: And how does that feel to know that?

H: Not very good… not very good.

J: Do they tell you how you will be able to deal with that?

H: No, they said that at first she would be very, very much like any other child. They said since this is your first child, you won't know the difference anyway. And I guess they were right... in a sense.

J: What were those things you were aware of, however?

H: She was really small, but that's not unusual for a baby. She didn't eat very well and she didn't feel, her skin didn't feel just right to me.

J: How did it feel?

H: It felt always quite cool. But she was healthy, and it felt a little spongy, not much, but it didn't feel like it should. I didn't want to think that it was different, but I didn't want to remember what they'd told me, either.

J: So what did you do with that memory?

H: I put it away.

J: When you looked in Marisa's eyes, what did you see?

H: I didn't see anything there. Just love, just like an ordinary child.

07-18-99 Regression with Helen.

J: And move forward again to the very first time you, Helen, were given the opportunity to be the mother of such a child, let your deeper mind be fully aware of how it happened... and tell me what you're aware of....

H: I'm on the exam table. I don't want to be there. They say we'll just give you a checkup. That's when I tell them I don't need a checkup, I feel good. Then the blue light, that's when I see the blue light.

J: Who's there with you, Helen?

H: The lady that I went for a walk with.

J: Is that Rosalind?

H: No, Rosalind is the doctor.

J: Is she there, too?

H: Yes, but I only see her for a minute. She's not very nice. And I can't move because the blue light is just brighter and brighter.

It pushes me down because I want to fight. I want to get off the table. I'm not tied down. The light comes closer and closer and then I can't... and it hurts... they say it's going to be over in a minute and you'll be fine. Then the light... that's all I remember, but when I wake up the light is not there. But the lady that I came with is.

J: And who is that?

H: I don't know her. I see her in the neighborhood... and I've seen her before, too. I've seen her at some of the dances we played for and some of the shows. She would be there and she would come over afterwards to me and say, how are you? I enjoyed you tonight. I'd say, thank you, and that would be all, but she would come. I saw her two or three times. I'd go for a walk sometimes and I would be down the street and she would always... people don't do that... they usually don't speak, but she always said hello, how are you? So she knew me.

J: And did you have a child, Helen, nine months after this experience?

H: Yes.

J: And who was born?

H: Marisa.

J: Helen, I want you to move forward in time to the very next time that you were inseminated or impregnated. Let yourself go there and be fully in the experience, telling me what happened.

H: That's when I think I am having a miscarriage. I think I am. I went to work. I didn't feel good. My stomach hurts but I go in because I need the money. I know I'm just going to bleed all over, I can feel it coming. So I go into the nurses' lounge and there's a cot in there. Well, maybe if I lie down on it I'll feel better, but I don't. One of the nurses comes in. I don't remember her name, but she sees what's happening and says, "I'll get you some help." And I think she's gone to call a doctor... well, she does call a doctor, I guess. But I did not go to the hospital. I should stay right there, but the next thing I know, I'm in the doctor's office again.

J: Which doctor is that, Helen?

H: Oh, it's Rosalind. And she said, "I'll take care of you." I say, "I need a D&C but you can't do that here." "Oh, yes, I can do anything I need to do... no, whatever I need to do, I can do that...," and she's saying this in her German accent—vatever I need to do. And I said....

J: Stay fully and completely in the moment.

H: I say... "I don't care. I just want to feel better," but the blue light comes again and I know they should be doing something different than they are. Because I know how a D&C is... and it's sort of like that. She's taking something out, but she's really careful with it.

J: I want you to see what that she's taking out, Helen. Look at what Rosalind is doing and tell me what you see.

H: I'm not sure what the instrument is, but she's really, really careful, she uses two things. It's like something to go up inside and then something like a spoon. That's not it. It's something. She's really careful, she's not going to spill anything that comes out.

J: How does it feel as she does this? How are you feeling?

H: Well, by then, I don't feel very much because the blue light is there. Yet somehow I know she's doing more than she should be. And there's somebody else there that's not a doctor, but it's not a nurse, either. It's somebody, some lady with a gray suit and I become aware that this is really a strange thing. You shouldn't be wearing nice clothes in a place like that, because you would ruin them. But anyway, Rosalind takes both things out and she has something in the little spoonlike thing and the other lady has a little dish. She says, take this, you know vat to do with it. And I don't remember anything for a few minutes. When I wake up I'm on a little couch and Rosalind is not there. But the lady in the gray suit is. And now, it's the same lady that took me there before. She says I'll take you home now.

J: I want you to go into the blue light. I want you to ask for information now, Helen, about how hybrid children are created. What is it that you know about the creation of hybrid children? And when you're clearly aware of that information, tell me what you know, let the blue light speak through you with that knowledge.

H: It happens sometimes when you think you're having a miscarriage. They like to have a fetus already started, but then that makes it difficult because they have to change it.

J: How do they do that, Helen?

H: I don't know exactly. They take out, they remove some... I don't know what DNA... they take some DNA out sometimes, but not very often. Usually they insert some, what they do most often is take the egg from the woman and mix it in a dish with... just like we do with artificial insemination. Then sometimes they put it back in the same woman they got it from because then it'll grow okay. When they can't, when circumstances aren't right, they have to do it in the tanks after it's too big for the dish. I don't like to think about it.

Helen has had three or four apparent miscarriages. Each one occurred during the latter part of her first trimester. There were no obvious reasons for the losses.

Chapter 37

Raechel's Origin

Helen consciously remembers being given information that Raechel was not from Earth, and that she didn't seem to have a real mother and father. Exploring this further revealed an interesting and startling turn of events.

10-03-98 Regression. When Helen first meets Raechel.

H: That was when I thought I was having a miscarriage... and I went to this lady doctor.

J: Was this your regular doctor?

H: No, she wasn't. I knew her because she was a doctor where I worked at the hospital. I don't know why I went to her. I should have just had one of the docs there take care of me, but I didn't. Anyway I went to her office and it was a funny room, too. Not much furniture, but tables and things, not much in there, and it was really old. She said, we have to do a D&C, and I said, I want to go to the hospital. And she said, no, we're going to do it here. I said I don't want to do that. I work there, I can just go and you can... we'll just do it there. No, I have to do it here, and I have to do it now. She pushed me back down on the table. It was cold and hard. I guess it was her nurse that held me down and strapped me down. I thought they just did a regular D&C, but I don't think so. I think they took out what turned out to be Raechel later on.

J: What symptoms were you having before you went to see the doctor?

H: A lot of cramps and my stomach hurt. I was kind of nauseated, too... but I guess I was probably at least two months.

J: Did you know you were pregnant?

H: I thought I was, but I wasn't sure, then I started to get cramps and a backache, and started to bleed a lot. I don't know why I went to her. She wasn't my doctor. I should have stayed right in the hospital because when it started I was already there and I worked for the operating room. But I had gone in the nurses' lounge and I laid down on the couch and somebody said... well, you just lay down... you just lay there and keep your feet up, and I'll go get the doctor. And I thought that they were going to get my doctor. And then I don't remember going to her office, but I was there, her office was maybe three or four blocks away.

J: Had you ever seen this doctor before?

H: Oh, yes, several times. She did a few little surgeries there. Nobody liked her very well. She was not very pleasant, but I think she was a good doctor. She just wasn't a very nice person. And she wasn't very nice to me. After we got through in her office I laid down for a little while on the couch until I felt better. Then I walked home... and I never went to see her again. I saw her again, but I never went to her.

J: Where did you see her?

H: In the hospital. Where I worked.

J: Did she acknowledge you when you saw her?

H: Not really. She would say, hello, how are you? Just like you would speak to a stranger.

J: Helen, I'm going to ask your deeper mind a question here. And I'd like your deeper mind to answer with your fingers before you speak about it. Deeper mind, I'd like you to go as far inside of this experience of having carried Marisa and carried Raechel, and I want you to tell me if you have knowledge of why you were allowed to give birth to Marisa, but that Raechel was taken from you and raised somewhere else. Do you know why it was done that way? Let your fingers know. Do you know anything about the difference in possible cell or tissue or DNA between Raechel and Marisa?

H: No.

J: Were you ever told by Raechel or the colonel or anyone else why Raechel was taken from you and then reintroduced to you when she lived with Marisa?

H: Yes.

J: Tell me about that.

H: That day in the kitchen when I talked to Raechel, when she talked to me. She said... I... have... never... had... a... mother... I... do... not... know... what... a mother... is... supposed... to... be... but... Marisa... talks... about... you... all... the... time. She said that she wished that I was her mother, and I said, I really can't be, what happened to your mother? And she said, I... never... had... one. Where... I... come... from... we... do... not. I... want... to... be... like... Marisa... and... have... a... mother. I... think... you... would... be... a... good...mother. And I said, "Raechel, I am not your mother," and then she said, "Well, maybe you do not remember.... No," she said, "someday you will remember." I said, "I don't want to talk about this any more." And that is when she said, "Well, let me show you where I live," and that's when I went to the window place. It's ridiculous. I didn't want to talk about it with her because I didn't think I was her mother but yet, I knew I was.

Later in the regression, Helen reveals more about Raechel's early years.

J: Did they tell you how they sustained Raechel's life at all?

H: She was raised in a vat, like an aquarium.

J: With liquid, you mean?

H: Yes, yes, with liquid. I don't know what kind.

J: How do you know that?

H: It's more information I got. I don't know who gave it to me. I think she did.

J: When would that have been?

H: That would have been that day I went behind the windows.

In another part of the same session, more information on Raechel's youth emerged.

H: ATIC wanted, insisted that he adopt her and raise her as a human. He had no idea of what to do with a child, never been around children. He didn't know if he could do it and he laughed, not laughed, because he wasn't a person that laughed, he kind of smiled. Then with sort of a smile, he just looked, just riveted his eyes on mine and all of a sudden, all this other information that would have taken at least a couple of hours to tell in words, all of a sudden it was there.

11-07-97 Interview with Helen telling of a telephone conversation with Marisa.

"She called me at work and was very upset at what had happened. I told her I would try to make some phone calls and see what I could find out about the father, if he had disappeared also. I did, and found out that he had disappeared without any apparent trace.

"She had called the college and there was no record of Raechel ever having been there. All her files had mysteriously disappeared, too. They said that all her records had disappeared. She didn't call administration. They were aware that Raechel was a student there, and they were surprised that the records had disappeared."

Worried about Marisa's safety, Helen calls Jim, a friend who works in security at Highland Air Force Base, asking him to check on Colonel Nadien. At this point she takes a piece of paper and jots down Jim's name and phone extension number. She also takes notes as she talks with Jim. By sheer chance, at the end of their conversation, she tucks the note away, rather than tossing it in the trash. More than twenty years later Helen runs across this note hidden in some other papers. This note provided the researchers with valuable leads, including the base extension number that was still in use. The following is a transcript as she remembers it, when Jim calls back with the information he has found.

Jim (J): I hope you're sitting down for this. The colonel and the daughter came here from Four Corners. He was attached to one of the black projects much, much higher than Blue Book. He was there for a long time and was commander of the detachment. Your suspicions about the daughter are probably true, but I can't tell you that for sure—you know what I mean. The whole thing is pretty exotic, the outfit he was working for, ATIC, Aerospace Technical Information Center. And the men you mentioned, sounds like Men in Black, almost like something connected to the Nation of the Third Eye.... I don't know. But I couldn't say if I did, either.

H: Are you sure about ATIC? I've never heard of it, and as we're talking, I'm trying to find it in my listing of acronyms, but it's not here.

J: Yes, I'm sure that's it, and I'm sure, too, that you won't find it listed anywhere because it's not supposed to exist, but take my word for it, it does. And take my word for it, too, that that girl living with your daughter is most likely something the colonel got out of one of those craft that come to Four Corners. And something else, too. If you ever mention one word about this conversation to anyone, ever, I'll deny the whole thing. I have no choice.

H: I really appreciate your honesty, Jim, and I can't imagine who I would ever tell this to, or what I'm going to do about the situation, either. I guess nothing for the time being.

Upon searching the base archives it was verified that Jim did work in security at that time. An Internet search and examination of the property tax records, old telephone directories, and other databases in the California State Library revealed Jim's present-day address.

05-30-98 Summary of a telephone interview with Jim.

Jim said he retired in 1987 from Highland Air Force Base, after spending 24 years as a criminal investigator, "same desk for all those years," in the base security police. He said he did some routine background investigations, but was primarily occupied with theft of government property cases.

When asked if he remembered Helen having asked him to verify Colonel Nadien's position, etc., at Masters, he said he had no recollection. He said every secretary from time to time wanted him to check on something, and that it could very well have happened, but that he had "no memory." He said he had the Masters base directory and was in its base personnel office every week or so reviewing personnel lists/records so that questions like that were referred to him. When pressed again on the name Colonel Nadien, he said he "might have seen—had a vague memory of—" a colonel with a name like that.

07-26-98 The following is a summary of a joint in-person interview with Helen, Jim, and the investigators.

Jim appeared to be a recovering alcoholic and of average intelligence. During the interview he was stoic, smooth-talking, and blank-faced. Everyone present agreed he was capable of stonewalling the investigators. He remembered Helen and was cordial in his greetings. When asked about their conversation years earlier he replied, "I can't remember," allowing for the fact he actually may not remember the incident, whether by his choice or someone else's. In the sequence of the conversation, Jim then said he'd been thinking about this all week. He then followed up by the mention of his pension not stretching far enough.

On two occasions, he broke eye contact when being questioned, and at this time added short asides that only Helen would understand based on their friendship years earlier. After the interview Helen admitted Jim may have wanted to impress her in his role as a "lady's man," knowing full well her marriage was in trouble at the time. He had been a frequent house guest at Helen's and Jon's home. She felt he was fully capable of going through the interview and convincing us of whatever he wanted. In view of his years of work in dealing with people in a security capacity, we had to agree it was a possibility.

Chapter 38

The Blue Lights

Blue lights seem to have accompanied Helen throughout her life's journey. Only after repeated questioning does Helen begin to understand and reveal the significance of their visitations.

10-03-98 Regression.

June (J): So, what happened when you touched the blue light as a child?

Helen (H): I was told... you don't belong in the family. You don't belong where you think you do. I said, well, it doesn't matter, they take care of me. They said, but they don't love you, and I said, I know that.

10-04-98 Regression.

H: The first time I ever saw the blue light they asked if I wanted to have a baby, and I told them no, I do not want to have a baby. I'm too young. They said, we could wait. I thought that was the end of it, but it was just the beginning.

J: I want you for a moment to concentrate on your aunt who was your real mother. I want you to make contact with her eyes and I want you to ask or pull information from her concerning whether or not she had made any agreements about her life in regard to other beings, and tell me what you're aware of.

H: Yes...

J: What is it you're aware of, Helen?

H: She did make an agreement, sort of...

J: What kind of an agreement?

H: To continue on.

J: What does that mean?

H: Because her mother had made an agreement, too. She, my aunt was from that... she came out of that agreement.

J: What are you aware of?

H: She thinks she didn't have a choice. She could have, but she didn't.

J: What do you mean, she could have but she didn't?

H: She could have said no, but she was afraid. She just went on.

J: And did you come out of an agreement?

H: Yes, because I was part of her agreement, but she couldn't have any other children.

J: Are you saying, Helen, that her agreement involved you, but at no level of awareness, spiritual, physical, or mental, did you give an agreement to be involved?

H: That's what I'm saying. I guess I didn't make it clear when they asked me if I wanted to have a baby. I said I was too young. I can't have a baby. I should have said no, I do not want to have a baby, and maybe they would have understood. I didn't say it that way, so I guess I was agreeing.

J: Who was it that asked you, Helen, if you wanted to have a baby?

H: It was not something I could see, it was not a shape, not a form, it was like a presence that I could feel.

J: I want you to be there right now, feeling into that presence. I want you to see the blue light, I want you to see and feel the presence, and I want you to be aware of who it is that's speaking to you, or what it is that's speaking to you.

H: Oh, my head hurts, the light... it's... I can't see anybody, there's no shape... it's just this light.

J: Go into the light...

H: I don't feel... I don't hear anything. I just know what is coming out of it, but I don't hear it.

J: It's not necessary that you hear it, Helen. How do you know it?

H: It's put it in my mind!

J: As you're becoming aware of it, I want you to ask... what is it or who is it that's giving me this information through the light? What is the light, and who is giving me this information?

H: Um...

J: Feel yourself in its presence.

H: They want me to feel so warm and so comfortable and just accept what they say, what they want. I can't see them and they don't say who they are.

J: I want you to ask. I want you to concentrate, make contact and ask who they are... you can do that, Helen.

H: They don't want to tell me where they are, but they're not from here.

J: Do they have a name, Helen?

H: They don't tell me the name. They say I would not understand yet.

J: Did the light or the energy of these beings touch you in any way?

H: Yes. The blue light did.

J: Where did it touch you?

H: My hand.

J: And how did it feel as it touched you?

H: Kind of tingly and warm, it didn't hurt.

J: I want you to feel it now, Helen. I want you to experience the light touching your hand. You're there, re-experiencing in the moment, what happened. I want you to be aware what's happening by the touch of the light. I want you to be aware of your surroundings. I want you to tell me where you are. What do you see around you besides the light?

H: I was in that special place that I would always go to when I wanted to be alone.

J: Where was that?

H: Not very far from my house, in the woods. It had a little stream that ran through it and a lot of trees, ferns, a lot of rocks, just a little stream. My horse is there, she didn't see the light, I guess. She wasn't afraid, so I guess she didn't see it.

J: In this particular time when you were touched by the light and asked if you wanted to have a baby, how old were you?

H: I think I was eleven or twelve... eleven.

J: And how many times before had you seen the light there?

H: I don't know, maybe... five or six, maybe seven.

J: I want you to move back in time and let yourself go to the earliest memory you have of the blue light, and as you're doing that, I want you to feel yourself becoming younger... feel your body so that you can know how big you are, how old you are... tell me about that very first time.

H: I was eight. That's the first time that I saw the blue light. The other time, when they asked about the baby, I was older then.

J: What happened that very first time when you saw the light? Did it touch you then?

H: No, it didn't come too close. I could see it just a little ways away. It just kind of sat there not on the ground, but not up in the sky. It was up a little, just off the ground. It wasn't very big. I looked at it and I'm not afraid. I should be because I never saw that before.

J: Tell me when you last saw the blue light.

H: I can't remember. I don't think I saw it before. I keep seeing it....

J: What do you mean, you keep seeing it?

H: It can't be the same one. It's the same color, it looks the same and it feels the same.

J: And where are you seeing it?

H: Just before I had Carl, they said I died and they brought me back. While I was gone I saw the light and it felt the same... warm, beautiful. It wanted to pull me in, but I wouldn't go.

J: What do you mean, you died and they brought you back?

H: Pre-eclampsia, I was really, really bad and I didn't care whether I lived or died. It hurt so bad and I was so sick. I was in the hospital and they were doing all they could to keep me going, but I guess I got tired of fighting. I let go for a minute. I should have had that baby sooner, I just couldn't seem to have him. I had this problem, and finally just let go. It would have been so easy to just go, just go with the light but I wasn't ready yet.

J: Did you tell anyone that?

H: Oh, yes. I told the doctor, and he said don't talk about it, people will think you're crazy. I told my mother, she said the same thing. My husband didn't care one way or the other, but he thought I was crazy, too. Finally I didn't tell anybody because they all thought I was crazy. I was not crazy. It did happen, and that was the same light.

J: What do you think the light did at that time? Why did it come?

H: Because I needed some help.

J: And it gave you help?

H: It gave me strength to get through what I had to do. I didn't even know what that was then.

J: What is it that you know now about what that was?

H: What I'm doing now.

J: How soon after this experience was the baby born?

H: I think two or three days. I got better and they let me out of the hospital. I went home, then right back in, and that time I did have him.

J: What are you thinking about right now, Helen?

H: Thinking that this thing is so complicated.

J: I'm going to touch your knee in a moment, Helen, your left knee, and when I do, you're going to have a deeper and deeper understanding of the purpose of all of this which is happening to you. There's going to be another letting go deep within yourself... to a much greater understanding and a pulling together of all the things that have happened... there'll be no more struggling to understand... but a much deeper acceptance to just know without all of the answers, knowing they will come... and allowing yourself at a very, very deep level to tune into the original plan... and to the originator of that plan... to begin to identify with the plan... in a way that doesn't keep you separate from it... and every time or any time I touch your knee in this way, you'll go to a deeper, deeper level... of letting go into... that acceptance and that knowing... the blue light has been with you throughout your lifetime and continues to be with you... learn to speak to it and receive from it. When was the last time you saw the blue light?

H: Last spring. (Jan. 10, 1998)

J: And where were you?

H: In my home.

J: And what were you doing?

H: I had just gone to bed, turned out the lights, and I could see a blue light reflected in the bedroom window. It should not have been there. I looked outside and of course, there was nothing there. So that meant it was in the house, it was in the hallway that goes from the bedroom to the living room. I could see from the bed, I could see the reflection in the window, but I could also see a faint, shimmering light in the hallway. I got up and I grabbed my big flashlight for protection, not for light. And I walked down the hallway with my flashlight in my hand and as soon as I stepped into the hallway, it was there, about three feet away. It just kept shimmering and changing shape. I forgot about protecting myself with the flashlight and I just stood there and looked at it. It kept changing shape, folding in on itself, and it got smaller and smaller. It went away, just disappeared in front of my eyes. But after it went, I could see like little sparkly light particles in the air. Then those went out like little lights, too.

J: And how were you feeling after your visit with the blue light?

H: Really good, and not afraid. I felt really stupid with the flashlight but I just turned around and walked back into the bedroom, got into bed, and went to sleep. I don't know why I accepted that.

J: Hadn't you been accepting it all your life?

H: Yes, I had so I guess it was no different. It had a little different shape, but the light, the warmth, the color was the same.

J: What was different about the shape?

H: Before it's always been quite round, like a ball... it had depth to it, but this was kind of... well, it didn't have a shape. It had depth to it, but it was kind of amorphous, is what they call it. It kept moving around, it would be high on one side and then that would go down. Then it would be low, and be high on the other side. Not alive, but more movement than the other ones.

J: Had anything happened, Helen, that day that was different, or anything happened after you saw the light that was different?

H: I don't think so. Well, maybe, it was before I came here to see you. We'd been talking about this, Jean and I were talking, not that day but near that time... and I was concerned.

J: What were you concerned about, Helen?

H: Well, how the sessions would go, how you would feel about me. How I would feel about you. I think it was that time when the light showed up.

J: Does the light often show up when you need help or reassurance? Is that a time it shows up?

H: Well, sometimes. If that's its purpose I need it. I need it a lot more often. Maybe it's just big things... when it comes.

J: So seeing the blue light is comforting.

H: Right.

07-16-99 Regression. Blue lights at age 13.

J: Tell me what it looks like.

H: It just shimmers, it's a beautiful blue, like the sky.

J: How big is it?

H: Not very big, it changes, it moves around, it's sort of round but kind of moves in and out.

J: What do you mean, in and out?

H: It goes like in on itself and then back out. It's kind of wavy-looking, like it's alive. Not like breathing in and out, it just changes its shape so it's not quite round all the time. What's so unusual is that it shimmers, it's such a beautiful shade of blue. Even though it shimmers, it doesn't hurt your eyes. It's just soft. And it feels warm.

J: What do you mean, it feels warm?

H: It feels warm like when you get in a warm tub.

J: So the area around where the light is feels warm?

H: Yes, and how can that be? It's in the woods and even though there's sunlight, sun and shade, it's not that kind of warm. It's not warm from the sun, I don't know how to describe it. It's just a warm, comforting feeling.

After Helen touches the blue light.

J: Then just let yourself feel those tingles and that warmth. Be totally involved in the experience, touching the blue light, feeling the tingles, the wonderful feeling of it, and let yourself move very slowly into the next moment and tell me what happens.

H: I took my finger away. That was when they asked me again did I want to have a baby. And I said no, I still don't want to have a baby. I have to go to school. I thought that was a good excuse and I guess they thought so, too. They said well, that's all right. We can wait. I was younger, maybe ten. I should have been thinking... the whole thing was ridiculous. A blue light asking me did I want to have a baby... but I didn't think so then, except that I didn't want to do that.

J: So was it the first time that you saw the blue light and that you were asked if you wanted to have a baby that you touched the blue light, or was it the second time?

H: It was the second time. I guess I was braver then. I still had the feeling I shouldn't have touched it. But I couldn't seem to stop. I don't really know why it all happened.

J: Just let yourself go into the touch again, Helen, and let yourself know what happened. Let yourself move very slowly through the experience, remembering what happened.

H: That was the time when they said that I would sooner or later, I would have one... and when I did... it would look like me but it would be like them.

J: Who is them, Helen?

H: I didn't see anybody, it wasn't voices, and it wasn't eyes. It was like the thought was in my head. I wasn't saying anything, either. That's when I learned to do it with thoughts, the first time with the blue light. I learned to communicate with my thoughts.

J: And did you have ongoing communication of that kind after that as you grew up?

H: With the blue light?

J: Either with the blue light or without.

H: I didn't do it for a while, but I could do it with Marisa.

J: Tell me about that.

H: When she grew up, we could just do it back and forth over the distance. Didn't even need a telephone. We did talk on the telephone but usually it was to confirm something we'd already talked about with the thoughts.

J: Was she also aware of that?

H: Oh, yes. I'm not sure if she could do that with anyone else, we never talked about that.

J: Was there anyone besides Marisa that you could communicate that way with?

H: I can do it with the boys sometimes, my boys.

07-18-99 Regression.

J: And when you look at when the light comes, does something different usually follow what happens? Anything significant happen after you've seen the blue light?

H: Yes, always. But it does not always have to do with the project, like the time I saw it before I met you. You're involved in the project now, not that project, you're involved in my project.

J: Which is also part of....

H: It's also part of the other... so it was like a sign not to be afraid or apprehensive.

J: So besides being significant to letting you know about the project, is the blue light also a source of comfort and trust with you?

H: Oh, yes... always.

J: So it's a gift that lets you know you're guided and well helped. Helen, I want you to reach out and touch the blue light. Let it be there. Reach out and touch it because I'm going to ask you to go back in time, not forward, but back in time. So let yourself reach out now and touch the blue light, and let me know when you're touching it.

H: Hm....

J: Good. And let yourself just become one with the blue light. Feel your entire body enveloped in it. Feel the wonderful sense of well-being, wonderful healing that takes place in every cell of your body, your mind, and your spirit. And now, Helen, I want you to be fully engaged in the choice, fully aware of what's happening and tell me... what it is that you're doing and feeling....

H: I'm in the light, it's all around, it's in front.... It's all around me, but I have my own separate light. I'm... I'm aware that... I have an opportunity....

J: What is that opportunity?

H: It will be a difficult one. I can be part of awareness. I'm not sure what that means.

J: Just let yourself go to that place inside that you do know what that means, Helen. Deeper and deeper, back to the very source of being that you've carried with you from the beginning, from the very first, and let yourself know fully... what that awareness is and what your opportunity is to be a part of it.

H: They say I could be an educator, and I don't know what that means. And I'm not a teacher. I thought that's what an educator was. I'm not pressured....

J: Go to your own place of commitment and awareness, Helen. What is it that you choose to do?

H: I choose to be an educator. I do it in a way that is different.

J: What is that way, Helen?

H: I choose to be part of this project.

J: For what reason do you choose to be part of this project, Helen?

H: Because... people need to know.

J: What it is they need to know?

H: That this is not the only civilization or universe. That there are other ways to do things, to be....

J: And Helen, what it is you're being given to help you to carry through this commitment you've made?

H: Strength, I'm given the strength. I understand that it's really difficult sometimes to make some hard choices, but I have the strength to do it now... with the light now.

J: Helen, when were you first given the blue light?

H: The first time I really remember is at nine or ten years old. I remember before... when I made the commitment. When I was older, nine or ten, I didn't make the commitment. It was already done.

J: What does that mean, Helen?

H: That I made it before I was born, well, it had to be me, nobody else could make it for me.

J: I want you to ask the blue light, Helen, just ask it when it first came into your being-ness, no matter when it was.

H: It was when they took the egg from my real mother... and did something... it hurt me... they did something with me. Then I'm inside of the person I thought was my mother. It didn't hurt very long because the light was there... but the light came from my... oh... I'm so mixed up....

J: Just be with the light and it will let you know. Just become one with the light.

H: It was with my aunt, my real mother. I think somehow the light... the light stayed with me... when I went into the... they're carrying me, but now I don't remember the light until I was older... maybe I didn't need it... until then.

J: Just be with the light now. Be at inception with the light... feel the light and see the light... the way in which an embryo can see the light. Let all thoughts of why or understanding fall away. Let yourself be in the experience of knowing the light. Let all doubt and concern fall away....Helen, I want you to go back into the experience of the blue light, enveloped in the light. I want you to feel the peace and contentment... I want you to be aware of the deep satisfaction and gratitude for the work that you've done, for the bravery and the courage, for the willingness to follow through on your commitment and the willingness to bring this investigation to this place. Just let that deep appreciation and awareness of how much good work you've done fill every cell in your body, and be aware that from this moment on you are still very, very open and appreciative of any new information that will come in. There's no need to push or be afraid, or to try to analyze or figure out why this is happening, because you know why it's happening. You know that you're part of something more and you'll be given that information, that you've asked each individual person in the project to come forward with more material when it's available. You've restated your commitment to witness what you have experienced and to bring that forward as a teaching. Be aware of the fullness of your love and of your courage... and bring that same love and courage to yourself and to the healing that's taking place, and be aware that all of the work that you've done is in the process of integration, and the deep, deep healing is continuing and will continue on all levels of your being... with every breath that you take, you breathe in... love, courage, and deep appreciation for all that you've done and all that you will do. Envelop yourself in that love. Let every breath you take continue the life force within you, continue the healing process, and renew your spirit... connect you with all there is... and keep you safe... and at your own speed, taking all of the time that you need, gently begin to bring yourself back, back from all of the places that you've been today... all of the feelings and physical experiences, knowing that you are healed and healing, that you are held and safe, and that you'll bring it all back with you... So make your way back into this room... It's Sunday morning, July 19, 1999.... Feeling wonderful, healed, full of love... feeling the life force in every cell of your body... feeling the strength and the energy coming back into every cell, every bone, and every fiber of your being. And not until you're completely ready do you need to open your eyes. Welcome.

Chapter 39

Men In Black

Numerous accounts concerning interaction with extraterrestrials include mention of the famous Men in Black. In the *Reader's Digest* book, *UFO:The Continuing Enigma*, Men in Black are described on page 118 as, "men dressed in conservative dark suits, often with white shirts, black ties, and dark hats, call at the witness' home. They look like FBI agents from a Hollywood B-movie... claiming to be from some obscure-sounding government department. They usually travel in threes, frequently the third man stays in the car, while the other two conduct the interview. The cars the MIB drive are odd, too. In the classic encounter they arrive in a brand-new car, although the model in question may have been out of production for twenty years or more. They are always prestige models. The license plates, when checked out, are unissued numbers."

10-26-97 Interview with Helen about her encounter with the Men in Black.

"Their car was shiny, extremely shiny and black, and long, with long sloping fenders, and big lights. It was really a striking looking automobile. Four-door. And it had brass or gold handles on the doors. I guess it wasn't gold, it was probably brass.

"They came in threes, and I did see those men face to face. I came up the stairs to the apartment one day as they were coming down, I stood way over to the right-hand side of the stairs and they rushed down, almost knocked me over, very rude, very threatening looking.

"They were probably about 5'8" to 5'10" in height, all of them, a little variation to the height. Real stocky-built, not fat but very muscular looking. And they were wearing black suits and black hats. Their clothes didn't seem to fit right. They didn't look comfortable in their clothes. The fedora kind of hats they wore didn't look like they belonged in that time frame at all. I just sensed that they were some dangerous people.

"They had small, dark eyes, and their complexions were kind of pasty and whitish. They looked like they didn't get out in the sun enough, and had fat faces for the rest of their size. Nothing seemed to match, the clothes, the body, the face, and the aura they gave off... nothing seemed to go together."

Interview with Marisa's husband concerning the Men in Black.

"The strange gal, Raechel, and these two strange men, Marisa said she never saw it, but they came in and there was some ruckus going on... hollering and noise. She kind of got scared.

"When Marisa started really pushing for her to get out of there was when the guys in black, she described them, came up and started... she heard a bunch of noise and everything in the bedroom and then I guess basically they just pushed their way... came right in and pushed their way into there, and there was some hollering and screaming going on...

"There was something weird about the license plate, she was looking at it. She said something about it being a sedan with some weird license plates, they weren't license plates from California."

04-20-98 Excerpt from a letter written by a former roommate of Marisa's.

"I do remember her saying something about odd visitors at the apartment. Odd in that the people who came to see Raechel were not other students like whom Marisa and I had friendships with."

10-03-98 Regression.

J: The only time you saw those men was on the stairway?

H: It's the only time I saw the three of them, but I saw the one head-on. Then through the windows I saw the one, just a profile.

J: Was there anything different or unusual about the profile?

H: I thought he looked like George Raft. He had that gangster look, Mafia hit-man look.

J: Did you ever have reason to be afraid of them?

H: Not really, they didn't threaten me. I thought that they would push me backwards down the stairs if I didn't get out of their way. They were coming down, two abreast and one behind, and the stairs were not that wide. They were not giving me any room. They looked quite intimidating. I just felt that I would be hurt physically if I didn't move.

J: When you continued up the stairs to the apartment, who was there then?

H: The girls.

J: Both of the girls were there?

H: Um-hm.

J: Did they mention the men having been there?

H: Marisa mentioned it, I guess you must have run into Raechel's visitors. I said yes, but I got out of their way before I got hurt. I had to leave within five or ten minutes at the most. So we didn't talk about the men.

Chapter 40

Projects and Agencies

During our conversations, Helen mentioned many different "secret government projects" by name. The possible existence of some of these projects, such as MAJI, MJ-12, and MAJIC, has been controversial for many years. Some of the other projects mentioned were more obscure, but reference to most of them was found. Again, the existence of these projects has never been resolutely proven, but their speculated purposes seem relevant to Helen's explanations. These projects are presented below without any guarantees as to their veracity.

Project POUNCE-the project formed to recover all downed/ crashed craft and aliens.

Project LUNA-a mining operation and alien base on the far side of the Moon.

MAJI-is the Majority Agency for Joint Intelligence. All information, disinformation, and intelligence is gathered and evaluated by this agency, and it operates in conjunction with the CIA, NSA, and the Defense Intelligence Agency. MAJI is responsible to MJ-12.

MJ-12-(standing for "Majestic Twelve") mystery was sparked off with the 1987 publication of an alleged briefing document from ex-U.S. President Truman to president-elect Eisenhower in November 1953. The document dealt with government knowledge about UFOs, aliens, and above-Top Secret projects.

MAJIC-a security classification and clearance of all alien-connected material, projects, and information. MAJIC mean MAJI controlled.

Project PLATO-the project responsible for diplomatic relations with the aliens. This project secured a formal treaty (illegal under the Constitution) with the aliens. The terms were that the aliens would give us technology. In return we agreed to keep their presence on earth a secret, not to interfere in any way with their actions, and to allow them to abduct humans and animals. The aliens agreed to furnish MJ-12 with a list of abductees on a periodic basis.

Project AQUARIUS- a project which compiled the history of alien presence and their interaction with Homo sapiens upon this planet for the last 25,000 years.

Project GABRIEL-no reference was found to this project.

Project EXCALIBUR-is a weapon to destroy the alien underground bases. It is a missile capable of penetrating 1,000 meters of tufa/hard packed soil such as that found in New Mexico with no operational damage. The device can carry a one megaton nuclear warhead.

Project GARNET- the project responsible for control of all information and documents regarding this subject and accountability of the information and documents.

National Reconnaissance Organization- The NRO designs, builds, and operates the nation's reconnaissance satellites. NRO products, provided to customers like the Central Intelligence Agency (CIA) and the Department of Defense (DoD), can warn of potential trouble spots around the world, help plan military operations, and monitor the environment.

Delta- is the designation for the specific arm of the NRO which is specifically trained and tasked with the security of these projects.

Area 51-Dreamland- is located at a corner of the Nevada Test Site, where highly classified national defense projects have been conducted for over four decades. Russian satellites have taken aerial photographs of this facility and sold them to the American public.

"Crawford" AFB- located in Lincoln, Nebraska, home of the Strategic Air Command (SAC), and the 20th Intelligence Squadron. This squadron is a subordinate organization of the National Air Intelligence Center (NAIC).

"Masters" AFB- a decommissioned Air Force base located near Sacramento, California. This base once housed a unit from SAC.

The acronym ATIC that Helen jotted down on a note, with the words Aerospace Technical Information Center written after, presented a challenge we couldn't solve. In the Acronyms, Initialisms, and Abbreviations Dictionary 1994, p. 332, ATIC has a similar sounding name, Aerospace Technical Intelligence Center. The Aerospace Technical Information Center (ATIC) is believed to be the original name of the Air Force Technical Intelligence Center (ATIC).

In response to a FOIA request, the Department of the Air Force replied in a letter dated 09-12-96, "From June 1947 through Dec. 1969 the Air Force was primarily responsible for investigating the UFO phenomena. That investigation was conducted by the Air Technical Intelligence Center (ATIC) at Wright-Patterson AFB, Ohio. That organization is currently known as the National Air Intelligence Center (NAIC)."

A thin, tenuous, and at times speculative thread seems to be connecting these projects, agencies, and places. It is wise to remember that for its size and weight, the thread of a spider's web is considered the strongest thread known to mankind.

Chapter 41

Symbols

The triangular insignia with three horizontal lines found on the food containers, water jugs, and license plates was a tangible logo that needed further examination. Searching sixteen source books on symbols ranging from symbol dictionaries, hieroglyphs, astrology, mysticism, mythology, and Chinese symbolism, a researcher found nothing definitive. A book on California license plates yielded nothing. An Internet search of the site www.symbols.com gave some hope, but not an exact match. Contacting the webmaster at this site with a query, Carl Liungman, the author of *The Dictionary of Symbols*, answered and gave some advice on how to proceed: "My tip is that you study the triangle and ideograms with lines at their bases and see which clues that may give you."

The related symbols and ideograms were found on this site, and combined to form the logo Helen drew. The resultant meaning of this combination was somewhat revealing.

A triangle can symbolize power, danger, God, the Holy Trinity, and fire. Symbols can have opposite meanings, in this case safety and success.

A triangle with one line is the most common sign for the element of air.

A triangle with two lines is the alchemists' sign for mixture.

The ideogram △ signifies similarity in one dimension. But ≜ means identity, a similarity so strong that there is no real difference.

It is quite logical that ≜ has been used in meteorology to indicate mist, i.e., an atmospheric condition where everything is identical.

The combination of these signs yields a symbol that could have the meaning signifying an organization filled with danger, and having godlike powers with those belonging identifying so strongly there is no difference.

Could the symbol seen on Raechel's food and drink containers, and on the license plates, symbolize this meaning? Could this be the purpose of the Humanization Project? Undertaking a project dealing with the genetic manipulation of the human race might be considered as assuming godlike powers. Their ultimate goal appears to be the mixing of two races creating a new race that is identical, no visible differences. The opposite sign holds true also, and could symbolize "safety" for the alien race, "success" for the project.

Chapter 42

Marisa

Marisa never lost sight of her goal to become a rehab counselor. She could have used her blindness as an excuse to give up; instead she turned it into an asset, using it as a way to reach and help others.

Marisa struggled through junior college and Golden State University. Never complaining about the inordinate amount of time necessary to do her homework, she just kept on until she was finished. With little time left for recreation she never complained about a thing.

Her acceptance of others no matter what they looked like or what they had done was illustrated time and again. From the time she saw and befriended the 'rat' baby as a young girl, she always stood up for the underdog, the underprivileged, and the lonely. She agonized over her increasing psychic abilities, and not being able to help the people she saw in trouble.

A peacemaker, she was constantly intervening in arguments and disputes between her brothers and friends. Usually she was successful in helping participants see all sides of the issue and reach a peaceful settlement. She had real compassion for the lonely. As an adult she opened her home to those away from home, with no place to go, or who would otherwise have been alone during the holidays and prepared gourmet meals for them.

The one item she kept her entire life was the picture of Jesus, given to her by her baby-sitter. The picture came to symbolize her "Bridge Over Troubled Waters," sustaining her during hard times. It was probably the one possession she treasured above anything else she ever owned.

Marisa fell in love, married, and had a child. Nothing could stop her from living the American dream. She had a goal, she was determined nothing could stop her, nothing did stop her.

Marisa's reaction to Raechel and the strange men dressed in black who visited the apartment is still remembered by her friends.

Marisa's husband.

"Marisa called Raechel strange and having problems with some of her strange friends. Marisa was frightened by at least one incident and wanted Raechel out of the apartment."

Marisa's friend and former roommate.

"I talked to Marisa about Raechel within the first month after she had departed. We had a little 'girl talk,' just the two of us, and I remember sitting on the steps outside the apartment, and being nervous and giggling about this strange experience. We were somewhat frightened, but treated it as just weird."

01-09-98 Interview with Marisa's brother Carl.

Jean (J): Did Marisa regain some of her sight?

Carl (C): She got it all back. She had a hemorrhage at the back of her eyes, and she was blind then, but before she died she could see.

J: Do you have any sense of when her sight started to come back relative to this period we're talking about, early 1972?

C: I have to say it got better right after that. I never thought about it. I was in the service and she was blind and the next thing I knew, she was seeing again.

J: And....all of a sudden she wasn't totally blind?

C: I never thought of it that way. It just got better like that, didn't it?

J: Of Marisa just before her death.

C: She was having the time of her life, she was happy, so happy, and so was he (her husband). It was just like a dream, then somebody just came along and stepped on it.

12-10-98 Synopsis of a telephone interview with an old boyfriend of Marisa's.

He had nothing but the highest praise for the work that Marisa accomplished in helping disadvantaged persons. "Marisa made a great difference in people's lives, and was an outgoing, helpful, caring person."

12-15-98 Second telephone interview with Marisa's old boyfriend.

"There was an awful lot that she could do and did do. I always remember Marisa being very realistic. The one thing that always kind of amazed me about her was that she was very accepting of what had happened. She didn't let it deter her or slow her down. She still had ambitions, goals, she wanted to achieve things and be somebody. She didn't let the visual impairment get in her way. I think she led a very full and active life at the time I knew her.

05/25/98 Interview with Marisa's husband.

"I went back to work and she started going to Golden State University for her Master's. She got everything done except for the project, which I still have all her research for."

He speaks of Marisa's psychic abilities.

"She could remember her dreams and a lot of times she would wake up and be scared. She'd start telling me about these dreams she was having, it was like she'd see things that had happened. She was there, but she couldn't do anything. She described it one time, "I saw this wreck and I was there, but I couldn't do anything about it. There was a man, and a woman, and a child in the car but I couldn't do anything." Then we get the paper and we start reading about it, the whole thing, a clipping of an accident where a man, a woman, and a child go off the road and somebody's killed. We started reading a little bit on leaving the body and stuff like that. I told her that it's possible for her to travel and that maybe she is leaving her body.

"She felt comfortable but sometimes uncomfortable because she couldn't do anything about it. She was an observer, watching what was going on, but couldn't do anything about it. The one thing we always agreed upon was if she had a bad feeling about something, we'd stop and wouldn't do it.

"If her intuition was, this doesn't feel right—okay, we're not going to do it. I felt comfortable with that. No matter what, if you say no, if your intuition tells you we're not going to do it, then we don't do it. There was an incident, we were driving back and she said, no, don't go that way...go this other way, and we did... and the next day we would read that there was an accident about that time where some people had gotten killed.

She felt frustration. I wish I could do something, sometimes she would cry because, "I couldn't do anything...I could only see them...I tried to...."

Foreseeing the unthinkable.

"There was a recurring dream that she started having, it seemed like for the last year. Then she started saying she wasn't going to be around next year. It wasn't direct enough for me. I said, 'oh, honey, you're going to still be around'. She said, no, I don't think so, and that's when we started discussing deaths and what are you supposed to do, and what I am going to do.

"We had bought a house, and were living in it. She was in her position as a teacher and we were remodeling the house. I was working on the house and she was helping with the work. Then she started dreaming more, and one recurring dream she had was waking up and telling me she was in the water and everybody was sinking, but a hand reached down to her and picked her up. And she took off walking across the water and she said... 'maybe it was Jesus, I don't know...., but a hand came down through the water and picked me up and I was able to walk across the water....' So on her gravestone it says, 'Friend, wife, mother—she could walk on water'."

Marisa's death on December 7, 1990.

"We were at my Christmas party at work, and we were sitting down with a friend. We were discussing death and my thing was that when I go, I'd like to walk out...I think the Eskimos have it right. You go out on an iceberg and let it float away and that'll be the end. We carried on this conversation because the couple that we were with, she was Native American Indian. We discussed this for a while, and then sat down and ate dinner. After dinner we were up dancing and she says, I feel kind of dizzy. I need some fresh air. So we walked out. She just kind of collapsed right there in front of me. I thought maybe she's having a reaction, I need some sugar...

"I figured the first thing I'm going to do is give her sugar and orange juice. I hollered, somebody get some help... somebody get me...and does she have a medical condition? I says, yes, she's a diabetic, get me some orange juice and sugar or sugar and water, something... and...basically I tried to give her some sugar and water and her teeth just collapsed on the glass and it just...broke it...in pieces...

"I was just trying to pour it into her throat a little bit to try to give her some sugar water. They tell me this was probably when she gulped back and everything filled into her lungs. What happened was that her lungs filled up. The way the doctor described it was heart arrhythmia and you gulp and everything goes into your lungs and fills the lungs up. There was no indication... I just feel faint. I didn't wait for the ambulance, I had a friend drive me. I tried to...I gave her mouth-to-mouth all the way to the hospital, and they told me that they took her and said they couldn't resuscitate her...that her lungs had filled up too much."

On the morning of her funeral, Marisa's students awakened with renewed knowledge, courage, and determination in their hearts. They had decided to show her their acceptance of the gift of freedom she had given them. They were no longer prisoners in their homes, always dependent on someone else. By refusing to yield to the limitations imposed by her blindness, she had inspired hope and given help to all of them. Saddened by her untimely death, her words echoed loudly in their minds, "Never give up, you can do it, set your goals high. Blindness is no more of a handicap than any sighted person saying 'I can't.' If you believe in yourself, you can accomplish anything."

She had given them the knowledge of how to get around town on the bus, how to interact with others, both blind and sighted. She had given them the courage to try and the determination to succeed. Filing into the funeral home as a group after arriving individually by bus, they knew it was what she would have wanted. It would make her happy.

05-25-98 Marisa's husband.

Have you had any sense of communication from Marisa since her death?

"Yes, I think so after her death. I don't know if it's communication or not, but sitting in the house up in Sandy Heights, it was like I said to her, I said to my son, I says, well...you know your mom's somewhere else now. I'm not religious, but I said she's somewhere else. I think she's still around. We were lying there together and I said well, honey, if you've got any kind of pull up there, why don't you let it start snowing...and it started snowing.

"The whole area got snowed on. I wasn't paying any attention to the weather and it started snowing and snowing and snowing. Finally I said, honey, if you've got any kind of pull up there, would you tell them to please stop."

Marisa's husband told those assembled at her funeral, "Not only was she a great teacher, but a wonderful wife, mother, and friend. I miss you, Marisa, we all miss you. I will always love you." With these words of goodbye, he walked over to the coffin and kissing his wife one last time, reached inside his suit coat and pulled out Marisa's favorite possession. Placing the faded, worn print of Jesus gently in her hands, he carefully closed the coffin lid.

"You know, she was a great lady...and she'll always be a great lady...."

Chapter 43

Contact with Marisa, Raechel and the Colonel

Contacting Marisa, Raechel, and the Colonel directly through hypnosis was discussed. It was decided that there would be nothing to lose, and possibly some interesting new ideas or leads to be learned. Trying to establish contact psychically sounded a bit extreme. However, June, with Helen's permission, agreed to see if she could elicit more information.

None of the three we attempted to contact, Marisa, Raechel, or the Colonel, would speak through Helen's voice. They did agree to communicate through ideomotor responses utilizing the movement of Helen's fingers. Frustratingly, this limited the questions to yes, no, and I don't know. The resulting sessions were long, and are summarized in the following pages.

Marisa.

Marisa has been trying to contact her mother through the various unusual incidents that have been happening to Helen.

Marisa confirmed the information that she was a hybrid, and knew this fact as a small child. She did not realize Raechel was a hybrid at first, but within a short time realized they were connected genetically.

She is still in contact with Raechel, who died shortly after leaving college, but not from natural causes. She was murdered by members of the military or government. The colonel, who is still alive, was aware this was going to happen and agreed it needed to be done. He did not participate in the immediate actions resulting in Raechel's death.

Marisa indicated she could communicate through her eyes. The unusual birds visiting Helen are trying to communicate with her through their eyes. She said that Helen has more information in her subconscious mind, but is not yet able to remember it.

Marisa assured us she had died of natural causes.

She indicated she has been warned not to give any further information about the colonel. She believes that she and others, including Helen, would be in danger if she reveals this information. Marisa will contact her mother when she feels it would be safe to tell more about the colonel. She wanted us to continue to investigate the case and feels the results of our investigation will be of positive use to the world.

Marisa indicates she has more information on the Humanization Project, but isn't able to tell us at this time.

Raechel.

Raechel confirmed that she had been taken from Helen's body and nurtured as an embryo in the large tanks. The colonel was her father, but he did not realize it at first. He decided to take care of her because she communicated this fact to him through her eyes. He conveyed much of the information about the base to Helen through his eyes.

Raechel said the colonel is still alive; that he was connected with, but not responsible for, her death. She had been killed about two years after leaving the apartment, because she was considered a threat to the project.

Raechel confirms she has been trying to communicate with Helen through the eagles. When Helen had refused to take care of the babies in the canisters, she had been given the job of making public the information on the project. The colonel is still involved in the project, which is still going on in the underground facility. At this time it is not safe for Helen to learn more.

Other members of Helen's family are involved in the project. The date Raechel had with Carl did not involve any sexual contact. Carl's inability to remember most of the date is because he was taken someplace or given information that made it important for him to forget the evening.

Raechel was created as a hybrid on Earth, and incubated on a spaceship. The ship left Earth and then came back when she met the colonel. Helen and the Colonel are fully human.

We explored the circumstances of Raechel's death through a regression with Helen.

07-17-99 Regression. During a regression it is learned that Raechel is no longer alive. That she died in a supposed accident.

J: What do you mean, supposed to be an accident?

H: She fell someplace... down a flight of stairs. She didn't fall, she was pushed. She didn't die right away but she was dead when they found her, when other people found her.

J: And why was she killed?

H: I'm not given that information...except she felt too much.

J: She felt too much? What do you mean?

H: She felt too much caring for me and for Marisa. She was only allowed to go so far. She went beyond the point. It wasn't time yet for that to happen.

J: What were they afraid would happen, because she felt too much?

H: They don't tell me that.

The Colonel.

The colonel does not want his true name to be known at this time. He feels it would be a danger for Helen to have this information. He is still monitoring Helen through other members of the project. He is aware of Raechel's and Marisa's contact with Helen, and is still in contact with Raechel. Although he is no longer working directly with the military, the project is still going on.

He had been taught to communicate through his eyes by the military, which in turn had been taught by the hybrids, and the ETs. People are still being taught this skill today.

The colonel no longer believes the project is for the good of mankind, but is in fact a danger. He feels if the information is made public, something could be done to halt the project. He indicated the hybrid project is being used in a way that is taking power away from mankind. Others in the military who are against this project are beginning to speak out. He does not feel the agreement between the aliens and the government is being honored, and that neither side is honoring the agreement.

He said more information would come forth after the book was written.

Nothing concrete was learned through these sessions that could be researched further. Contact with these individuals or spirits was interesting, but there was no way to verify that contact was actually made. It is included here as wait-and-see information.

Chapter 44

Currently Occurring Paranormal Events

Other than taking Raechel out on a date, Carl knows nothing of the story of Raechel and Marisa. He had recently moved to the area and was living with his mom until he found an apartment when some strange incidences occurred.

Helen continues to have experiences with the eagles which have appeared at odd times, exhibiting behaviors not indigenous to raptors. Once she saw two eagles hovering over her home as she came back from downtown. Another time two eagles kept abreast of her car for more than 100 miles as she drove through a particularly upsetting part of a journey. Eagles don't hover, and they certainly couldn't keep up with a car speeding down the highway. These events qualified as unusual, so Helen was asked whether she had ever had any other unusual experiences that she couldn't explain.

"An amorphous, shimmering light appeared in my bedroom the night my father died in 1977. He was in New York State and I was in Montana. It woke my cat which was asleep on the bed with me and she woke me and was very frightened. About three hours later, at 6 A.M., I received a call that he had died at about the same time the light appeared."

The following is a summary of some unusual events occurring since the investigation began in 1995.

An interview with Helen concerning unusual birds.

"I have a hard time at Christmas, because of my daughter's death being so close to Christmas. I was moping around Christmas morning, trying to watch the Macy's parade and cheer myself up. I noticed the big cat was sitting on the stool over by the window and was looking up underneath the overhang of the roof. I went to see what he was staring at and saw another bird like this weird thing that was at the office window a while back. It was hanging upside down, off the overhang of the roof, and was just kind of swinging back and forth. It was looking at me, but not in a piercing sort of way, it was more like it was there to cheer me up. I laughed at that one. I remember saying to it, you look so stupid, you look so stupid, but you made me laugh. It swung and it swung, and then the phone rang and I went to answer it. The bird was gone when I went back. But I know again that I didn't imagine it because the cat called my attention to it first. It isn't that my cats are so smart or anything, but they're really perceptive of anything out of the ordinary that disrupts their schedule."

06/22/98 Photograph.

Helen called and told me about a puzzling experience that occurred that morning. I urged her to write it down in as much detail as she could remember.

"I can see no logical explanation for what happened. I was gone about an hour and a half, returning at about 10:15 A.M. The minute I came into the kitchen I knew something had happened. Then just at the entry to the hallway off the living room I saw the wooden back to the picture of Marisa and her husband placed carefully and squarely on the floor. The front of the picture (glass, photo, and small picture of my grandson in the corner) was intact on the wall. When I picked the back off the floor, I realized it had a sort of lip to hold the glass in on the bottom as well as a hook on the top to hang the whole thing with, and that what was on the wall had nothing to hold it together or hang with. When I removed the glass and picture from the wall, it all slid apart and I was unable to get it together to hang back up. One cat was securely locked out on the deck and the other two were inside and acted quite nervous and didn't want to come close to the hallway or the wall for some time. They could not have carried out something like that. Both boys were at work all day (Helen's other son lived in the same town) and I had locked the house securely before I left. Nothing else had been disturbed that I could tell. When Carl came home I told him what I'd found. He took the picture apart and tried to hang it up without the back and it was impossible to do."

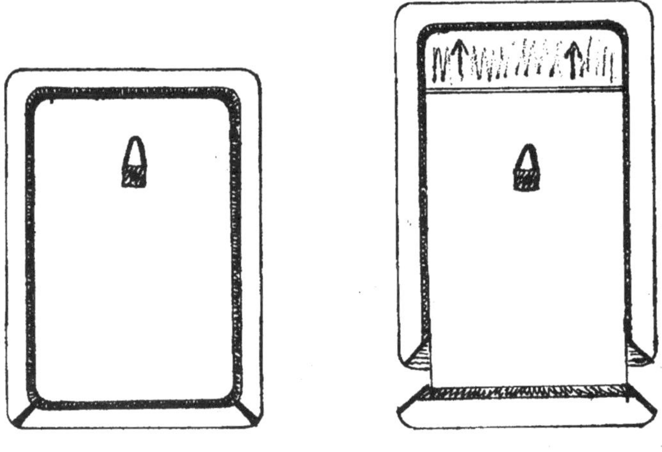

FIGURE 8. Drawings of Marisa's photo frame showing its deisgn and how it defied the laws of physics.

07-09-98.

After the photo incident whenever Helen and Carl walked into the kitchen they would look at the photo to see if anything else had happened to it. Imagine Carl's surprise when several days later the photo had started to move, once again defying the laws of gravity.

During an interview with Carl, he reveals his reactions, and his attempts to explain these unusual events.

"I got accused of doing that. Mom thought I was playing a foolish trick, but I didn't. I came home and she told me that the picture, that the back of Marisa's picture was out and lying down here.

"What she did was find it lying over here on the rug and the picture was hung back up. Without the back on it. Which is pretty hard to do. I can't hardly get it on there. And then a couple of days later, the bottom of the picture was slid out, this bottom part, again... which you have to... it was slid out like that on there."

Where was it the second time you saw it?

"It was not on the floor, but the bottom of the picture was slid down. It was on the hook, and the back is on the hook. So how can it slide...the picture has to slide up... which is kind of unusual. All the other pictures were nice and straight. I checked the backs of all the pictures. I thought maybe somebody broke in and was looking for... sometimes people hide things in pictures."

Did the photos fall off the wall or anything during the big earthquake?

"No, they didn't. And that was a good earthquake."

"I had thought of poltergeist phenomenon when this happened, but nothing else was disturbed and we don't have any teenagers."

You made absolutely sure the second time when you fixed it that it was hooked on the hook?

"I most certainly did. I did it. I put it up. None of the other ones had been moved. They all had cobwebs. I'm Mr. Gotta be an Excuse for Everything... not an excuse but an answer. The top slid up. That was the bizarre part of it. I could see the hook was on the frame and the top slid up. I had to inspect everything around here to see if I could duplicate it. There has to be an answer for everything, but there isn't."

After careful examination of the photograph and frame, it was agreed that there was not a logical explanation for what happened.

Footsteps.

At 8:20 A.M., carefully locking the door behind her, Helen left to go to some garage sales. Carl was sleeping in after working late the night before. Around 8:45 A.M. as he is beginning to wake up, he hears footsteps going from the kitchen, down the hall, and to the office. He assumed it was his mom. At 9:15 A.M. the phone rings, he ignores it thinking his mom will answer it. As the phone continues to ring, Carl finally gets up to answer it. It was then he noticed the photograph of his sister had slipped up again.

C: "I thought it was mom. I thought it was her. I was sleeping in, and I thought it was grandma sneaking around the house trying to be polite like she does when I work late. She kind of tiptoes around. Then the phone rang and it rang and it rang. I jumped up and came out and answered it, and she wasn't here."

H: But I'd been gone for quite some time.

C: "I got up because she didn't answer it. I figured, well, she must be out in the garden. I answered the phone and went out and looked for her. She wasn't there. Then I looked in the garage and the car was gone. She snuck right out on me. I thought it was her, I really did. I was really surprised when I came out and nobody was here. Very surprised."

06-22-98.

In the afternoon of the day the photograph came off the wall, Helen was listening to part of an earlier regression when she experienced yet another strange event.

"Off and on during the afternoon I would catch various scents throughout the house—pipe tobacco, chocolate, allspice, and perfume like Marisa used to wear. I don't own any of Marisa's perfume. No one in the neighborhood smokes a pipe, and I hadn't been cooking. The event affected me quite deeply, more than it really should have, and I felt quite agitated, much like the reaction from the eagles and other birds. There certainly wasn't anything threatening about it, just a real attention-getter."

Caller ID.

As the result of some nuisance calls, Helen purchased a caller ID device. She hooked it up, and it worked as advertised, for about a week. Then perhaps a chance request by Carl evokes a mysterious response by the machine.

Carl (C): Well, we were discussing if it was Marisa, or somebody was causing the falling photo. I said, "Leave a message in writing." I'd like to see something in writing on the bathroom mirror, like when you take a shower and you come out and you see something on the.... The phone rang, and the caller ID printed out, not a name, but, "Saturday June 29."

Helen (H): It happened on June 29th, the date was correct, but it showed Saturday. It printed out Saturday when it was really Monday?

C: And it printed out like somebody had called you, how they print the name out, it's in that spot, which is bizarre. I asked for a sign in writing, so we waited around for Saturday to happen.

H: Nothing happened?

C: Nothing happened.

H: I checked with the local repair service and nobody seemed to know much. They think the batteries went dead, but they said they never heard of the days of the week being printed out, and suggested I call U.S. West. I called their troubleshooter, and he'd never heard of that, either. The batteries weren't dead.

11-07-97 Helen sees the insignia again.

"I had just received some meditation tapes. I was really all upset because the boys had a lot of personal problems and they'd both dumped them all on me. I was just beside myself, so I thought, well, this is a good time to put on this tape, and I'm just going to lie down and listen. I won't have to deal with the problems for a while. I was playing this tape and I guess I did go into an altered state of consciousness, which you do with some of these tapes.

"I felt really fine, but I thought I was looking through a window. The first thing I saw... it was like looking out from the dark in through a lighted window, and I saw this trilateral insignia, but instead of being with the base on the bottom it was upside down. I looked at it, and I thought this is so strange, and this is not right. Then nothing else happened that I remember except I drifted for a little bit. Then I looked through another window and I could see the face of one of these men in black. I know it's the face that I saw originally. He looked like George Raft, wasn't he kind of a mobster/gangster type?"

Eureka Entities.

During her first regression, Helen referred to some strange-looking people watching her while she is dining at a restaurant in Eureka, northern California. She remarks that other people don't seem to notice how odd-looking they appear. Exploring this occurrence a bit further enabled Helen to better recall the experience and sketch the entities.

05-01-98 Helen describes the encounter in a note.

"The two of them looked identical. I saw them on September 20, 1996, in Eureka, northern Califronia, just outside a restaurant, at approximately 6:30 P.M. The entities walked deliberately to the window at my side and stared at me for approximately thirty to forty-five seconds. Then they entered the restaurant and sat at a table about fifteen feet away. They continued to stare at me. The waitress and I were apparently the only people to see them as the other diners appeared totally unaware of their presence.

"They were about 5' 10" tall, very thin, with disproportionately long arms and legs for the rest of their bodies. They walked stiffly, mechanically, in lockstep with abnormally long strides. Dressed in matching two-piece, sky-blue jogging suits with helmets, similar to bicycle racing helmets, on top of their heads.

"Their faces were elongated, egg-shaped, with the appearance of being artificially constructed. Their faces were covered with irregular patches of skin or with scales. My first impression was that of a botched plastic surgery, however, both their faces were identical. The color of the patches or scales was light brown, in variegated shades.

"Their eyes were like upright teardrops, very dark brown with a piercing gaze. They were solid brown with no pupil, iris, or white visible. Their ears were not distinguishable under their close-fitting helmets. The side surfaces of their heads appeared flat.

"They exhibited no change in expression on their faces during the ten minutes or so that I observed them. They seemed very ill at ease inside the restaurant and they did not move in their seats once they sat down."

Helen Tells of a Birthday Phone Call.

On my first birthday following Marisa's death, she'd been on my mind all day. I'd just gotten into bed that night when the phone rang in my office across the hall. Upon answering it I heard Marisa's distinctive voice say, "Hi, mom. I just wanted to let you know that I'm all right." Sure that someone was playing a cruel joke on me, I replied through tears, "Don't do this to me, this isn't right." As if the voice hadn't heard me, it continued, "I'm okay, mom, I just wanted you not to worry about me." Then there was a lot of hissing and crackling sounds like radio static, which gradually faded to complete silence and no dial tone. I slowly hung the phone up, picked it up again, and the normal dial tone had returned. I know that somehow Marisa had found a way to communicate with me electronically in this one-way conversation.

The Van.

On May 22, 1998, Helen and her son are having breakfast together one cloudy, rainy morning when they both get up to refill their coffee cups. Glancing out the window, they are surprised to see an official-looking van drive up and park, not in the driveway or at the curb, but on an unused strip of land adjacent to the front lawn. The van parked facing the kitchen window, and two sinister-looking men wearing sunglasses stared at the startled mother and son standing inside.

In the ten years Helen has lived at this address, only a handful of cars have parked in this spot. None have ever elicited the response this van did. In recounting the visit, both Helen and Carl have that telltale slip in logic that could indicate something more has happened than can be consciously remembered.

Helen and Carl are interviewed about the incident while it's still fresh in their minds.

06-06-98 Interview with Carl giving a description of the van and its visit.

"It was in the morning, probably 9 o'clock. My mother and I had just walked out to the kitchen and looked out the window when the van pulled up and stopped. There were two gentlemen in there.

"The men in the van looked like a couple of pilots, almost, real clean-cut, real concentrated. They just beaded in on us, just like we beaded back on them. I think they were 100%, the focus was on us in that kitchen. They had sunglasses on. I thought they had dark green uniforms on. They were both dressed the same. It wasn't like a regular military uniform... it was all over so quick.

"They had nothing in their hands at all. It was really strange because we had just walked out to the kitchen to get coffee. We just looked out the darned window and it was pulling up. They just stopped and looked straight at us.... I mean eye-to-eye contact. It was really kind of bizarre. I was going, what have I done wrong? What have you been doing wrong? It sort of looked like FBI, like an agency or something on that line. They just looked real professional, clean-cut. They kind of looked like pilots, with the glasses on, and really strange.

"They just stared at us, we stared at them, and then they backed up and turned around and took off.

"I felt pretty strange, just looking out the window and seeing a van like that pull up, and they did have their lights on. Then for them to stop and turn their heads in unison and look straight at us... looking in... made me feel pretty uncomfortable. I was trying to think, well I haven't done anything wrong, of any magnitude, and I know my mother doesn't do anything wrong.

"Their heads turned straight towards us. If they weren't staring at us, they'd be looking straight ahead instead of turning their heads to the left and looking towards us. And both their heads turned at the same time, made eye contact with sunglasses. Contact, how's that? You could feel that focus, you can feel when someone's looking at you. Just as quick as they pulled up and looked at us and we looked at them, they proceeded on their way. Not fast... just kind of moseyed on out of there. Then mom went to see if she could find them a couple of minutes later. They were no place to be found. They just looked too professional, sort of like a cross between a pilot and FBI, you know clean-cut... just real sharp... straight upright. They weren't sitting like I am....

"On the back of the van was a sign saying 'Caution. This vehicle makes frequent stops.' And the license plate started with an E, the same size as the numbers. The plate was orange, like the old Oregon license plates. The new plates aren't orange like that. It looked like an older plate on a new Dodge or a Plymouth full-size van. It didn't make sense because all new vehicles, you've got Oregon Trail, they've got three different kinds of plates, and they're not just basic orange with the black letters. Those are plates that are on older vehicles like twenty years ago... ten to fifteen years ago. The Oregon plates, you don't see them any more unless they're on an old vehicle and you buy it. Then when you re-license it, they give you the new plates.

"There were no markings at all on the van, other than the outdated license plate. It wasn't a private vehicle because I didn't see a sticker up in the right or left-hand corner for your registration.

"The plate looked like it was a state or government plate because it didn't have the little renewal stickers on it, just the E without anything in either corner.

"The color of the van was blue or silver. I've got to remember things when I see them like that or write them down. It's like when you're dreaming and you wake up and it's fresh in your memory, and five minutes later you wash your face and you want to tell somebody what you... forget it... it's gone. They were there couple of minutes at most.

"Police lights? Heavens no, there weren't any lights on that car. There was on top, but they weren't red and blue, they were all white. They went across the top of the van, on the top of the roof, about a third of the way back. They ran all the way across, and they were all clear lights."

Helen and Carl describe the visitors and the van.

Carl (C): Both the same, like the Bobbsey Twins.
Helen (H): They looked like goons, is what my impression was.

C: Like Joe Friday and his partner.

H: No, a lot worse than that, much worse. They had dark brown hair.... Nothing was quite right about it. They didn't turn the motor off. They looked in the kitchen window as if they were expecting us... which was the first time the two of us had stood in the kitchen window at the same time since I can remember. It was if they had sort of orchestrated the whole thing, and there we were and there they were, and they were just going to give us a stare-down. They just pulled in and looked directly in, they knew exactly how far to pull in so they would get that proper angle. It was as if they looked in and grabbed me, that was how I felt.

C: They looked in and they were looking for us. It was kind of powerful in a way. Just as quick as they locked on, they locked off, made like we weren't there any more, and just drove off.

H: They didn't look away at all.

C: Yeah, when they drove off, they weren't turning around or looking, or anything, like robots. We did what we came for and that's the end of that and they weren't looking at any other houses. That was the strange part, you'd think they'd come up and knock on the door, talk to somebody, or say, we're looking for so and so. There was none of that.

H: Well, those people were military of some kind or government.

C: You can't have a newer vehicle with one of the old plates like that, they're outdated, they don't use them any more. It wasn't labeled "First Presbyterian Church bus" or "Operation Head Start" or U.S. Navy, there was no labeling at all on it. They may have a "frequent stops" sign if they had a bus or something. It was just totally out of character, no insignia or a logo on the doors, nothing on it. That was the strange part, to have the one sign and the government plate.

H: And the E on the license plate seemed too big, the same size as the numbers.

C: I looked at one of the police cars and the E's a little bit shorter, down-centered, from the top and bottom. It's smaller, the E is smaller, not the same size.

H: I don't know why those men impressed me so much except I've seen that I've seen the eyes before, which doesn't make any sense as I'm saying it, but I have just the same. I've seen that same kind of face... really sharp, not thin, but just... chiseled, I guess you might say, sort of like George Raft used to be.

C: I thought the plate was a little extra long, a little oversize. I'd like to think that there was another number or two in it.

10-03-98 Helen is regressed to see if she can recall any details concerning the slip in logic she admits, but cannot explain.

June (J): How could you see his eyes when he wore sunglasses?

Helen (H): I don't know, but I could... you can't see through sunglasses... but I could see his eyes... and the glasses were black... real dark... I don't know how I could do that.

J: I'm going to count from one to three, and on the count of three, I want you to know if you had ever seen the men in the van without their glasses on. One, two, three.

H: The passenger I don't think I have, but the driver... his eyes were the same as the colonel's. They were a different color... how... how... I don't know, sometimes they're black and then I see the same eyes and they're a real bright shade of blue. I don't know... one person, how can they change the color of their eyes like that? It felt like it was the colonel looking at me through those sunglasses.

10-04-98 Regression.

J: I want you to move in your experience to the men themselves. I want you to go to their eyes, the way in which you know and have been able to go to their eyes through their glasses, through the windshield, and just let yourself be looking directly into the men's eyes... and as you do that.

H: They want to pull me in, but I won't go.

J: Where is it they want to pull you?

H: I don't know, but they want to pull me in. It's like I can feel somebody pulling on me physically. I won't go... I don't have to because I'm not alone today.

J: Have you had to go before when you were alone?

H: With the colonel... but I don't have to go, because Carl's here and he won't let me go. He doesn't know what's happening.... He knows something is wrong.

J: Is there any other way to go without going physically?

H: Oh, yes.

J: Tell me about that.

H: They can pull my mind right in, but this time I won't let that happen. I know what they're trying to do. I know what they're there for and I'm not going to go.

J: Have you ever gone there in your mind with any of the men from any of the vans?

H: No. I don't know what they want. I don't know what they want with me and I'm really afraid. I was not afraid of the colonel.

J: What's the difference here? Why are you afraid of these men?

H: I feel that they're very dangerous. I feel if I go with them... I won't come back.

J: Does that mean you won't come back physically? Or your mind won't come back? Or what is it that won't come back?

H: Well, they can't take me physically... but they can change my mind... to... I... I don't want to think like they do.

J: Who told you they could change your mind?

H: Nobody has told me, but I know they can. I don't know how I can know that, either.

J: Just be in that place right now where they are asking or pulling at your mind… just knowing that you can say no, but being at that place… I want you to ask them and I'm going to count from one to three, and on the count of three, I want you to ask what it is they're going to do with your mind. One, two, three.

H: They do not want me to tell what I know, and *I will tell what I know.* They can't harm me; the driver tried really, really hard and he was angry. I know he was angry because I resisted and he couldn't pull my mind in. I won't let him do that.

J: So something was different about the driver and the men in the van and the colonel.

H: Oh, yes.

J: What was that difference?

H: I don't believe the colonel meant me any harm…. I believe he… he had to do certain things. He had to… do the things he did… I think he had no choice… but he would not harm me, and I knew that. I felt that.

J: You said when he pulled you into his eyes, he gave you information.

H: Yes.

J: Did he also take information?

H: I don't think so. I don't think he did, he was not a cruel man, but the man in the van could be. He knew that he couldn't take me physically because I had someone else there. I think he just wanted… he would like me to change my mind and I will not change my mind.

07-16-99 Regression.

J: Have you ever looked into the windows of eyes similar to those that pulled you in?

H: Not really… the eyes were not the same, but the colonel… he didn't really pull me into his eyes. He told me a lot of things with his eyes, but the men that came in the van, the first time… the one man… the driver was trying to pull me in.

J: And how did you stop him from pulling you in?

H: I just told him he couldn't have me. I was not going with him. That he could try as hard as he wanted, but I'm not going with him. Because if I went, I wouldn't be back.

J: How do you know that?

H: He told me that.

J: What did he say?

H: He said you've gone too far.

J: What did he mean, Helen?

H: The project. I told him I haven't gone nearly far enough. I'm going to go all the way, and I'm not going with you. This time there's somebody else here and they saw what you're trying to do. He can't stop you, but he'll know what happened.

J: Who was that, Helen, that he saw?

H: It was my son, Carl, he was scared, really frightened… he really didn't know what happened and I've never really told him. I told him they were here because of what we're all doing, I didn't go into any detail. I told him it was a courtesy call from the government to try and make me back off. I told him I'm not going to do it.

07-17-99 Regression.

Helen: I don't know what they were, you couldn't tell. I'm not sure they were military, but they looked it… they were enforcers.

Was this a visit from two men lost in the neighborhood? If so, why didn't they look at a map, or ask directions of the two inside the house? Was it part of the so-called intimidation tactics of the Men In Black, only this time they wore green?

Lightning.

In August 1999, Helen experienced severe difficulty in breathing. She managed to call 911 and ask for help. The paramedics came and transported her to the hospital emergency room where the doctor examined her. He explained she'd had an arrhythmia attack, (one of the listed causes of Marisa's death), a condition in which her pulse rate had accelerated to a dangerous level. The condition is serious and the doctor prescribed an appropriate medication. As the weeks went by Helen still had some pain, felt weak and listless. Late one afternoon during a thunderstorm, Helen was in her office and heard a loud crash at the window. The window rattled and the floor shook. A blue streak of light went through the window and across the room. She immediately smelled ozone and then had a tingling feeling in her legs. She got scared, thinking this was it, she was going to die. All of a sudden a concussion wave hit her chest, quite hard, making her heart go thump. She continued to smell ozone for a few minutes, then it went away. The lingering pain in her chest disappeared and she's felt better, although not entirely well ever since.

Neither her computer nor any of the electrical equipment in the room was damaged. The home has underground wiring, with no power poles.

During her last regression, Helen and June were just starting the questions when something outside caught my eye. Out of their line of sight, a huge eagle dove down between her house and the neighbor's. Its wingspan momentarily cast a shadow filling the living room picture window, then it flew on. A few moments later one of the two plants hanging side by side next to the window began to sway. Not wanting to disturb the session in progress, I motioned to another person in the room to look. We both spent the next fifteen minutes trying to come up with a rational explanation for why one plant was swinging in a foot-wide arc, while the one next to it remained still.

Glowing.

A few days later Helen was talking to some friends in her front yard when suddenly the conversation stopped. The two women visitors were staring at Helen. One woman turned to the other and asked, "Do you see that?"

Helen, wondering what they were looking at, turned to see what was behind her. The women said, "No, no, not behind you, it's you. You're glowing."

Helen tried to convince the women that she wasn't glowing. The women were not convinced and left shortly thereafter.

Helen Tells About a Casino Episode.

Marisa and I had a tradition to go gambling on our birthdays whenever possible. On one of my birthdays a few years ago, I felt Marisa was very close and decided we should have our usual celebration at a nearby casino. The entire time I played the nickel slots I could feel her presence. A little after 11 A.M., hungry after having skipped breakfast, I was the first and only one in line for brunch. I handed a twenty to the Native American cashier and she asked if I was also paying for the young blonde lady behind me. I turned to see who was there, and seeing no one, told her, no, just for myself. The cashier's face blanched and she said, "I'm sorry, I must have made a mistake." I'm sure Marisa had been present momentarily in visible form just to reinforce what I'd known all morning—she was there for our customary birthday celebration.

Chapter 45

Epilogue

After five years of intensive investigation, visits to the college, the state library, hometowns, military bases, countless interviews, regressions, numerous book and Internet searches, all leads were exhausted. Despite eyewitness testimony attesting to the existence of Raechel and the colonel, on paper they did not exist.

In complete frustration, a private investigation company was hired. Their ad read, "No matter who you are looking for, we can help you find them. Our extensive data bank of information allows us to locate missing persons. Unlike other services that simply provide a list of names, we actually locate the person you're seeking." Better yet, they offered a "No Find-No Fee" guarantee.

A few days later, the company called saying, "We're sorry but you must have given us a wrong name, or perhaps you spelled it incorrectly."

When assured that the name was spelled correctly, they replied, "Are you sure? Either you're mistaken or it's a bogus name. We cannot find anyone with this name. Not in the entire United States."

"Well, we couldn't find anyone with that name either."

"It's not the same. You see, we have extensive databases and resources. This is what we do, we find people. Never, never in the history of our company have we come up with absolutely nothing.

With that they hung up.

We recalled the former intelligence officer telling us, "Doing extensive research and finding nothing is an answer, too. Never forget, 'no' is an answer, too."

Helen's heart arhythmia problem had worsened during the last couple of years and finally her doctor recommended surgery. She was quite worried about her upcoming operation. A few days before her surgery, she awakened to the sound of her cats frantically sneezing and the fragrance of Marisa's perfume permeating the room. Helen does not have any of this type of perfume in her home.

The morning after her operation Helen awakened early in the hospital. She was appreciative of the flower arrangements sent to her. A brightly-colored balloon floated in the window, a little weight attached to its string keeping it from drifting around the room.

No one came into the room, no fans came on, and no windows or doors opened. When she walked out of the bathroom she noticed the balloon had moved. It was at her bedside, with the weighted string wrapped completely around her bed rail.

I spent the first night home with Helen after her surgery, sleeping in the guest bedroom adjacent to the hallway. During the night I awakened to the sound of footsteps walking down the hall. I assumed if she needed help she would come in and tell me. I waited and when she didn't come in, I drifted off to sleep again. During breakfast I asked her if she had had a problem during the night. She replied that she felt wonderful and other than her cats being unusually restless, she had slept through the entire night.

The next day while working in her office she noticed her sleeping cats perk up and look towards the hall door. Turning down the tape she was listening to, she heard footsteps coming down the hall. Thinking it was Carl, she waited for him to come into the room. But Carl was at work across town. There was no one there.

Our investigation at a standstill, we decided to go with what we had, albeit a little circumstantial in parts, factual in others; but we felt we had built a compelling case for the validity of Helen's story.

Then, one day, while finishing up the investigation a letter arrived from an obscure department at the girls' college. It read: "This is official verification that Raechel Nadien was a student at our college in the spring semester. She was granted a leave of absence at that time." The year of attendance was also noted on the embossed college stationery. Tangible proof at last.

Several months later the department that sent us the note was contacted for further information. The woman who had signed the letter had been transferred. As far as the college was concerned Raechel had never attended the school.

In the early 1970s, when Marisa and Raechel were roommates, cloning, in vitro fertilization, DNA manipulation, and gene splicing were topics of wild conjecture and science fiction. Today they are facts of life and we wrestle with the ethical and moral issues concerning these scientific breakthroughs.

Thirty years ago, secret underground military facilities were figments of overactive imaginations. Today, satellite photographs of Area 51 are sold on the Internet. The revelation and subsequent admission of the government's involvement in the Tuskegee and other clandestine experiments confirms the fact of unsolicited, unwanted and, at the time, unknown secret military intervention in the lives of humans.

Watching the space shuttle landing on a dry lakebed in Nevada or California reminds us that others could land there, too. Screen memories and hypnotic blocks are only a step beyond a Las Vegas stage show act. Drugs are routinely used by doctors to help their patients forget the trauma of their operations. Native American and other cultures have legends and folklore telling of star people. Go to the desert, away from the city lights. Watch as myriads of stars,

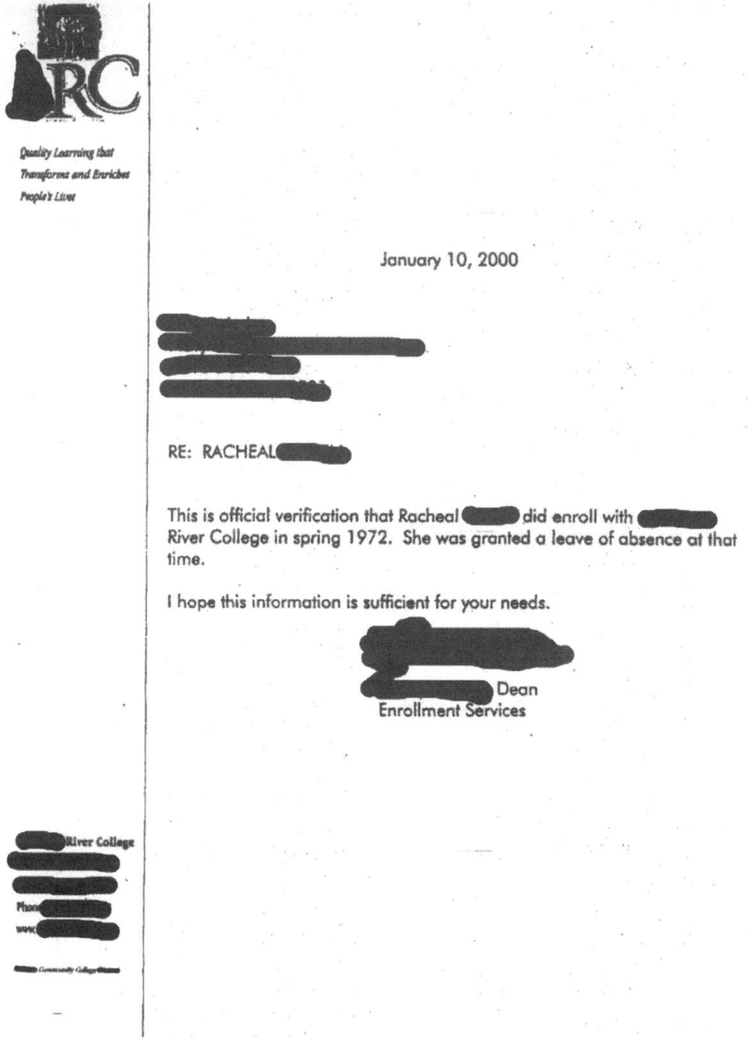

RC

Quality Learning that Transforms and Enriches People's Lives

January 10, 2000

RE: RACHEAL

This is official verification that Racheal did enroll with River College in spring 1972. She was granted a leave of absence at that time.

I hope this information is sufficient for your needs.

Dean
Enrollment Services

River College

Phone

www.

FIGURE 9. Official community college letter verifying Raechel's attendance there.

planets, and galaxies shine in the night sky, signaling, assuring us we are not alone.

For years rumors have hinted at government scientists working with ETs, crashed spaceships, back-engineering, human-alien hybrids, ETs eating green liquid food, and of humans having been given psychic gifts, enabling them to communicate with ETs.

When man first stepped on the moon, his ties with earth-bound thinking were loosed. Gazing heavenward, the astronauts saw Earth as she assumed her place in the cosmic family. Humankind's macrocosm suddenly became a microcosm in the universe.

Eyes are said to be the windows to the soul. Raechel's eyes are not only the windows to humanity's soul, but to a universal soul.

Helen's story may be the answer to why we don't see a spaceship landing on some world leader's lawn. We have already assumed our place in the cosmos and are standing side by side looking heavenward together. Raechel is not only Marisa's sister, she is our sister, too. We are them, they are us.

About the Authors

Helen Littrell is Marisa's mother. She operates a home-based medical transcription business in addition to performing freelance editing and consulting for a major medical publisher. She is also the author of six medical terminology word books on various medical specialties that have been distributed world-wide. She lives in a rural area of southern Oregon with her three cats.

Jean Bilodeaux is a freelance writer, photographer, author, newspaper correspondent, and businesswoman who has had articles published in various local and nationally distributed newspapers and magazines. She lives on a ranch in a remote section of northeastern California.

Granite
Publishing
Group